The world as we experience it is fi _____
radical thesis that no physical object ı._____ , _____ __ _____
it as having. The author provides a unified account of colour that shows
why we experience the illusion and why the illusion is not to be dispelled
but welcomed. He develops a pluralist framework of colour concepts in
which other, more sophisticated concepts of colour are introduced to
supplement the simple concept that is presupposed in our ordinary
colour experience.

The discussion draws on philosophical and scientific literature, both
historical and modern, but it is not technical and will appeal to a broad
range of philosophers, cognitive scientists, and historians of science.

Colours

CAMBRIDGE STUDIES IN PHILOSOPHY

General editor Ernest Sosa

Advisory editors JONATHAN DANCY, GILBERT HARMAN,
FRANK JACKSON, WILLIAM G. LYCAN,
SYDNEY SHOEMAKER, JUDITH J. THOMSON

RECENT TITLES

WILLIAM G. LYCAN *Judgment and justification*
GERALD DWORKIN *The theory and practice of autonomy*
MICHAEL TYE *The metaphysics of mind*
DAVID O. BRINK *Moral realism and the foundations of ethics*
W.D. HART *Engines of the soul*
PAUL K. MOSER *Knowledge and evidence*
D.M. ARMSTRONG *A combinatorial theory of possibility*
JOHN BISHOP *Natural agency*
CHRISTOPHER J. MALONEY *The mundane matter of the mental language*
MARK RICHARD *Propositional attitudes*
GERALD E. GAUS *Value and justification*
MARK HELLER *The ontology of physical objects*
JOHN BIGELOW AND ROBERT PARGETTER *Science and necessity*
FRANCIS SNARE *Morals, motivation and convention*
CHRISTOPHER S. HILL *Sensations*
JOHN HEIL *The nature of true minds*
CARL GINET *On action*
CONRAD JOHNSON *Moral legislation*
DAVID OWENS *Causes and coincidences*
ANDREW NEWMAN *The physical basis of predication*
MICHAEL JUBIEN *Ontology, modality and the fallacy of reference*
WARREN QUINN *Morality and action*
JOHN W. CARROLL *Laws of nature*
M. J. CRESSWELL *Language in the world*
JOSHUA HOFFMAN AND GARY S. ROSENKRANTZ *Substance among
other categories*
PAUL HELM *Belief policies*
NOAH LEMOS *Intrinsic value*
HENRY S. RICHARDSON *Practical reasoning about final ends*

Colours

Their nature and representation

Barry Maund

University of Western Australia

CAMBRIDGE
UNIVERSITY PRESS

CAMBRIDGE UNIVERSITY PRESS
Cambridge, New York, Melbourne, Madrid, Cape Town, Singapore, São Paulo, Delhi

Cambridge University Press
The Edinburgh Building, Cambridge CB2 8RU, UK

Published in the United States of America by Cambridge University Press, New York

www.cambridge.org
Information on this title: www.cambridge.org/9780521110129

First published 1995
This digitally printed version 2009

A catalogue record for this publication is available from the British Library

Library of Congress Cataloguing in Publication data
Maund, Barry.
Colours : their nature and representation / Barry Maund.
p.   cm. – (Cambridge studies in philosophy)
Includes index.
ISBN 0-521-47273-3
1. Color.   2. Colors.   3. Color vision.   I. Title.   II. Title:
Colors.   III. Series.
QC495.M37   1995
111′.1 – dc20   94-23287

ISBN 978-0-521-47273-9 hardback
ISBN 978-0-521-11012-9 paperback

For Connie and Harry

Contents

Acknowledgments

This work belongs to a wider project on perception, one that I had been engaged on for some time, and which was driven, largely, by the thought that certain traditional thinkers such as Descartes and Locke deserved a better reception for their views than they had received. A central part of that projected book concerned colour and colour perception. As my interest in colour grew, so did this part of the book, so much so that it took on an independent life. Part of the stimulus for this turn in events was the publication in 1988 of the excellent book on colour by C. L. Hardin, *Color for Philosophers,* which demonstrated how important it is for us to develop an adequate philosophy of colour. My debt to Hardin will be evident to the readers of this book, especially of Chapters 6 and 9.

The major influence on the shape of the book, however, was the work on meaning by Gareth Evans. It was at a weekly seminar presented by John McDowell at Pittsburgh University, in late 1986, that I came to appreciate the significance of Evans's ideas on reference, as expressed in his *Varieties of Reference,* edited by McDowell. This led me to make use of some of Evans's views in formulating an account of colour, in a way that neither he nor McDowell, I feel sure, would have approved.

I am grateful for my colleagues at the University of Western Australia and at other universities in Perth, for their patient attendance and helpful comments at talks and research seminars at which topics from the book were discussed. I owe a special debt of thanks to Paul Green-Armytage, of Curtin University, whose intimate knowledge of colour and the appearances of colour has been invaluable. I should also like to thank audiences at papers read at the following universities: Murdoch, Pittsburgh, Queensland, St. Andrews, Stirling and Australian National University.

Much of the work for the book was done while I was given study leave grants from the University of Western Australia, and part of it was done when I had a visiting fellowship at the Center for Philosophy of

Science at Pittsburgh University. I am grateful to both of these institutions for their suppport.

I have drawn on some material that I have already published in journal articles. Chapter 1 incorporates most of the paper 'The Nature of Colour', which appeared in the *History of Philosophy Quarterly*, 8 (1991), while parts of Chapter 6 rework some of the material from 'Colour: A Case for Conceptual Fission', in the *Australasian Journal of Philosophy*, 59 (1981). I wish to thank the editors and publishers of those journals for permission to make use of this work.

Finally I would like to thank my wife, Dolores, and my sons Gavin, Chris and Jeremy, for their love and support.

Introduction

The status of colour has for long been puzzling. Almost everyone agrees that physical objects have colours: that sunsets are golden or red; that bananas are yellow; that claret is purple; and so on. Everyone agrees that objects are perceived as coloured. Where there is disagreement is over the nature of the colour physical objects have and the nature of the colour we perceive objects as having, and indeed whether the two are the same.

Modern opinion over the nature of colour of physical objects is divided between those who think that colour is a dispositional property which is perceiver-dependent in some way, and those who hold that it is an objective property whose nature is obscured from us. Each opinion implies that the 'commonsense view' is false, i.e. the view that colour is an objective property of physical objects, a property whose nature, so to speak, is written on its face.

It is possible, I argue, to formulate a 'mixed' dispositionalist account of the nature of physical colour which can combine elements from both the dispositionalist and objectivist doctrines. The more interesting question, however, concerns what is the nature of the representation of colour, i.e. the colours objects appear to have. It is interesting in its own right, it is important for understanding colour perception, and in any case it is necessary for being clear about what, if any, colours physical objects do have.

I hold that the colour we perceive objects as having is an 'objective' quality, but a virtual one. That is, it is an intrinsic, nonrelational property of physical objects but one which no object in the actual world has. It is a property whose instances are in other possible worlds. It is a property objects might have had if the world had been different from what it is. Colour is a virtual property in the way phlogiston and caloric are virtual natural kinds. There is, however, a significant difference. In the case of colour, unlike the other natural kinds, there is a significant dispositional property: the power to appear a certain distinctive way, that is, to appear crimson, yellow, olive, purple and so on.

Although colour is a virtual quality, we can, nevertheless, say much about it. We can describe the way colour appears, we can recognise colour truths, we can identify causal statements involving colour and so on. Above all, we can order virtual colours into systematic colour arrays, and we can describe this structure. More than that, we can explain why the system of colours should have the character that it does. We do so by appealing to phenomenal qualities. Very roughly, virtual colour has two central components:

(i) It is a property of physical objects having causal powers
(ii) It has qualitative content

No actual properties have both components. The explanation for why we have formed virtual colour concepts is that phenomenal states have the qualitative content, and physical structural properties have the causal powers. Simplifying greatly, each of us, in experiencing virtual colours, has visual states which have qualitative character. We are caused to have such states by physical features which do not have collectively the structure of virtual colours.

The theory of virtual colours implies that physical objects do not have the colours they are naturally perceived as having. The paradoxical flavour of this remark can be removed by the consideration that we can distinguish between two kinds of colour: colour as it is in physical bodies and colour as it is represented. The virtual-colour theory is a theory of the latter. For a theory of what colour is as a property of physical bodies, it is possible to develop a pluralist framework for colours within which there is space for different kinds of colour concepts. One of the most important concepts among these is a dispositional concept, where the disposition is a power for the object to appear in distinctive ways to perceivers.

The position outlined above falls within an important tradition that stretches back at least as far as Descartes and John Locke, and which includes most of the great physicists who thought about colour: Galileo, Newton, Maxwell and Helmholtz. The thinkers in this tradition distinguish between colour as a property of physical objects and colour as we experience it, regarding the former as the power to produce, in the right circumstances, the latter. Where I differ from these thinkers is on how these two kinds of colour are to be characterised. For the right formulation, we are indebted to the ideas of one of the great colour scientists, Edward Hering.

In defending my position, I examine and argue against rival accounts of colour: objectivist and analytical-dispositional views. In so doing I draw substantially upon the writings of Gareth Evans on meaning and reference, though I doubt that he would have approved of the use to which I put them.

The book contains a discussion of claims to describe what colours are essentially, of the significance of the natural concepts of colour and of the importance of colour appearances to those concepts. Emerging from this discussion are an argument for the recognition of phenomenal colours and a defence of such qualities against the strongest objections.

Part I

The representation of colour

Interestingly, the ideas central to the Descartes-Locke tradition on colour have not found great favour among philosophers of the twentieth century. Indeed, they are commonly held to result from confused thought. I believe, however, that with a little sympathetic reading, the tradition is the best source for insights about colours and colour perception, and that it is possible to extract from the tradition a set of doctrines which are important for thinking clearly and correctly about colours.

Unfortunately, such are the ambiguities found in the writings on colour, both by thinkers in the tradition and by their critics, that there are difficulties in extracting and formulating those doctrines. The people in the tradition often appear to contradict themselves: sometimes they express themselves by saying that colours are not in the physical objects and sometimes by saying that the colours in the objects are nothing but powers to induce sensations of colour. And yet again, the colours in the objects are spoken of sometimes as powers, sometimes as 'textures' and sometimes as ways of affecting light. Additionally there is an ambiguity in speaking of 'sensations of blue' or 'ideas of blue'. The reference to 'blue' can be taken either as the colour objects are represented as having or as a sensory or sensuous quality, that is, a quality of or 'in' the experience, what I shall call 'colour-as-it-is-in-experience'. Ambiguities, we should note, are not restricted to writers in the tradition. Its critics sometimes write of the colour 'that is perceived' as the quality in the physical object and sometimes as the property objects appear to have. It may well be that this is a distinction without a difference, but it should not be assumed without argument that it is.

Despite the undoubted difficulties, it is possible to extract from the tradition certain central truths about colour perception, and certain claims which are interesting and illuminating, even if not happily formulated. One important truth, perhaps the crucial truth, as John Cottingham recently put it (in his 1990 Aristotelian Society paper), is that in colour perception, when we perceive through the senses the colour qualities of objects, we perceive, as it were, through a glass darkly. A visual sensation of redness, say, is the sign of some property of the external object, but it tells us little or nothing of the nature of that property. This is a significant feature about colour perception which is such that it, whatever else Descartes and Locke and their fellow theorists are wrong about, remains true. There is much else that they are right about, or so I shall argue.

Associated with that major truth, however, are certain claims which are more controversial. The problems with such claims, however, have more to do with the way in which they have been formulated, e.g. by Locke and Descartes, than with the spirit that lies behind them. For thinkers in the tradition there are two striking theses. The first is:

T1 When we see physical objects as having colours, those objects do not have the colours that we experience them as having. That is, in perceiving what we naturally take to be coloured objects, we are subject to a mistaken tendency to attribute to objects colours which they do not have.

This view, that no physical object ever has the colours it is perceived as having, is often known as The 'Error Thesis of Colour Perception'. It needs to be stressed that thinkers in this tradition do not and need not deny that, in some important sense, Sigourney Weaver's hair is red (and not silver) and Paul Newman's eyes are blue (and not pink). Indeed the tradition is normally marked by its commitment to a second central thesis:

T2 We can and need to make a distinction between
    (a) colours as they are in experience
and
    (b) colours as they are in physical objects.

The first set of colours are subjective qualities, that is they are sensory qualities or features intrinsic to sensations or experiences. The second type of properties are dispositional properties: powers or dispositions to produce in perceivers or subjects colours in the first sense, colours as we experience them. Eyes are blue in the sense that they have the power to produce the appropriate experiences. (As pointed out earlier, people in this tradition speak of colours in the object sometimes as powers and sometimes as 'textures' or ways of affecting light. This apparent inconsistency can be resolved by treating the writers as holding a 'mixed' dispositionalist account. See 'Clear and Confused Representations', section 5 of Chapter 1, and the conclusion to Chapter 7.)

As far as Descartes, Locke and most people in the tradition are concerned, there is a link between T1 and T2. The colours physical objects are experienced as having are subjective qualities: they are features of our sensations, i.e. they are features intrinsic to sensations or experiences, and they are conceptually basic or prior to colours as they are in physical objects.

I wish to defend both T1 and T2, but at the cost of breaking this link. There is in fact a third thesis that is implicit in the Descartes-Locke tradition:

T3 We can identify a colour as it is represented, that is the concept of colour that is embodied in one's colour experiences, in such a way that we can draw a distinction between (i) a naive concept and (ii) a sophisticated concept.

The point here is that when we make colour judgements and have colour thoughts about objects, e.g. as expressed in

My bedroom wall would lift if I changed it from peach to lime

those judgements and thoughts employ a concept of colour, and depending on our degree of sophistication, that concept can be either a naive concept or a sophisticated concept. As far as Descartes and Locke are concerned, there is a link between this last thesis T3 and the other two theses which can be expressed as follows:

T4A The error in colour perception occurs through the application of the naive concept of colour: we judge objects to have colours (as naively conceived) which they do not have.

T4B The naive concept of colour is of colour as a subjective quality, as a feature of our sensations, as a feature intrinsic to our sensations or experiences: 'colour as it is in experience'.

This last claim I wish to reject. I wish to defend all the other major theses: 1, 2, 3, and 4A. There is a naive, natural concept of colour, but it is not as those in the Descartes-Locke tradition have supposed it to be: it is not a concept of colour as a subjective quality, as a feature of a sensation or experience. On the contrary, the naive, natural concept of colour is such that:

3

> Colour is an objective, perceiver-independent intrinsic property of objects, usually (but not exclusively) of physical surfaces, located in objective physical space.

What I propose is that colours are virtual properties: surface colours are colours located in space on the surfaces of objects. They are virtual in that although I locate them in space they are not there. The surfaces do not have the colours I or anyone perceives them as having. The colours are virtual colours.

Although Descartes and Locke were wrong in the formulation of their thesis, their instincts were right. There are phenomenal colours. That they have the character they do is part of the explanation for why virtual colours have the character that they do. It is the aim of this book to give substance to these instincts. But first it is necessary to reformulate the Cartesian-Lockean thesis.

1

Colour-as-we-experience-it

The philosophical and scientific tradition to which Descartes and Locke belong holds that there is a need to distinguish between two kinds of colour, between, say, the yellowness that (in some sense) is in our experience or sensations, and the yellowness that physical objects actually have.[1] The latter is nothing but a power or disposition, albeit one having a physical basis in the relevant object: a power to induce in perceivers a certain kind of experience, an experience of yellow-ness. Physical bodies do not have colours in the first sense. Despite this, there is a natural tendency for us to think otherwise.

That we are naturally subject to this mistaken tendency, as confused as it may be, is a view shared by Descartes and Locke. In explaining their own position they both feel constrained to argue for it, or at least to defend it. They concede that we naturally think of physical bodies – leaves, trees, flowers, animals, etc. – as having colour in the nondispositional sense. They feel their own position to lack plausibility and to require defence. Part of their approach is to explain how we come to form the natural conception and how it is an understandable, if mistaken, view to take. And both of them attempt to draw an analogy between pain on the one hand and perceptions of colour and warmth on the other, arguing that we should be no more surprised to find that the red we experience is no more part of the tomato, say, than that the pain experienced when we cut ourselves with a knife is in the knife. They try also to explain how we are inclined to swallow the mistaken view. The view that Locke and Descartes find natural, if mistaken, is also one to

---

1 R. Descartes (1954), *Philosophical Writings*, trans. G. E. E. Anscombe and P. Geach, London: Nelson, pp. 194–5, 234; J. Locke (1961), *Essay Concerning Human Understanding*, ed. J. Yolton, London: Dent, Book II, chs 1–9 (esp. 8, 9). The material in this chapter is substantially the same as that presented in J. B. Maund (1991), 'The Nature of Colour' in *Hist. Phil. Quart.*, 8, pp. 253–63. There are some small but significant changes, especially near the beginning.

5

which they see certain philosophers and scientists, by virtue of their theories, to be committed.

1. COLOUR AS IT IS EXPERIENCED

Is it so clear, however, what this yellow-as-it-is-in-experience is? For some people, it seems obvious that we experience colours as qualities of the surfaces (and sometimes of the volumes) of physical bodies. It seems to be intrinsic to the nature of our visual experience that we normally experience colours as occurring in objective space, usually as the intrinsic qualities of physical bodies. This view need not be intended to commit us to the view that colours are always experienced in this way: after-images and hallucinations appear to be experienced in objective space, but other colour experiences, e.g. those had with the eyes closed and so on, will need special treatment.

When we do experience colours as occurring in objective space, we experience a coloured body that has other properties, e.g. that is also shaped, and we do not experience a body visually as shaped unless it is also coloured. The colour is experienced as an intrinsic quality of the body just as much as is its shape. This does seem to be an important fact about our colour experience.

Some philosophers, however, would think that this way of describing visual perception goes too far already towards conceding the Cartesian-Lockean position. They would be wary of allowing that we can rightly be said to 'experience colours in space'. The set of complex issues which lie behind this concern will take some time to unravel. One, however, can be dealt with quickly. It is possible to express the Cartesian position without begging the question in its favour. It is surely unexceptionable that our visual experiences are typically experiences of coloured, shaped objects located in a three-dimensional space. Such visual experiences have representational content, i.e. they have conceptual or intensional content which can be expressed as follows:[2]

(1) There are red tomatoes on a brown table (before me);
(2) There are green leaves on a densely foliated tree (before me);
(3) There are yellow stockings with a black suit (before me), and so on.

But to identify the conceptual content in this way leaves us with the problem of saying with respect to the concepts *red, green, yellow,* etc.

2 To attribute this kind of conceptual content is not necessarily to deny that the experiences also carry nonconceptual content. See articles by Tim Crane and Christopher Peacocke in Tim Crane (ed.) (1992a), *The Contents of Experience,* Cambridge: CUP.

which concepts of colour are being used. (Some philosophers, e.g. Sellars and Dretske, have argued that experiences have nonconceptual content,[3] but if that is so, it will not affect the point that we are interested in the concept of colour expressed in the sorts of judgements described.)

Descartes's view, as I understand it, is that with respect to our colour experiences it is possible to identify a quality intrinsic to our sensations or experiences, and this is the concept of colour expressed in the colour judgements above. Crucially, physical bodies do not have colours in this sense. Nevertheless, he contends, there is *a natural tendency* for us to think that physical bodies do have colours in this sense – and that thought is a confused one. Descartes and Locke also hold of course that there is a sense of colour in which physical objects are coloured, where this is a dispositional or power sense of colour. This set of views may be mistaken, but it does seem possible to set out the position without begging any important questions.

There is, however, an ambiguity hidden in many formulations of the views of Descartes and Locke which it is important to resolve. For someone who holds those views and distinguishes between colour-as-we-experience-it and colour-as-it-is-in-physical-bodies, there is an ambiguity contained in the use of 'colour-as-we-experience-it'. This can mean either of two things: (i) the colour as an intrinsic quality of the experience and (ii) the colour objects are represented (by the experience) as having. This ambiguity is hidden because Descartes and Locke want to say these are the same. At least for them they are the same, as far as naive perceivers are concerned, and for all of us in our naive moments. The thought is that our colour experiences represent physical objects as having colours, where those colours are aspects of our sensations or experiences. The ambiguity is brought into the open, however, when they present to us their picture of the sophisticated perceiver – someone who becomes aware that physical bodies do not contain colours but instead possess powers – to induce experiences of the appropriate kind.

My reading of their position is that we must first distinguish between colour-as-the-representational-content of our experience and colour-as-an-inherent-feature of the experience. We must then make a further distinction between two kinds of representational content. The first is a confused representation: it is an expression of the natural mistaken ten-

3 W. Sellars (1968), *Science and Metaphysics,* London: Routledge and Kegan Paul, ch. 1; F. Dretske (1981), *Knowledge and the Flow of Information,* Cambridge: MIT Press, ch. 6. For an excellent discussion, see essays by Crane and Peacocke in Crane (1992).

dency. The second is a sophisticated representation: colour is the power to make us experience the object as coloured.

Some commentators, sympathetic to Descartes and Locke, would reject the interpretation offered here. They hold that Descartes and Locke use expressions such as 'sensation of blue' and 'idea of blue' and that this is consistent with not taking 'blue' to apply to a sensory quality. Instead we can read them as merely ascribing to sensations and ideas representational or intensional content. But if we follow this path we need to specify what that content is. That is, we need to be able to say what the concept of 'blue' is that is being used. It cannot be the disposition or power concept, for that would make nonsense of the efforts by Descartes and Locke to show that our tendency to ascribe to physical objects the blue contained in the sensation is mistaken. For now it would mean that we have no mistaken tendency at all. Alternatively, if 'blue', in the sensation of blue, is meant to apply to the unknown physical quality in the physical object, then once again there is no room to describe the mistaken tendency. One thing, however, Locke and Descartes are clear about: physical objects do not have the colours which they appear to have and which we naturally ascribe to them.

The reasons why Descartes and Locke hold this belief are controversial. Recently John Cottingham has argued that Descartes's views on the nature of causality are crucial, although the application of them to sensations leads Descartes into contradiction.[4] My belief is that Descartes and Locke simply took it as obvious that colours could not be in physical objects, or at least that, if they were, we could have no reason for thinking they were there. Descartes says that we have a clear idea of what blue is if we restrict ourselves to considering it as it is in the sensation, but we have only a confused idea if we think of it as a quality of physical objects. (See the passages from *Principles of Philosophy*, quoted in section 5 of this chapter.)[5] I take the talk of 'confused idea' to mean not that the idea is unintelligible, but that we have an idea of something 'whose nature is unknown'. Once we are clear about what is the quality of blue that is in the sensation, and clear about what kinds of physical properties are causally effective, then it is obvious that there is no causal role for colours such as blue to play. Being themselves convinced that such colours are not in physical objects, Descartes and Locke then feel constrained to defend the view, to show that it is not absurd, and so on.

4 John Cottingham (1990), 'Descartes on Colour', *Proc. Arist. Soc.* 64, pp. 231–46.
5 R. Descartes (1954), p. 194.

2. THE NATURAL VIEW OF COLOUR

Descartes and Locke, I am maintaining, hold two views: (1) there is a certain view of colour which it is natural to take; (2) that view is incorrect. Many people, including many philosophers, have found the position defended by Descartes and Locke to be very threatening. In so doing they question not (1) but (2). Many would sympathise with Whitehead in his characterisation of the scientific philosophy:

Thus the bodies are perceived as with qualities which in reality do not belong to them, qualities which in fact are purely the offspring of the mind. Thus nature gets credit which should in truth be reserved for ourselves; the rose for its scent: the nightingale for his song: and the sun for his radiance. The poets are entirely mistaken. They should address their lyrics to themselves, and should turn them into odes of self-congratulation on the excellency of the human mind. Nature is a dull affair, soundless, scentless, colourless; merely the hurrying of material, endlessly, meaninglessly.[6]

Philosophers sympathetic to Whitehead would agree with Locke and Descartes on the naturalness of the view of colour but endorse rather than reject the view. It is possible, however, to provide a radically different response to the set of Lockean-Cartesian claims: to argue first, that the view that they hold to be natural is not at all natural, and secondly that the view, far from being plausible, is actually incoherent.

Such a response has been given in recent times by various philosophers: Michael Dummett, Gareth Evans, John McDowell and Colin McGinn.[7] These writers are agreed that the correct characterisation of the colours of physical objects is in dispositional terms, and in this they are in agreement with Locke and Descartes. Where they differ is in refusing to allow that this dispositional view is anything but a natural one to take. For them, the natural view and the commonsense view are the same as the dispositional view. Not only is the allegedly natural view, which Descartes and Locke take some pains to combat, not the natural one, nor part of common sense, it is said to be incoherent. That is, the thesis is not so much false as incomprehensible. It is, so it is claimed, impossible to understand what is meant by anyone who thought he or she was asserting such a thesis.

6 A. N. Whitehead (1925), *Science and the Modern World,* Cambridge: CUP, p. 55.
7 M. Dummett (1979), 'Common Sense and Physics' in G. Macdonald (ed.), *Perception and Identity,* London: Macmillan, pp. 1–40; G. Evans (1980), 'Things Without the Mind' in Z. van Straaten (ed.), *Philosophical Subjects,* Oxford: OUP; J. McDowell (1985), 'Values and Secondary Qualities' in T. Honderich (ed.), *Morality and Objectivity,* London: Routledge and Kegan Paul; C. McGinn (1983), *The Subjective View,* Oxford: Clarendon.

That the thesis is not simply false but incoherent should not distress Locke and Descartes. They are trying to argue that it is false. If it is incoherent, it is still false. It was not part of their task to provoke common sense or to challenge our natural inclinations – it was simply that certain counterintuitive theses were consequences of what they took to be the truth. To be shown that the consequences are not, after all, counterintuitive or unnatural, should not bother them. Moreover the views they opposed were not understood simply as 'natural' ones to take (i.e. before reflection) but also as ones implicit in certain rival philosophical doctrines, and therefore it was important to show that such views were false or even incoherent. If the latter, so much the better.

This being said, it is still difficult to read Dummett and Evans without thinking that Locke and Descartes, and similar scientific-minded philosophers, are being criticised – as if it is somehow an objection to Locke and Descartes that the view that they thought was false and had to be disputed was not simply false but was incoherent. Evans, after explicitly discussing Locke, goes on to point out that

> these remarks are equally directed against those 'hard-nosed' philosophers who wish to maintain that 'science has shown that objects are not really red'. Such a position would equally require the intelligibility of a non-dispositional concept directly fashioned from experience, which I am trying to deny.[8]

In the next footnote, he commends Berkeley for drawing out unacceptable consequences from Locke's contention that we can form an idea of a world existing independent of observers out of the ideas of primary properties which . . . remained sensory concepts.

It should be noted that this assumes Locke's brand of empiricism to be sensationalist, and as at least one philosophical historian, Aaron, points out, there is another interpretation that makes more sense of Locke's overall position.[9] Moreover sensationalism certainly does not describe Descartes's position. It is also relevant to cite Aaron's discussion of the fact that Locke makes no serious attempt to face the problem of how we know that the ideas of primary qualities do resemble the qualities themselves. Instead Locke concentrates on arguing that ideas of *secondary* qualities do not.

> To Locke's contemporaries the view that any ideas in the mind given by the senses were not resemblances of things or of their qualities was apparently somewhat novel and needed to be defended.[10]

8 Evans (1980), p. 99, n.30.
9 R. I. Aaron (1971), *John Locke,* 3rd ed., Oxford: OUP, pp. 109–10.
10 Ibid., p. 119.

If we turn to Descartes we find a view that acknowledges the Evans-McDowell-Dummett point about incoherence. Nancy Maull points out that the view Descartes opposed, one that located colours (as well as tastes, odours, sounds, etc.) in bodies, was held by him to be 'ineradicably obscure and confused'.[11] The view, however, was one actually held by Kepler: 'Kepler's theory suggested that physical bodies are truly coloured and not merely perceived that way.' Kepler held that pictorial images are transmitted from physical object to one's visual apparatus and thence to the mind. Descartes rejects this view, arguing that it is not necessary that pictures or images resemble the objects that they represent. Maull ascribes to Descartes an important motive for not accepting Kepler's view: it would be to concede that nature is not fully intelligible, or at least it is not fully intelligible in geometrical terms.

Indeed that the view that Locke and Descartes take themselves as having to combat was a widely held view with a distinguished pedigree is brought out by Henry Guerlac in his article 'Can There Be Colours in the Dark?'.[12] He quotes Epicurus writing in a letter of external things that

[they] would not stamp on us their own nature of colour and form through the medium of the air which is between them and us, or by means of rays of light or currents of any sort going from us to them, so well as by the entrance into our eyes or minds . . . of certain films coming from the things themselves, these films or outlines being of the same colour or shape as the external things themselves.[13]

It is well to remember that even if a thesis is incoherent it may be necessary to argue against it. For it may be either widely held or held by influential thinkers, and its incoherence may not be at all obvious. That what I have termed the 'natural view of colours' is widely held can be gauged by the common response to the quotation from Whitehead.

The point that views that are logically unintelligible may still be important is brought out by E. Gellner in his discussion of some of the issues raised by P. Winch (and others) about the Azande of Africa.[14] As Gellner points out, some social practices and beliefs may be logically incoherent but yet serve a social function; not only that, but it may well be that their logical incoherence is essential to their serving that social

11 N. Maull (1980), 'Cartesian Optics and the Geometry of Nature', in S. Gaukroger (ed.), *Descartes: Philosophy of Mathematics and Physics*, Brighton: Harvester, pp. 23–40.
12 H. Guerlac (1986), 'Can There Be Colours in the Dark?', *J. Hist. Ideas*, 47, pp. 3–20.
13 Ibid., p. 9, quoting Diogenes Laertius (1925), *Lives of Eminent Philosophers*, trans. R. D. Hicks, London: Heinemann, II, p. 579.
14 E. Gellner (1979), 'Concepts and Society' in B. R. Wilson (ed.), *Rationality*, Oxford: Blackwell, pp. 18–49, esp. 42.

function. We need to draw a distinction between two kinds of incoherence. A concept may be 'incoherent' because it is contradictory, or it may be incoherent because it makes no sense whatsoever, not even enough to count as contradictory. The natural view that Descartes and Locke see themselves as opposing is perhaps logically inconsistent, but it is not gibberish.

3. COLOURS-AS-WE-SEE-THEM

The philosopher who has provided the most persuasive arguments that the thesis that I have called the 'natural view' is incoherent is Gareth Evans: 'All it can amount to for something to be red is that it be such that if looked at in normal conditions it will appear red.' Philosophers have, however, tried to provide a different account of what it is for a colour ascription to be true. 'They have tried to make sense of the idea of a property of redness which is both an abiding property of the object, both perceived and unperceived, and yet "exactly as we experience redness to be".' This view is flawed, he believes, because it involves an impossible task. By concentrating on one's experience of colour, one is supposed to know what it is for an object to have this property, a property it can have independent of being experienced. The task is hopeless because it involves

an attempt to make sense of an exemplification of a property of experience in the absence of any experience. We may ask a philosopher who claims to find intelligible the idea of an objective property extracted from our experiences of colour in this direct way, whether or not such a colour property can characterize an object in the dark. He can hardly say 'Yes' since it would be quite obscure how a 'colour-as-we-see-it' can exist when we cannot see it, and how our experiences of colour would enable us to form a conception of such a state of affairs.[15]

This argument is extremely puzzling. One reply to it is to say that we should find the idea just as intelligible as thinking of a shape-as-we-see-it or a number-as-we-see-it existing when we cannot see it. The reply can be deepened by pointing out that the expression 'colour-as-we-see-it' is not intended to define the kind of colour in question but to identify it, i.e. to refer to it. There is no more problem in thinking of such colours-as-we-see-them existing when we do not see them, e.g. in the dark, than there is of thinking of 'the man whose hand I am shaking' as existing when I am not shaking his hand.

15 G. Evans (1980), pp. 98, 99.

Moreover, even if one holds that colours-as-we-experience-them are *essentially* contents of experience in the way that water is essentially H_2O, there is surely no more problem in someone's *thinking* that such colours are not contents of experience than there was for some early scientists' thinking that water was not H_2O but HO, and some earlier ones' thinking that water was a basic element (with fire, earth and air).

People such as Descartes and Locke may believe that colours-as-we-experience-them are essentially contents of experience, but they are well aware that there are many people who do not think of colours in this way. For one thing, there are many people who disbelieve that we have *experiences* of colour. Some are like Ryle in believing that terms such as 'experience' and 'sensation' have a limited application and in particular do not apply to 'colour experiences' or 'colour sensations'. Some are people, possibly not philosophically sophisticated, who simply have no concept of 'experience', 'sensation' or even of 'perception'. Indeed, as Wilfred Sellars has argued, there could exist a culture which didn't have concepts for mental states.[16] (The members do have mental states; they simply get by without talking or thinking about such states.) All Locke and Descartes need say is that the colours such people are aware of in experience are contents of their experience, only they are not aware of them *as such,* i.e. as contents-of-experience.

Locke and Descartes do not believe that colours-as-we-experience-them are intrinsic qualities of physical bodies. Can they allow nevertheless that this belief could be true? In other words, can they allow that it is intelligible? Surely they can. Surely all that is required is that we imagine that perception works not just differently from the way we believe it does, but in the way that many people have actually supposed that it does. Secondly, we might further imagine that physical bodies have, by virtue of their respective colours, causal powers that currently they do not have. In our world colour is not a primitive concept used in physical laws. Nor has it a place in higher-level physical and chemical laws. It is controversial whether it has a place in biology and psychology. (See 'The Causal Role of Colour' in Chapter 6.) We might, however, imagine a world in which colour terms do play a part in causal laws. Perhaps there are such laws as 'like colours repel'. Perhaps in that world colour is a primitive irreducible property possessed by large-scale physical

16 W. Sellars (1963), 'Empiricism and the Philosophy of Mind', *Science, Perception and Reality*, London: Routledge and Kegan Paul, pp. 127–96.

objects, i.e. not by photons and electrons, and, let us suppose, there is no theory of microstructure available.

In this hypothetical world colours have causal powers. In addition, and this is crucial, the process of perception whereby perceivers see these colours is that process which many philosophers have described as 'direct realism'. Some philosophers have believed that it operates in the actual world. They are wrong about our world, but, I maintain, there could be a world such that *in that world* their theory is true. In that world, perception of colour works as follows: the colour of a body is one of the things that modify light. Instead of electronic states' acting to modify incident light, the causal laws in this hypothetical world are such that it is by virtue of a body's colour that light is selectively absorbed or reflected. Red and blue bodies selectively absorb different ranges of wavelengths. Given this, how does a perceiver perceive colours? One important difference between the hypothetical world and ours is that in that world the causal mechanism is an enabling mechanism: it operates so as to enable the percipient to perceive the coloured world. The mechanism acts so as to reveal the world, the world as it really is independent of perceivers, in all its Technicolor glory.

A theory which is close to the hypothetical one just described is discussed in M. Burnyeat's paper 'Conflicting Appearances', in which he discusses certain problems in perception raised in ancient Greek philosophy.[17] The theory is referred to by him as the 'window model' of perception: the perceptual process is likened to opening a window so as to see things as they are. The model, Burnyeat claims, underlies the thinking, sometimes unwitting, of many philosophers about perception. The reason for that lies in the plausibility, however superficial, of the model.

A similar theory is that version of Direct Realism that was popular in American philosophy in the early part of this century and went under the title of 'New Realism.'[18] Leading exponents were Marvin, Holt, Montague, Perry, Pitkin and Spaulding. A quotation from Holt indicates the position:

---

17 M. Burnyeat (1979), 'Conflicting Appearances', *Proc. Brit. Acad.*, 65, pp. 69–111. The major problem is that of conflicting appearances; the problem of how we should respond to the fact that the same thing appears differently to different perceivers.

18 See the Introduction to the book *Thomas Reid's Inquiry and Essays*, ed. K. Lehrer and R. Beanblossom, 2nd ed., Indianapolis: Hackett, 1983, for a brief discussion of this movement.

Nothing intervenes between the knower and the world external to him. Objects are not represented to consciousness by ideas; they are themselves directly presented.[19]

A third description of this kind of view can be found in J. J. Ross's *The Appeal to the Given*. He describes what he calls the 'Object Theory' of the given, the view that we are presented in perception with 'things' and 'objects' themselves and not with any such sensible particulars as 'ideas', 'impressions' or 'sense-data'. The sense in which things are presented is not that they are thought about, but rather that they are presented in perception, to be objects of judgement. Ross writes that investigation shows that this view was held by many great philosophers in antiquity and also in modern times, as well as being part of 'untutored commonsense.'[20]

4. THE INTENSIONALITY OF PAIN

Those in the Descartes-Locke tradition hold that there is a certain feature intrinsic to our colour experience, 'colour-as-it-is-in-experience', which we experience in physical space, typically on the surfaces of physical bodies. Some opponents, as we have seen, hold that this belief is simply unintelligible and that Descartes and Locke have misconstrued our natural beliefs about colours.

These opponents, however, are wrong. It is false that the belief is unintelligible. To see why, let us turn to a different question: do we experience pains in physical objects? It is clear that we don't experience pains in fires or in cutting swords or in thorns in rose bushes, so pains are not experienced as features of ordinary physical objects. It is just as clear, however, that we experience pains in our body, that we locate pains in feet, teeth, heads, bowels, necks and spines.

It is interesting that though, broadly, Wittgensteinian ideas on the philosophy of mind are in ascendancy over Cartesian ideas (though possibly this is superficial if John McDowell's analysis of much contem-

---

19 E. B. Holt et al. (1912), *The New Realism*, New York: Macmillan, p. 2. See also p. 10, where Holt associates the new realism with 'that primordial common sense which believes in a world that exists independently of the knowing of it, but believes also that the same independent world can be directly presented in consciousness ...'
20 J. J. Ross (1970), *The Appeal to the Given*, London: Allen and Unwin, p. 23.

porary philosophy of mind is right),[21] nevertheless Descartes is more Wittgensteinian on pains than is Wittgenstein. Descartes stresses that pains are located in the body (arguing that this shows the confused though usefully confused character of the sensations), whereas Wittgenstein concentrates on expressions such as 'I am in pain', 'he is in pain'.[22] If one does that, it is easy to overlook the fact that pains are essentially located in the body. One doesn't just feel a pain: one has a headache, a toothache, a pain in the foot, an ache in the wrist and so on. Secondly, it is very unusual for people to make claims such as 'I am in pain' or 'I have a painful sensation.' Normally we tell people about the pains in their bodily location. Moreover in teaching children the language of pain, one does not train them initially to say, 'I am in pain' or 'the dog is in pain' but rather to use such expressions as 'sore foot', 'sore head', 'my arm hurts', and so on.

Pains and aches are certainly experienced in the foot, in the head, in the wrist and so on. Two questions: (1) Where are the pains located? Are the pains in the bodily locations? Is an ache-in-the-wrist actually in the wrist, never mind where it is experienced? (2) In what sense are pains experienced in the wrist? Many people are prone to deny that the pain is in the foot or in the elbow. These people have an obligation to provide us with a theory that does two things: (a) it tells us where, even if it is nowhere, the pain is; (b) it explains what it is for us to experience a pain in the elbow, foot, etc. That is, an interpretation has to be given of 'I have a pain in my foot'. If pains are not ever in one's foot, what makes such claims true? Or, putting it another way, if I believe that pains are never and can never be in my foot, what am I saying, what claim am I making if I say 'I have a pain in my foot' or 'Lucinda has a pain in her foot'?

As far as the second question is concerned, there is no doubt that what is experienced in the wrist is the felt pain: that is where the sharp pain, the dull ache is felt. From the point of view of the person in pain, it is in the head or the foot or the elbow that one feels the pain. If I can be said to feel movement in my elbow, I just as clearly feel pain in it.

The difficulties were neatly exposed by Michael Bradley in his article 'Two Objections against the Identity Theory'. Here he argued that

21 J. McDowell (1986), 'Singular Thought and Inner Space' in P. Pettit and J. McDowell (eds.), *Subject, Thought, and Context*, Oxford: Clarendon, pp. 137–68, esp. 152–61.
22 R. Descartes (1954), pp. 194, and 122–3; L. Wittgenstein (1967), *Philosophical Investigations*, 3rd ed., trans. G. E. M. Anscombe, Oxford: Blackwell, paragraphs 244–6, 250–63, 271, 283–9, 300–25, 393, 403–8.

sentences making such claims as 'I have a pain in the arm' should be interpreted as making claims literally about the bodily location of pains, failing an alternative interpretation of such sentences.[23] His examination of the plausible candidates indicated that each was defective. Nor do later attempts seem to be any more successful.[24] (See Chapter 8, where the intensionality of pain is taken up with respect to the very different discussions by Harman and Perkins.)

If claims about bodily locations of pains are taken literally, it would seem that they are all false. That pains are not literally in the legs, arms, etc. was argued by Descartes.[25] He had two major reasons. The first deals with phantom limbs: the girl with the amputated leg felt pain in that leg, but since she no longer had the leg, the pain could not be there in the leg. The second is based on the claim that a person who was experiencing pain in the leg would no longer feel the pain, were nerve signals from the leg to the brain diverted or stopped from proceeding to the brain. Let us not evaluate those arguments but ask: where else might the pains be, and what is it that makes a certain pain one in the left leg rather than the right? For Descartes, the pains are in the mind, wherever that is. Other answers are: in the brain, in the person, nowhere. Someone who argued that pains are simply in the person would be in partial sympathy with Descartes, differing from him, however, in thinking that a person's mind is simply located where the person is. On such an account, pains, emotions, beliefs etc. have no specific location. They have location only in the sense that the person possessing them has location.

Again, let us not try to decide which of these answers is correct. Instead let us concentrate on the question of what it is for a pain to be a pain in the left leg rather than in the right. Whatever the answer to where the pain is located, this problem remains. If pains are located in the brain, it could be that all or many of the different pains are located in the same place in the brain. As far as brain states are concerned different bodily locations might be registered by qualitative differences at the same brain location.

As I understand Descartes, his answer is in terms of the representa-

23 M. C. Bradley (1969), 'Two Objections Against the Identity Theory' in R. Brown and C. D. Rollins (eds.), *Contemporary Philosophy in Australia*, London: Allen and Unwin, pp. 173–89.
24 For a subtle and sophisticated account of the experience of pain, especially of its content, see Moreland Perkins (1983), *Sensing the World*, Indianapolis: Hackett, esp. pp. 25–56.
25 R. Descartes (1954), pp. 122–3, 113.

tional content of the pain sensations. The pain sensation can be thought of both as having certain qualitative features and as having certain representational content. Part of the representational content, or what we might call the intensional content, is in terms of the bodily location: '. . . in the right foot', '. . . in my arm', '. . . above my eye'. So far so good, but how are we to fill in the blank? One possibility is a phrase such as 'a pain' or 'a throbbing pain', 'a dull ache', 'a splitting headache' and so on. This will not do for Descartes's purposes. He needs the sensation to point beyond itself. His answer is suggested by what he says about colours:

When we say we perceive colours in objects, it is really just the same as though we said that we perceive in objects something as to whose nature we are ignorant but which produces in us a very manifest and obvious sensation called the sensation of colour.[26]

By analogy, we might suppose a pain sensation to have the following kind of representational content:

I am aware of a dull pain in my left arm   iff
I am aware of the presence of the sort of condition in my left arm which typically causes me to have a dull pain.

Unfortunately, this has the consequence of taking the bodily location away from the pain of which it seems to be an essential part. Moreover it is surely the pain one is aware of, not the bodily condition. It may be that the pain is one's way of coming to believe there is something wrong in one's arm, but it is because one thinks that the pain is in one's arm that one thinks that there is something wrong with one's arm. The point surely is that it is not so much that the bodily condition is identified as the cause of the pain, as that a *pain in the arm* is identified as the kind of pain typically caused by a condition in the arm.

It must be remembered that this representational content is an intensional content: one need not be aware of the condition which actually is causing the pain – it may be a referred pain, or the limb may be amputated. The 'aware' is aware in the intensional sense. Possibly it is true that in the case of a referred pain, say, where a pinched nerve in the spine causes a pain in the upper part of the arm, one is materially aware of the pinched nerve, but what one is intensionally aware of is a condition in the arm: it is the sort of condition that typically causes that kind

26 Ibid., p. 195.

18

of pain. What kind of pain? – The one characteristic-of-a-condition-in-that-part-of-the-arm.

This account may seem circular. It is not. The description of the pain is descriptive of the qualitative character: it is not an attributive description. It is functioning as 'Victorian' does in 'Victorian attitude' or 'Caesarian' in 'Caesarian birth'. A surgeon in a casualty ward may become very expert in recognising types of wounds: gunshot wound, knife wound, chain saw wound etc. In describing these wounds with such descriptions, he can use the descriptions to describe either the intrinsic character of the wound or the causal history of the wound – or possibly both. There is no circularity involved in saying that gunshot wounds are wounds caused by gunshots if the first description describes the intrinsic character of the wound. Likewise the term 'pain in my left foot' can be used both to describe the character of the pain and to describe its causal history: pain caused characteristically by a condition in my left foot. Accordingly, when I experience a pain, that pain-token, i.e. that instance of a pain, has both an intrinsic qualitative character and a representational content. Qualitatively, it is a token of the type pain-in-my-left-foot. Its representational content can be expressed as follows:

> There is in my left foot a bodily condition causing a pain of the type 'pain-in-my-left-foot'

What is crucially retained in this account is that what is represented by the pain is a condition in the foot. What is also shown is that nothing need be known (without further investigation) of what this condition is, except that it is the one causally responsible for the pain. And for many purposes, that is the crucial information.

5. CLEAR AND CONFUSED REPRESENTATIONS

The characterisation of the representational content of a typical pain experience given above may strike many people as unnatural or implausible. Surely, it will be said, we don't think normally of our pain experiences as having that content: we simply think of them as pains in the foot or in the arm etc. Indeed, but that is the problem. That we do normally think of pains in this way is the puzzling fact that we need to explain. To explain it, we need to distinguish between two representational contents of the experience: a confused one and a reconstructed one. It is just such a distinction that Descartes relies on to provide this explanation in *Principles of Philosophy*:

19

Pain, colour and so on are clearly and distinctly perceived when they are considered merely as sensations or experiences (cogitationes). When they are judged to be realities existing outside our mind, their nature is quite unintelligible; if someone says he sees colour in a body, or feels pain in a limb, it is *just as though he said* he saw or felt in that place something of a completely unknown nature . . . It is true that if he is careless he may easily persuade himself that he has some notion of what it is, because he may suppose it to be something like the colour or pain of which he is aware within himself. But if he examines the question of what is represented by the sensation of colour or of pain, *which looks as though it existed* in the coloured body or the painful part, he will see he is wholly ignorant of this.

A little later he concludes:

Clearly then, *when we say* we perceive colours in objects, *it is really just the same as though we said* that we perceive in objects something as to whose nature we are ignorant, but which produces in us a very manifest and obvious sensation, called the sensation of colour.[27]

Descartes, it seems to me, is distinguishing between two contents a given experience may have: a confused, inadequate one and a reconstructed one.

The assumption that the same experience can have more than one representational content will strike many as unacceptable. But why should it be? Something can have representational content in two ways: (i) it is apt to represent *X;* (ii) it is representing *X*. The difference is between having a disposition and exercising that disposition. Even if there is a problem with something's representing two things at the same time to the one person, there is no similar problem with its aptness to represent.

If a reader reads a sentence in a book, then her reading with understanding means that the sentence succeeds in representing some possible state of affairs. The sentence may, however, be ambiguous, capable of being understood in different ways. Indeed, it may be deliberately ambiguous, e.g. being in a children's book designed to be read by adults to children, or it may be part of a book meant to be understood one way by the invaders of a country and another by the patriots.

In fact I doubt that there is even a problem with something's representing two things at the same time to the same person. That the children's book should represent one thing to children may be an essential part of its representing a different thing to an adult (or possibly vice versa). That a historical play such as *Coriolanus* or *Richard II* should be

27 Ibid., pp. 194, 195.

interpreted as saying something about a current political situation, or *Little Dorrit* about a social situation, depends on the audience interpreting it also in its own terms.

The same point may be made about visual experiences. Given that cubical bodies have, as they undoubtedly do, characteristic appearances, it seems to me to be just as clearly true that a certain visual experience can be characterised in two ways, i.e. in terms of two representational contents:

(i) In terms of there being something intrinsically cubical
(ii) In terms of there being something with the power to look cubical, i.e. something dispositionally cubical.

Given that we can, for simple qualities such as shape and size, and more complex properties such as being metallic or being rusty, distinguish between the intrinsic quality and the dispositional quality – in such a way that a given visual experience, say, of shape, can represent either an object with intrinsic squareness or dispositional squareness – why should we not also be able in the case of colours (and analogously for sounds, odours, flavours and so on), to distinguish between intrinsic redness and dispositional redness? Furthermore, why shouldn't the same experience of redness have as its representational content either intrinsic redness or dispositional redness? It is hard to see why colours and sounds, in principle, should not be in the same position as shapes and sizes. Accordingly, if I have visual experiences with content that can be specified as

It is with me as if I am seeing red tomatoes on a white tablecloth

then we would need to distinguish between two possible contents in terms respectively of 'seeing red$_I$ tomatoes' and 'seeing red$_D$ tomatoes'. This leaves it open for there to be no objects that actually have the intrinsic-redness property. Indeed there may be strong arguments to show that no objects do have the property. This suggests a way of thinking about the (naive) representational content that goes beyond that of Descartes and Locke. In the next chapter I propose to explore it. For the moment, it is important to be clear that their position is coherent.

The position of Descartes and Locke is best understood in the following way. When we think about sensory ideas or sensory representations (which Locke and Descartes discussed), we need to distinguish two aspects of the ideas or representations. First, the ideas or representations have a certain content; they represent something. Secondly, they have certain qualities by virtue of which they do the representing. Accordingly, when we think of an idea or representation of colour we need to distinguish between

(a) Colour-as-it-is-represented

and

(b) Colour-as-it-is-in-experience

According to Locke and Descartes, colour-as-it-is-represented takes different forms, depending on whether one is a naive perceiver or a sophisticated perceiver. For the naive person it is simply the same as colour-as-it-is-in-experience. For the sophisticated person it is a power to produce colour-as-it-is-in-experience.

Having distinguished in the case of experiences, both of colours and of pains, between the intrinsic character of the experience and its representational content, there is the further question of the form the representational content should take, in particular why the sophisticated content should be thought of in dispositional terms rather than as the condition which is the causal basis for the disposition. Descartes's position, as I understand it, is that the experience gives us knowledge only of the power, not of the intrinsic condition itself. I further take it that his reason for holding this is that the experience does not reveal what the physical condition is *essentially*. By contrast, experiences of shape, motion, number etc. do reveal the essential properties.

The question about what colours are essentially will be discussed in the following chapters. As far as pain is concerned, Descartes's position could be defended as follows. Whatever the bodily location of pain, we can and do identify resemblances and differences among pains: pains can be sharp, broad, pulsating, throbbing, dull, intense, mild and so on. Certainly at the time of Descartes's writing one could say: we have no knowledge of what the specific physical causes are, but the knowledge that we do have makes it unlikely that the physical causes satisfy those descriptions; furthermore, it is plausible that the same kind of pain, say a dull, flat one, will be caused in different parts of the body by quite different physical causes. Given this, it is very reasonable to conclude that what the experience represents is a power to induce experiences of a certain kind, rather than any specific physical condition.[28] We might note as well that insofar as our knowledge has changed, it has changed to support the implications that I have attributed to Descartes.

---

28 See Cottingham (1990) for a similar point.

22

6. CONCLUSION

Descartes and the others were right to think that colour can be treated as analogous to pain. Just as phenomenal pain, the experienced pain, is felt in the leg, so phenomenal colour, the experienced colour, is experienced on the surface of an object.

We normally think of colours as being on the surfaces of bodies in the same way as we think of pains being in the foot or in the arm and so on. To those who say that it is unintelligible that colour-as-it-is-in-experience can be experienced on the surfaces of physical objects, we can reply that it can be so experienced in the same way as felt pains are felt in physical objects, such as legs and arms. Everyone agrees that pain is an experience or a sensation – whatever one's theory of pain and of experiences. And everyone should agree that we experience the pains as having a bodily location, as being in the foot, the arm, etc., and more-over that it is the felt pain, the pain-as-felt, that is experienced as being located in these physical objects. If that is the case with respect to pains and other bodily feelings, then there is nothing incoherent about the claim by Descartes and Locke that colour-as-it-is-in-experience is both

(i) A feature of our experience,

and

(ii) Experienced as being located in physical space, typically on the surfaces of physical bodies.

If we feel that intuitively there is something wrong with this claim, the objection surely is not that colour is an experience or sensation and therefore cannot be experienced in physical space, on a physical body, but rather that we do not normally think of colour as an experience or as a feature of experience. But this presents a different problem. The solution to that, I shall argue in the next chapter, depends on establishing that colour-as-it-is-in-experience is an aspect of experience but is not normally thought of as such. This requires, as we shall see, an important amendment to the Descartes-Locke position.

There is an interesting consequence of my analysis. Although Descartes and Locke explicitly drew an analogy between colour and pain, they drew it in the wrong place. They were right, but for the wrong reasons. They argued that it is no more unreasonable to deny that colour-as-it-is-in-experience is on the surface of a physical body than it is to deny that a pain from a hot stove is in the stove or a pain from a stabbing knife is in the knife. Their motivation of course was to get us

23

away from thinking of colour as on the physical surface. But this is the wrong analogy. There is no tendency for us to think that the pain is in the stove, unlike the case of colour, where we are prone to think that colour *is* on the physical surface. The proper analogy is to point out that, just as we are prone to think that colour is on the physical surfaces of objects, so we are prone to think that pain is in a physical object, the foot or the knee. And just as the felt pain is not actually in the foot, neither is the colour-as-experienced on the physical surface.

2

Colours as virtual properties

Central to the tradition that I have referred to as the Descartes-Locke tradition are two theses about colour. One has to do with the viability and importance of the distinction between colour-as-it-is-in-experience and colour as a quality actually possessed by physical objects. The second important thesis in the tradition is the 'error theory' of colour perception. The claim is that we have a natural but mistaken tendency to think that objects have a certain kind of colour which they do not in fact have.

Put in its most basic terms, the error theory consists of the claim that we perceive physical objects as having colours that they do not have. Putting it more carefully, it is that we naturally or naively perceive objects as having colours that in fact they do not have. It could be that as we become theoretically sophisticated we take a different view of what colour is, but the idea is that prior to such sophistication – or alternatively, when the sophisticated mood lapses – we unhesitatingly and straightforwardly perceive physical objects as having colours which in fact they do not have.

As far as both defenders and critics of the tradition are concerned, there is a vital link between these two major theses. The natural, naive concept of colour is taken to be the same as the colour as it is in sensation or experience. It is this nexus, however, that needs to be broken. Descartes and Locke overlook the possibility that the natural concept of colour might be different from the concept of colour as a subjective quality. Despite that, they are nearly right. They are right in holding an error theory and right in claiming that we need to make a distinction between colour as a phenomenal quality and colour as a quality of physical bodies. What is crucial is how we interpret the error theory and in particular how we characterise the natural concept of colour.[1]

1 The work for this chapter was completed before I discovered the book by Charles Landesman (1989), *Color and Consciousness*, Philadelphia: Temple U.P. Drawing upon considerations similar to mine, Landesman comes to a conlusion that is significantly

1. A PROBLEM IN STATING THE ERROR THESIS

There is a problem in stating the error theory, a problem which some critics seize upon. How we state it will depend on what theory of perception we adopt. It is no doubt incompatible with some theories of perception, but the theory can be stated in different forms to accommodate different theories of perception or, more specifically, different theories of visual experience.

One view of visual experience is that it is something which has representational (or intensional) content. My visual experiences are experiences, say, of red, square, dancing, spatially located objects. If so, to experience something as red is to require the application of the concept 'red'. In such a case the error theory takes the form that, given the concept of red that is contained in the representational content, no physical object is red in that sense.

An alternative view of visual experience draws a distinction between the experience and the judgement based on that experience. Here the judgement involved in colour judgements normally employs a concept of colour, but, so the error theory implies, these colour judgements, applied to physical objects, are false. The idea is that there is a natural concept of colour that we tend normally and naturally to acquire through having colour experiences but which we mistakenly but understandably apply to physical objects.

On both views of experience, we naively and straightforwardly acquire a natural concept of colour, and we perceive objects as having colour in this sense, but, as it happens, no physical object has any such colour. We can thus see that the error theory has two components:

(i) A characterisation of what the natural concept of colour is;
(ii) The thesis that no physical object has colour in this sense.

As it happens, the other major thesis, about the need to distinguish two kinds of colour, also has two components based upon how we characterise each kind of colour:

(i) Colour as it is in sensation (i.e. in experience) is a subjective, phenomenal quality;
(ii) Colour as a modification of matter is a power or disposition to induce colour experiences.

(note 1 continued)
different. The thesis that he argues for is what he calls 'colour skepticism'. (See his ch. 8, 'Colour Skepticism'.) As I explain in Chapter 4, Section 10, this thesis is sharply different from the virtual-colour theory defended here.

Whichever theory of perception and of perceptual experience is adopted, the error thesis can be intelligibly formulated.

2. COLOUR EXPERTS ON COLOUR

The Descartes-Locke tradition is one that contains many scientists and scientifically minded philosophers, e.g. Newton, Maxwell, Helmholtz, Broad and Smythies, but it is one that is less well received generally in philosophy. Indeed, it has been very unpopular recently. The view expressed by Westphal in his book *Colour* is not uncommon: he attacks what he calls 'the gibberish of Newton and Maxwell', particularly as expressed in the following quotation from Maxwell:

It seems almost a truism to say that colour is a sensation; and yet Young by honestly recognizing this elementary truth, established the first consistent theory of colour.[2]

Gareth Evans, as we have seen, sees his attack on the coherence of the intrinsic colour-as-it-is-in-experience as undermining those 'hard-nosed philosophers who wish to maintain that science has shown that objects are not really red':

Such a position would equally require the intelligibility of a non-dispositional concept directly fashioned from experience which I am trying to deny.[3]

Without in the least suggesting that it is a clinching argument, I think it is worthwhile to note, however, that things are very different in the sciences which deal with colour – physics, physiology and psychology – and even more so in those fields in which people work with colour, e.g. in art and design. There the Descartes-Locke tradition is firmly entrenched.

Gerald Wasserman, for example, in his book *Colour Vision* (1978) describes what he terms 'the foundations' of the science of color vision as comprising a grand plan laid down over 300 years ago in a 'brilliant series of insights contributed by Newton'. Central among these insights is the distinction between the outside world (which is the domain of physics) and the inside world (which is the domain of psychology and physiology). What made it intellectually difficult for us to recognise the distinction, says Wasserman, is the pervasiveness of naive realism, a

2 Jonathan Westphal (1991), *Colour: A Philosophical Introduction*, Oxford: Blackwell, p. 11.
3 Gareth Evans (1980), p. 99.

27

viewpoint which denies this distinction. 'It was Newton who was largely responsible for establishing the difference between a stimulus and perception, between light and colour, between stimulus and sensation.'[4]

G. A. Agoston in *Color Theory and Application in Art and Design*, after distinguishing between two concepts of colour, colour as a property of materials and colour as a property of light, adds:

The concepts of color as a property of materials and of light serve numerous practical needs in daily life, the most important of which are those of survival. The concepts serve well in a host of ways in commerce, art, science, and technology. For these reasons, it comes as a surprise to many people that these concepts are incorrect. Perceived color is incorrectly given as a property of materials and as a property of light.[5]

Other illustrations of the Descartes-Locke tradition are widespread. K. Nassau in *The Physics and Chemistry of Color* writes:

The term color is properly used to describe at least three subtly different aspects of reality. First it describes a property of an object, as in 'green grass'. Second it describes a characteristic of light rays . . . And, third it describes a class of sensation.[6]

Chamberlin and Chamberlin, in *Colour: Its Measurement, Computation and Application*, would no doubt qualify the following statement, but it is clear where their heart lies:

There is no such thing as colour in the absence of an observer; 'colour' is in fact a subjective sensation, experienced by an observer through the light-sensitive receptor mechanism of the eye.[7]

W. D. Wright, in *The Rays Are Not Coloured*, quotes Newton with approval when he distinguished between colours in the object, colours in the rays and colours in the sensorium, and proceeds to say that colour is subjective:

Our sensations of colour are within us and colours cannot exist unless there is an observer to perceive them. Colour does not exist even in the chain of events between the retinal receptors and the visual cortex, but only when the information is finally interpreted in the consciousness of the observer.[8]

---

4 G. Wasserman (1978), *Colour Vision: An Historical Introduction*, New York: Wiley, pp. 8–40, esp. 8–10.
5 G. A. Agoston (1987), *Color Theory and Application in Art and Design*, Berlin: Springer, p. 50.
6 K. Nassau (1983), *The Physics and Chemistry of Color*, New York: Wiley, p. 3.
7 G. J. Chamberlin and D. G. Chamberlin (1980), *Colour: Its Measurement, Computation and Application*, London: Heyden, p. 1.
8 W. D. Wright (1967), *The Rays Are Not Coloured*, London: Adam Hilger, p. 20.

Hurvich begins the second chapter of *Colour Vision* by considering a range of questions leading from: what is colour? Is colour something that inheres in objects themselves? Is it related to the light falling on an object? Is it a photochemical event that occurs in the receptor layer of the eye? Is it a neural brain-excitation process? Is it a psychical event? Hurvich's answer is 'Colour is all these things.'[9]

D. R. Hilbert in *Color and Color Perception* argues for an objectivist (realist) account of colour. It is interesting that, as Hilbert concedes,[10] two of the scientists whose work he appeals to in defence of his position, E. H. Land and S. Zeki,[11] are squarely in the Locke-Descartes-Helmholtz tradition. Zeki, for example, writes:

The nervous system, rather than analyze colours, takes what information there is in the external environment . . . and transforms that information to construct colours, using its own algorithms to do so. In other words it constructs something which is a property of the brain, not the world outside.[12]

Hilbert, in pointing out how Land believes that colours are the creation of brain mechanisms that compute colour descriptions based on retinal stimuli, quotes Land:

What we know as reality is the experience at the terminal end of this computation. Since we all use the same computation mechanism, we share the terminal experiences. We name them, talk about them, train ourselves to relate to them and to handle them.[13]

Such views are not confined to colour. They find expression likewise in regard to sound, including music. In Alexander Wood's *The Physics of Music* we can read the following passage:

Pitch is the characteristic of a sound in virtue of which we describe it as 'high' or 'low'. More exactly it is 'that subjective quality of a sound which determines its position in the musical scale'. It has long been correlated with frequency of vibration.[14]

In the opening chapter Wood distinguishes between sound-as-sensation and sound-as-external-cause-of-the-sensation. Although his book is largely concerned with the latter, 'it is the character of the sensation

9 L. Hurvich (1981), *Colour Vision*, Sunderland: Sinauer.
10 D. R. Hilbert (1987), *Color and Color Perception*, Stanford: Center for the Study of Language and Information (C. S. L. I.), pp. 1, 9, 17.
11 E. H. Land (1983), 'Recent Advances in Retinex Theory . . .', *Proc. Nat. Acad. Sci.*, 80, pp. 5163–9; S. Zeki (1983), 'Colour Coding in the Cerebral Cortex . . . ', *Neuroscience*, 9, no. 4, pp. 741–81.
12 Zeki (1983), p. 764.   13 Hilbert (1987), p. 17.
14 Alexander Wood (1962), *The Physics of Music*, 6th ed., London: Methuen, p. 42.

which determines whether a sound is musical' and hence comes within the scope of the book. In similar vein, Robert Donington, in *The Instruments of Music*, writes:

Sound is the raw material of music. Paradoxically enough, although we always think of sounds as reaching us from the outside, sound is something which only exists in our minds. Strictly speaking, sound is the name for what happens to us mentally when certain physical events occur within range of our hearing faculties ... When *sound-vibrations* reach our ears, we feel them through the response of our aural nerves, and this response as our mind experiences it is *sound*.[15]

3. PERCEIVED COLOUR AND VIRTUAL COLOUR

Among those who work on, and with, theories of colour it is common to distinguish between colour as a property of physical bodies, i.e. psychophysical colour, and colour as a subjective quality. Psychophysical colour is the property specified by dominant wavelength, excitation purity and luminant reflectance (for physical surfaces). The waters of this neat classification are muddied by the common practice of talking about 'perceived colour', where this seems to be related to the subjective colour. The problem raised by this practice is that it is plausible to take the 'perceived colour' to be the colour-perceived-as-an-objective-property. But if we do that, then it becomes hard to see how this colour can also be the subjective quality in the sense of being the colour-in-the-experience.

I take it that this is the thinking behind the worry expressed by Gareth Evans and like-minded philosophers who argue that 'colour-as-it-is-experienced' or 'phenomenal colour' is incoherent or unintelligible. To forestall misunderstanding, it needs pointing out that such thinkers do not make the outrageous mistake of believing that we do not experience colours. No one questions that we do. What is being opposed is a certain way of understanding 'colour-as-it-is-experienced'. What is being claimed is that in the only intelligible sense of this expression, the only one that makes sense, the colour that is experienced is a colour of objective entities, usually physical objects in the physical world, often their surfaces, sometimes their volume: tomatoes, ice cubes, lightbulbs, atmospheres and so on. I take it that the force of this objection to the Locke-Descartes tradition is that the sense in which colours are experienced is such that my experience is something with conceptual content,

---

15 R. Donington (1962), *The Instruments of Music*, London: Methuen, p. 1.

and the relevant concept is a concept of colour as an objective property of physical objects.

To say this, however, requires that we specify what this concept of colour is. Evans and Dummett and others hold that it is a concept of a dispositional quality. In Chapter 1, I argued briefly against that view. In this chapter I want to develop more positively the view I sketched as an alternative. In doing so it will be instructive to draw upon the ideas of the German physiologist Hering, who is one of the leading figures in the history of colour science. He is particularly interesting for his points of agreement and disagreement with the tradition of Locke, Descartes and Helmholtz.

One of the major points of agreement is expressed in Hering's description of the psychologist who distinguishes the physical processes underlying the subjective phenomenon of colour and the phenomenon itself:

If he speaks of a green leaf, of a green radiation, of a green excitation of the inner eye, then he is aware that he may do this with about the same right that one speaks of a wine vine, a bunch of wine grapes and a wine flask.[16]

According to Hering, we must accordingly distinguish strictly between colours as visual qualities, or so-called subjective phenomena, and the more proximate or remote physical conditions or causes of these phenomena.

Unlike those who work with colour or on it, many philosophers are resistant to the move made by Hering. For many, identifying colour with something subjective is the last thing, or one of the last, they want to do. Many see talk about colour-as-sensation as showing a deep-rooted confusion, one that of course needs to be eradicated. Two examples are Gareth Evans and Jonathan Westphal. Instead these philosophers, each with his own programme, seek to identify colour with some other objective property, be it some disposition to modify light, e.g. reflectance or a disposition to produce some standardized response typical of human observers and so on.

Certainly the inference made by Hering that we must distinguish between colours as subjective phenomena and their physical causes does not follow from the original analogy between green and wine. I omitted a further sentence: 'Just as the beverage wine is not a common ingredient green is not a common property.' Someone might agree that colour was not a common ingredient and yet balk at the claim that colour is

16 E. Hering (1964), *Outlines of a Theory of the Light Sense* (1920), trans. L. Hurvich and D. Jameson, Cambridge: Harvard U.P., p. 3.

essentially subjective. It could well be that colour, essentially, is something objective. The dispute between Hering and his opponents, as I have characterised it, is a dispute over what colour is essentially. Each side to the debate wants to specify what colour is essentially while allowing that the leaf or the radiation or whatever can be coloured, in a secondary or derivative sense.

There is, however, a further remark made by Hering, one that shows that his position is not so easily dismissed as is suggested by the criticism I offered: 'It is not consistent with the original meaning of the word "sensation" to call colours sensations.' Hering contrasts the way we talk of sensing pain, pleasure, warmth and cold with our perceiving white, red or black:

Sensations mean in our language something that one perceives in or on one's body, but colours always appear outside of our body and especially outside of our eyes.[17]

We might respond to this comment that colours are sometimes perceived as on one's body, e.g. my hand is a lightish creamy-brown. Hering's point, however, surely is that insofar as our sensations are associated with our sense organs, the sensations are located on or in the body, and as far as the organs for vision, the eyes, are concerned, there is a vast difference between the colours perceived by the eyes and the sensations of the eye. The sensations are typically smarting sensations, e.g. if the light is dazzling or very bright or if one rubs one's eyes with the fingers after peeling onions or cutting up chillis, or yet again if the eye is scratched. Hering is quite right. Colours are not sensations as they are ordinarily understood. On the other hand, for those philosophers and psychologists who do speak of colours as sensations, the term 'sensation' functions as a technical term. In this technical sense, not only are colours sensations but so too are ordinary sensations: pains, tickles, feelings and so on.

Nevertheless, Hering's wish to speak of colours not as ordinary sensations but as visual qualities that are in some sense subjective, but are perceived as outside our body or at least as external to the eyes, shows that he is not guilty of the sort of confusion that critics such as Evans and Westphal want to foist on those who maintain that the subjective aspect is essential to colour.

There are important parallels between Hering's views and those of one of the modern authorities quoted at the beginning of section 2. In *Color Theory and Application in Art and Design,* Agoston wrote that per-

17 Ibid., p. 6.

ceived colour is incorrectly given as a property of materials and as a property of light. He explicitly denies, however, that colour is a sensation. Rather we are said to have certain sensations that make us aware of certain characteristics of physical materials or of light, and these characteristics constitute colour.

This may seem confusing. What Agoston is doing, however, is making a distinction between two kinds of colour concept: colour as a characteristic possessed by light or by materials, and colour perceived to be a property of light and of materials. These concepts though they 'bear a strong resemblance to each other', are different: 'The difference is that, in the former concept color is a set of data and, in the latter, it is a subjective judgment of an aspect of appearance.'[18]

One way of understanding Agoston's point is by putting it in terms of the philosophical distinction between material objects and intensional objects of perception. The characteristics of materials or of light – the spectral reflectance characterisations – are the material objects of perception; they are what the sensations make us aware of. They are not, however, aspects of how things appear – these are the properties of objects or of light, and these constitute the intensional objects of perception.

It is well known that there are different modes of appearance for colour. That is, we perceive colour as a property of different kinds of objects: of surfaces of opaque bodies, and as properties of light sources, of illumination, of transparent volumes and of films. Though Agoston in the quoted passage concentrates on two of these, he is implying that for each mode of appearance we can pick out a range of properties, e.g. hue, brightness, saturation, and for each there is a corresponding characteristic of the relevant physical object. He then goes on to point out that

the characteristic (color) of the light is its spectral power distribution (wavelength composition) and the characteristic (color) of an opaque material is its spectral reflectance distribution, considered along with the characteristic (color) of the light illuminating the material. Color characterized in these ways is given by numerical data or curves representing the data.

Hering writes that the strict distinction between real objects and seen things as colour forms – between the real world and the visual world that is built up from colours and shapes – is an indispensable prerequisite for understanding the visual function and its laws. Thus the subjectivity of colours is not the subjectivity of sensations – at least not straightforwardly so.

18 Agoston (1987), pp. 9–10.

33

However, Hering's view is primarily about perceived colour: colours are visual qualities that are both subjective and spatial. It is this view that I wish to defend. There is no question that colours, at least typically, are qualities perceived as in space and external to the eye, i.e. as located at a distance from the point of view that I occupy, the place from which I look. What I propose is that perceived colours are virtual properties: surface colours are colours located in space on the surfaces of objects. They are virtual in that although I locate them in space they are not there. The surfaces do not have the colours I or anyone perceives them as having. The colours are virtual colours.

4. COLOUR AS A VIRTUAL PROPERTY

Our colour experiences are experiences that represent objects as having colours, where this colour is a visual quality, i.e. an intrinsic quality of physical objects. This presupposes that our experiences of colour are experiences with a certain conceptual content. The latter way of putting things will appeal more to those who think that talk of representational content favours a representative theory of perception. Such a thought would be mistaken. A direct realist could admit that my cognitive states and my perceptual states are states which represent objects as having properties. The difference between representative realism and direct realism (at least this version of it) depends heavily on the form the representation takes.

To say, however, that visual experiences and in particular experiences of colour have conceptual content requires us to say what concept of colour is employed. The relevant concept, I am proposing, is a concept of a nondispositional, intrinsic quality of physical objects.

I take it as obvious that when we experience coloured objects we experience, typically, a physical body that has other qualities than colour. If I see a red cricket ball, then I see a cricket ball that is round, is shiny on one side, is located in space, is distant from my eyes and is red. As far as the quality of redness is concerned, there seems no difference between it and the other properties of the ball: its shape, its shininess, its spatial location, its number, its state of motion or rest and so on. I see the ball as red in the same way as I see it as round, shiny etc. The onus to prove their case must be on those who deny this.

Whatever is the right account of colour, everyone agrees that for each colour there is a characteristic appearance. That is to say, objects can be grouped according to whether they look red or look yellow or look

34

chartreuse, etc. Clearly, to have such an appearance is to have a dispositional property: the power to look red or look yellow and so on. I claim that we can distinguish between this red in the dispositional sense, red_D, and red in the intrinsic sense, red_I.

This distinction between the intrinsic and dispositional senses of red can be thought of as matching a parallel distinction that needs to be made with respect to other qualities: square, circular, rusty, obese, metallic and so on. Things that are square can (and do) look square, things that are metallic can look metallic, things that are obese look obese and so on. Obviously, properties such as being square, being metallic, being obese, being rusty etc. can be defined independently of how things look: they are intrinsic, nondispositional properties. Nevertheless we can also define a dispositional sense of square, metallic, obese, rusty and so on.

x is $square_D$	iff	x has the power to look square
x is $metallic_D$	iff	x has the power to look metallic
x is $rusty_D$	iff	x has the power to look rusty
x is $obese_D$	iff	x has the power to look obese.

If we look at the right-hand side of these definitions, however, we should be confronted with the question of how the terms 'square', 'metallic', 'rusty' and 'obese' should be understood. To avoid circularity, it would seem that these terms should be understood as applying to the intrinsic, nondispositional qualities. Given the way the world is, we know that there is a certain appearance (a look) that obese bodies have, a different but characteristic appearance that rusty bodies have, another that metallic objects have and so on. In like manner we can define a dispositional sense of red in terms of an intrinsic sense:

x is red_D iff x has the power to look red_I

It is consistent with this account that there are no things that have the redness that many things look as if they have. That is, no objects are red_I, but many are red_D: ripe tomatoes, certain apples, fire-engine trucks, pillar-boxes, sunsets and so on. If one has doubts about this, consider the claim that in certain films, James Bond looked satanic or Jack Nicholson looked satanic: one does not have to believe that Satan exists in order to accept that someone truly does look satanic. Likewise, for people to look demonic, to look divine and to look angelic, it is not necessary to believe that there are demons, heavenly beings or angels.

Being red_I, I claim, turns out to be like being satanic, being demonic or being angelic rather than like being square. Never mind, the important thing for most purposes is that certain things are red$_D$ (sunsets), and other things are blue$_D$ (skies) and so on. What this means is that intrinsic colour is a *virtual property*. It is a hypothetical property, one that objects might have but do not, a property that in some possible world they have, but not in this one. In other words, colours such as red, yellow, turquoise etc. are virtual properties, unlike such real properties such as squareness, rustiness, obesity etc. Just as in optics we can distinguish between real images and virtual images, so we can distinguish between real properties and virtual properties.

To be clear, what I am suggesting is that intrinsic redness, as opposed to dispositional redness, is a virtual property, just as phlogiston is a virtual natural kind, and so is caloric. The important difference between red$_I$ and phlogiston is that for redness there is a significant dispositional property, the power to look red$_I$, whereas for phlogiston (and caloric) there is no comparable dispositional property. The dispositional reds, yellows and blues have a crucial role to play in our social and biological lives. For those who disbelieve in Satan, demons and angels, the property of redness$_I$ is analogous to being satanic, demonic and angelic. Like those properties, there are many objects that are not red$_I$ but have the power to look red$_I$.

But to say that intrinsic colour is a virtual property is to say what colour is not rather than what it is. Can we say more? At one level it would seem that at least we can indicate what the property is. Most people would say that typically redness is a quality in (or possibly on) the surface of physical objects: it is an observable, objective feature (of things) in a public time and space. Take a cricket ball: we experience it as spherical, as shiny, as located in three-dimensional space and as red. The cricket ball has all these properties, and we experience it as having them. The redness seems to be just as much a property of the surface as does its shape and shininess.

Some philosophers, e.g. Michael Dummett, claim not to understand what can possibly be meant by saying that colours are in (or on) the surfaces of physical objects.[19] Many of us, on the other hand, find it hard to understand what Dummett could possibly mean. Most of us will find ourselves only too willing to agree with the physiological psychologist Richard Boynton when he writes in 'Color in Contour and Object Perception':

19 M. Dummett (1979), 'Common Sense and Physics' in G. Macdonald (ed.), *Perception and Identity*, London: Macmillan, pp. 1–40, see 21–3.

36

From early childhood we are easily able to recognize a property of objects, usually associated with their surfaces, that we call color. No child, and relatively few adults, will doubt that color is on (or sometimes in) objects.[20]

It seems only too clear that we experience the redness of a ripe apple as an objective quality of the apple, the redness being in an objective space just as much as are the shape, the contour, the texture of the apple. It is just this point that is so tellingly made in this passage by Hering:

When we open our eyes in an illuminated room we see a manifold of spatially extended forms that are differentiated or separated from one another through differences in their colours . . . Colors are what fill in the outlines of these forms, they are the stuff out of which visual phenomena are built up; our visual world consists solely of differently formed colours; and objects, from the point of view of seeing them, that is, *seen* objects, are nothing other than colors of different kinds and forms.[21]

Let us look at Dummett's reasons for what he says. Dummett describes what he takes to be the plain man's view of colours.[22] It is how a moderately thoughtful person might conceive of the visual qualities of objects if he were quite innocent of scientific knowledge, and relied only on facts of everyday experience:

On a quite ordinary understanding of colour predicates, as applied to opaque and transparent objects, they stand for dispositional properties: no one who has ever noticed – and who has not? – the varied appearance of a uniformly coloured surface, from one area to another, as light from different sources strikes it, as parts lie in shadow and other parts are tinged by reflections from nearby objects, could conceive of them otherwise.[23]

This is a strange argument. First, it ignores that we are told ad nauseam that white papers appear white in all sorts of lighting and shadows: that the paper continues to look white as the illumination changes, and across shadows. That is, many psychologists and philosophers insist upon what is called 'colour constancy'. Now, it may be, as I would argue, that there are problems with what is often maintained about colour constancy: that the facts are wrongly interpreted. However, the fact that colour constancy is so widely believed is surely evidence that what the plain man believes is captured not by Dummett's hypothesis, but by Boynton's. Perhaps the plain man ought to believe what Dummett holds that he does believe, but that is not what we are considering. Perhaps the reason

20 R. Boynton (1978), 'Color in Contour and Object Perception', in E. C. Carterette and M. P. Friedman (eds.), *Handbook of Perception*, vol. 8, New York: Academic Press, p. 175.
21 Hering (1964), p. 1.   22 Dummett (1979), pp. 27–9.   23 Ibid., p. 28.

the plain man believes what he does is similar to the reasons Aristotle had for not believing that all bodies fall at the same rate. A colleague of mine was puzzled by Aristotle's holding this belief, because he and his five-year-old daughter had, by pushing coins over the edge of a table, discovered that different coins fall at the same rate. How could Aristotle not have noticed a fact like this?

There is a second problem with Dummett's argument. Those reasons do not require a dispositional account of colour. At least they leave it open for us to distinguish between a dispositional concept and a concept of an intrinsic property. This is the distinction drawn by Keith Campbell between standing colour and transitory colour. My hand has a standing colour that is mottled pink and cream, but under sodium lighting it has a transitory colour of a sickly yellow. The standing colour is the transitory colour it would have under some suitable standard conditions, and hence is dispositional. The transitory colour is the colour had under whatever illumination the object is placed in. It is, at least plausibly, an intrinsic property. To show that in fact it is dispositional requires extra argument, and not the facts of everyday experience mentioned by Dummett. Moreover, as we shall see in Chapter 6, even Campbell's distinction between standing colour and transitory colour does not rule out the possibility that there might be good reason to identify a third kind of colour, identifiable with the causal basis for the standing colour.

5. IDENTIFYING VIRTUAL COLOURS

What else can be said to identify this virtual redness? Well, it is the property shared by (or appeared to be shared by) ripe tomatoes, jackets of Grenadier Guards, hair of Sigourney Weaver, sunsets in Perth, dirt in Kalgoorlie, blood, raspberry juice, tomato sauce, and so on.

Pointing to facts such as these makes a beginning, but only a beginning. There is something deeper to virtual redness that has not yet been taken account of. To see what it is we need first to address ourselves to a problem that would seem to confront any account of virtual colours.

For anyone defending a theory of virtual colours, i.e. of properties that do not exist, and who claims that this is the natural concept of colour possessed by those who are colour-competent, there arises the problem of how we would know of anyone that he or she possesses the concept in question, given that no physical object has the colour quality.

The key to the solution to this problem rests on the recognition that although physical objects do not have the colour qualities in common, there is something else that they share: the power to *look* as if they had the properties. For purposes of acquiring a colour language and being taught colour terms, this will do. It is enough that objects *appear* to have the qualities: it is not necessary that they actually have them. We can readily appreciate this if we consider how we would learn the colour terms if we supposed that physical objects actually did have the colour qualities in question. In those circumstances it would still be because red objects *looked* a certain characteristic way that we would come to know that they were red and to understand what it is for something to be red. Given this, it should not be surprising that, if it turns out that in fact things are not red but only look red, people should still acquire the same facility with colour terms.[24]

The defender of virtual-colour properties can present an account of the historical development of colour terms. Historically, language-users begin by being taught to describe objects as yellow, white, brown and so on. It is at a later stage that there arises a distinction between being red and appearing red, and at a yet later stage it is discovered (I claim) that in fact there are no reds.

The fact that physical objects have the power to affect different observers in such a way as to lead them to agreement in their colour judgements enables us to be more specific about what virtual colours are. With respect to people who make colour judgements, we can order and systematically arrange both arrays of physical objects, e.g. colour chips, and arrays of lights in such a way that we can construct ordered colour systems in which individual colours are systematically arranged along different dimensions. According to the system we adopt and the domain of objects that we are interested in: surfaces, lights, light waves, volumes etc., we can order the objects in a three-dimensional array:

Lights: hue, brightness, saturation
Surfaces: hue, lightness, chroma or
           hue, blackness/whiteness, chromaticness

Reference to such colour arrays and systems enables us to construct what might be called a descriptive *phenomenology of colour*. A particular presentation or sample of colour (say, of a specific hue, degree of chromaticness and degree of whiteness/blackness) has a particular place within *that system* (and possibly a different place in a different system). A

24 A similar argument is presented by Landesman (1989), pp. 103–5.

person's understanding of colour terms can be gauged by that person's capacity to participate in such colour-ordering practices. (This allows us to make room for the possibility of a blind person's using colour names though that person's use is dependent on the primary use of colour-perceivers.)

Bernard Harrison in *Form and Content* argued that the meaning of each specific colour term depended on its unique place in the ordered complex colour array:

What entitles us to refer to something as coloured is the possibility of assigning that thing to some place in the complex system of internal relationships that characterize the colour array. Colour then is simply the aspect of things under which they stand in these relationships to one another.[25]

As tempting as this account is, before we endorse it we need to resolve some of the problems contained within it. Harrison suggests that there is a unique colour system and that each colour presentation (of specific values of hue, saturation and tonality) occupies a unique place in that colour array. This suggestion must be rejected. First of all, there is one colour array applicable to surfaces of physical objects and quite another to the light reflected from the surfaces. The second system will be built up in terms of the colours objects appear to have when viewed through narrow apertures. Such colours are referred to as 'aperture colours' or 'film colours' and are different from the surface colours of objects. For one thing, they are quite often different: browns will be seen only as surface colours and not as film colours. For another, the film colour is seen not as a colour of a surface but as the colour of a film.

In the second place, there is not a unique system even with respect to the colour of physical surfaces. If we are thinking of film colour, then the three dimensions of the colour system are hue, saturation and brightness. If we turn to the colour systems applicable to surface colours, e.g. colour chips, then we have different possible systems, none of which correspond to the system applicable to film colours. Brightness, for example, is associated with film colour, whereas for surface colour the corresponding dimension is either lightness or whiteness, depending on the system. Likewise, the second dimension, even if it is called 'saturation', corresponds to different properties: it is defined differently and variously. For the Swedish Natural system the corresponding dimension is chromaticness; for the Munsell system it is chroma.

There is a second problem with Harrison's account. It lies with

25 B. Harrison (1973), *Form and Content*, Oxford: Blackwell, p. 86.

whether and if so how a colour's occupying a certain place in a colour array determines the meaning of the corresponding colour expression. Given the variety of colour systems and the complex nature of each colour array, it would be difficult to hold that a person's understanding of that colour term requires understanding that the colour occupies that role, i.e. is interrelated in that systematic way to the whole range of colours.

The question of how the meaning of colour language is determined is taken up in the next chapter. For the moment it is sufficient to overcome the problem I elicited from Harrison's account in the following way. Colour-naming practices are to be thought of as linguistic practices which enable language-users to latch on to certain colour properties. These properties are ones which stand together in the systems of relationships that constitute the various complex colour arrays. In this way we can understand how the users of colour language can refer to colour properties without possessing detailed knowledge of the complex set of relationships.

Reference to the 'three-dimensional colour array' therefore needs to be kept in its proper perspective. The systems of colour samples are used to order colours and to test people's capacities to make colour discriminations. Very few people with an understanding of colour terms in their natural language have any knowledge at all, let alone any precise knowledge, of any such system. Nevertheless there are broad features of the system that capture principles implicit in natural language. Central among these are the following:

(a) The division between chromatic and nonchromatic colours
(b) The existence of the unique psychological primary colours: yellow, blue, green and red
(c) The broad ordering relationships as expressed in judgements such as x is a deeper red than y, v is a darker blue than z, u is a paler green than w, b is a richer red than k, and so on.

What I am claiming is that the use of colour terms in natural language presupposes certain broad principles which are captured and fleshed out and refined within various colour systems. Actually to say this is to make a substantial assumption about colour experience. The question of whether it can be defended is taken up in Chapter 9, especially in Section 1. Part of the task of such systems is to provide structure and systematic order to natural colour judgements and to their underlying principles. As far as the colours' being virtual is concerned, there is no problem in understanding the colour terms: the agreement, the principles, the systems are the same whether the properties are possessed or only appear to be possessed.

6. TWO KINDS OF QUALIA

The important point about perceived colour, i.e. colour as it is represented, i.e. our concepts of colour, is that the different colours can be systematically ordered and arranged in terms of a colour system or, as it is sometimes known, a colour solid. The systematic relationships that hold between these various colours have such a structure that there are no physical features that stand together in the right kinds of relationships. For example, if we think of surface colour of physical bodies;

(1) There are no physical properties of surfaces
(2) There are no qualities of light waves, e.g. reflectance curves
(3) There are no dispositional physical qualities in terms of the response curves in relation to light-sensitive retinal cells

that stand together in the right kinds of relationships. In other words, surface colours are virtual properties.

Specifying virtual colours in this way, however, enables us to identify an important relationship between such virtual colours and what have standardly been known as 'colour qualia'. Qualia, I take it, are defined in the following way:

Qualia are the qualitative or phenomenal features of sense-experience in virtue of having which the sense-experiences resemble and differ from each other qualitatively in the ways that they do.

Defined in this way, their existence is controversial. Some philosophers find it obvious that they exist. Many of these would sympathise with C. I. Lewis, who wrote that only a madman could deny them. The more careful qualia-supporter would phrase this differently: I would have to be mad to deny that *I* experience them. Other philosophers, however, reject them or reduce them or eliminate them. It needs to be clear that it is *my* qualia (and *yours*) that these imperialists and carpetbaggers wish to reject or reduce or eliminate.

There are two significant characteristics of qualia as defined above. (1) They are universals or properties; what I experience are tokens or instances of qualia. (2) They are phenomenal features either of experi-

42

ences or of phenomenal objects. Given these two characteristics, it seems to me that we need a wider term than 'qualia'. Qualia are the qualitative features in virtue of having which objects (tokens) qualitatively resemble each other and differ from each other. We ought to define a wider term that leaves it open whether or not these qualitative features are features of *phenomenal* objects or experiences, or alternatively of *physical* events or states. Take colour, for example; it strikes me as obvious that the relations of similarities and differences that are said to hold between colour qualia *might* hold with respect to physical objects. It is commonly believed, and has at least initial plausibility, that there are objective physical states of objects that have the right kinds of features; that is, they qualitatively resemble each other and differ from each other in the right way. Even if it turns out to be false, this belief is plausible. And it requires argument to show that it is false.

Let us use the term 'open-qualia' to apply to those features which are so defined as to leave it open whether instantiations of them are physical or phenomenal. Let us use 'phenomenal qualia' to apply to the phenomenal features, if they exist. Clearly an instance of a phenomenal quale will also be an instance of an open-quale, but not vice versa.

In saying that it is possible that physical objects may be instances of colour qualia, I take myself to be stating as a possibility what many people take to be the truth. Most people would say that typically redness is a quality in (or possibly on) the surface of physical objects: it is an observable, objective feature (of things) in a public time and space. Some philosophers would, like Dummett, reject the claim that this reflects the natural view of colour, but as we saw in the last section, such a rejection is highly implausible.

But in any case it is not so much what people take to be the truth that is crucial. The point is that there is a set of practices whereby people order colour samples in systematic arrays. Whether the samples are lights or chips, they appear to have features that stand together as a whole in the relationships of similarities and differences that are alleged to characterise phenomenal qualia. It is this set of features that are open-qualia.

It should be pointed out that this 'natural view', according to which colours are both objective and are open-qualia, is not that view which Gareth Evans claimed to be unintelligible. Evans was wrong on this, but in any case the view he attacked is not the natural view. If I am right, the natural view is closer to Hering's view than to that of Descartes and Locke.

43

7. VIRTUAL COLOUR AND PHENOMENAL COLOUR

The right view of the natural concept of colour, which is not the same thing as the view of colour that unreflective people would give if asked, is given by the following. The term 'golden' that functions in sentences such as 'that sunset is golden', 'Michele's hair turned golden from grief', 'that jockey's silks are mostly golden', expresses a concept of the following kind:

(a) Golden is an open-quale of objects
(b) It is a property possessed by publicly accessible objects such as sunsets, hair, rings . . .

To these two conditions I would add a third:

(c) It plays a causal role in perceivers' perception, i.e. in their recognition and identification of the colour.

I have not presented any argument for making (c) a requirement. However, it is included here to foreshadow an argument presented in the following chapter. Of course for some people such an argument would be unnecessary. They would take such a condition to be obvious.

The force of (b) is that *golden* is the property possessed by objects that makes true such sentences as 'that sunset is golden'. This is the concept of 'golden' that is contained in the representational content of colour thoughts or colour judgements. That is, for sentences using 'golden' (red, yellow, blue . . .) it expresses what is understood by someone who has full understanding of the sentences. It is possible for a language-user to use the term without full understanding, as someone can use the term[26] 'gauss' without full understanding. (Only it is rarer for 'golden' than it is for 'gauss'.)

However, it turns out that nothing exemplifies this concept. Nothing has the colour property, so defined. This kind of colour is a virtual property, just as caloric and phlogiston are virtual natural kinds. Thus Descartes and Locke were only partly right when they claimed that

(i) Our visual experiences represent objects as having colours that they do not have;
(ii) The concept of the colour that objects are falsely represented as having is the concept of a feature or aspect of our experience.

They were right in the first claim but wrong in what they took the colour concept to be. That is, they were wrong about what the natural

---

26 Gauss is the centimetre-gramme-second unit of magnetic flux density.

concept is. Nevertheless they were on the right track. Their instincts were right. For after we have decided that the colours-as-they-are-represented are virtual properties, there is a lot of work still to do

(a) To explain why we have this concept;
(b) To explain why the concept is so valuable;
(c) To show us how to proceed: what is the right way to think of colour.

The key to these questions is the recognition that even if colour is a virtual property, there is a significant and important dispositional property: the power to induce sensory representations which represent objects as having (virtual) colours. Although objects do not have these virtual colours, it does not matter. At least for many purposes it does not matter. For these purposes, 'it is as if they had these colours'.

The answer to the third question is the most difficult to provide. To give it is one of the aims of the final two parts to this work, and I shall say no more here about it. The second question, to explain why the concept is valuable, is the easiest to answer. There are two major functions for colour concepts. One reflects an epistemological purpose: colours are signs used to indicate the presence of objects of interest. The purpose is equally well served even if objects do not have colours. All that is needed is that they are represented as having them. The second major purpose of colour concepts is aesthetic, understood in the widest sense. Colour is significant in painting, decorating, clothing, theatre, make-up, advertising, showing off, sexual appeal and so on. It matters not in the least that objects do not have these properties. All that is required is that they be represented as having them.

The first question is more difficult. To answer it we need to mount a story that provides the best explanation. One of the factors that constitute the virtual-colour concept is that colours are open-qualia. No physical features of physical bodies are in fact open-qualia. However, our sensory representations which represent virtual colours have features which are qualia. That is, they are phenomenal qualia. But of course, being phenomenal qualia they are also open-qualia. It is because we experience these phenomenal qualia in a three-dimensional space and on the basis of this experience judge that, say, this watermelon is green or that that sunset is red and so on, that our concepts of green, red, brown, etc., contain the quale element. Contrary to what some philosophers believe, there is no more problem in experiencing phenomenal qualities in such a way than there is in feeling a pain in a foot or an elbow. However what prevents the quale element in the virtual-colour concept from

45

being a phenomenal-quale element, that is, what makes it an open-quale element, is that in the case of colour we are not, normally, naively, aware of the phenomenal feature as phenomenal. We take colour to be an objective quality of physical objects.

This explains why the quale element belongs to the virtual-colour concept. What explains the contribution of the other components? To explain them we need to reject any notion that our story is committed to concept empiricism. Descartes was not. If Locke was, he was not consistently so. But in any case the important point is that the representationalist does not need to be committed to it. The right answer is something like this. When my visual experiences represent to me three-dimensional objects located in time and space, it is to a conscious person with developed conceptual resources and powers that they represent such objects. That person is also someone who has (possibly limited) command of a language with which he communicates with his fellows. The explanation of the contribution of these elements to the concept requires placing perceivers within the matrix of conceptual practices that they share with other perceivers. The right account of this matrix will, I suggest, be heavily indebted to the kind of story told by Gareth Evans.[27] Where I differ, crucially, from him is about the place in the story that I want to establish for phenomenal experience.[28] In the next two chapters I shall draw upon Evans's account to sustain the theory of colour that I have proposed here.

8. REVIEW

We are now in a position to provide a reconstruction of the view on colour in the Descartes-Locke tradition. Central to that tradition were two theses about colour:

(i) That it is important to draw a distinction between
    (a) Colour-as-it-is-in-experience and
    (b) Colour-as-it-is-in-physical-objects
(ii) 'An error theory', as a theory of normal perception

The colour-as-it-is-in-experience is thought of in subjective terms, as a quality of an experience or sensation. The colour that is in physical objects is nothing but a power or disposition to excite the first kind of

---

27 Gareth Evans (1982), *The Varieties of Reference*, Oxford: Clarendon.
28 I should add that the account of perception developed by Moreland Perkins (1983) sits very easily with the account of colour set out here.

colour experience – or as it is sometimes put, a power to appear in characteristic ways to perceivers.

How the error theory should be interpreted is controversial. The best way of making sense of it is in terms suggested by Descartes's use of 'representations'. These terms were used in the last chapter, where I provided a reconstruction of the Descartes-Locke position on ideas or representations of colour. This account stresses that in thinking about sensory ideas or sensory representations we need to distinguish two aspects of these items. First, the ideas or representations have a certain content; they represent something. Second, they have certain qualities, by virtue of which they do the representing. Accordingly, when we think of an idea of colour we need to distinguish between

(i) Colour-as-it-is-represented
(ii) Colour-as-it-is-in-experience

According to Locke and Descartes, colour-as-it-is-represented takes different forms, depending on whether one is a naive perceiver or a sophisticated perceiver. For the naive person it is simply the same as colour-as-it-is-in-experience. For the sophisticated person it is a power to produce colour-as-it-is-in-experience.

This means that in order to clarify the Descartes-Locke view we have to recognise, in addition to the two kinds of colour identified above, (a) and (b), a third kind of colour:

(c) Colour-as-it-is-represented-in-physical-objects

With respect to (c), we need moreover to distinguish between a confused representation and a clear one:

(c_1) The colour represented is the same as that in (a), i.e. the same as as colour-as-it-is-in-experience
(c_2) The colour represented is a power to produce colour-as-it-is-in-experience

The view of colour which this description of the confused representation is meant to capture is thought to be the 'natural view' of colour, the mistaken view that we are in the grip of as unreflective colour-perceivers. Our visual experiences, it is claimed, represent objects in the world as having properties that they do not have: colour properties. Thus we have an 'error theory' of colour.

Whereas Descartes and Locke are right in holding the error theory, or some version of it, there is something wrong in their formulation of it. We need to modify what they say in order to come up with the right formulation. It needs to be stressed that 'colour-as-it-is-represented' can

47

only be represented for a perceiver with appropriate cognitive powers. The right way to characterise colour-as-it-is-represented, at least in the naive form, is to say that colour is represented as a primary quality, i.e. as an intrinsic quality of surfaces that has a characteristic appearance (as do shapes) and that has appropriate causal powers (as do shapes). Our visual experience represents objects as having such colour qualities, just as it represents them as having shapes and sizes. It turns out, however, that objects do not have any such colour qualities. Instead they have shapes, sizes and textures and a wide set of causal powers.

Accordingly we can improve on their position (that is, on my first reconstruction of it) by modifying the sense of colour as it is expressed in (c_1). I think that their specification of (c_1) is incomplete. It needs filling out by saying that this conception of colour, the colour that experience represents objects as having, is a property that has three aspects to it:

(C_1^*) Colour is an intrinsic nonrelational property of objects (e.g. of surfaces) which has the following features:
   (a) It is an open-quale
   (b) It is the property possessed by objects which makes true the colour-sentences
   (c) It plays the right causal role in the perceiver's recognition and identification of colour

From this characterisation it follows that colour is an intrinsic nonrelational property which:

(i) Appears in a way characteristic of colours
(ii) Plays an appropriate causal role vis-à-vis that characteristic way of appearing

This characterisation of colour as a primary quality is a description of the naive version of 'colour-as-it-is-represented'. Physical objects do not possess these colour qualities, but for many purposes this does not matter. For even if they do not have the properties, they appear to have them. For many purposes, *it is as if they have* these qualities. For those purposes, appearing to have the colour qualities is just as good as really having them. For these reasons, it is possible to formulate a more sophisticated concept of colour: colour as a disposition to appear in the appropriate way. It is the use of the sophisticated concept, for example, that allows us to say that the following sentences which ascribe colours to physical objects are true: lettuce is green, dirt in Kalgoorlie is red, skies in Wiluna are always blue, the moon tonight is yellow, the Perth sunset last night was golden and so on.

48

Given these modifications, there is still a role for colour-as-it-is-in-experience or phenomenal colour to play, but it is not the role envisaged by Descartes and Locke. It is not, as they supposed, that our visual experience represents physical objects as having the same colour that is intrinsic to our visual experience. Rather physical objects are represented as having intrinsic colour properties which, it turns out, are virtual properties. Nevertheless it is part of the correct explanation for why the concept of the (virtual) property has the character that it does that the visual experiences have the character that they do. The phenomenal relationships that form part of the virtual concept do not hold true of any physical properties, but they do hold true of aspects of our visual experiences.

The relationship between colour-as-it-is-in-experience and the virtual-colour properties is as follows. It is through experiencing colour-as-it-is-in-experience that one typically believes physical objects to be coloured. Colours-in-experience represent for me virtual colours. They do so by having certain of the features that one takes virtual colours to have. It is because the phenomenal colours, the reds, pinks, whites, oranges, etc., stand in certain relations to each other that the virtual colours stand in similar relations. Unlike virtual colours, phenomenal colours do not have the causal features that virtual colours would have if they existed.

3

What colours are essentially

Opposition to the Descartes-Locke tradition comes from a variety of quarters. Of particular interest are two rival views which, despite their differences, share an important assumption. The first treats colour as an objective physical property: possibly relational and dispositional and certainly complex. The second treats colour as a dispositional property, the power to appear in certain distinctive ways to perceivers of the appropriate kind. According to this approach, the natural concept of colour is a concept of this dispositional property. Clearly with such an approach one is rejecting the Descartes-Locke account of the natural view of colour. Although it is not so obvious, it is also the case that the objectivist essentialist account should be understood as presupposing a rival account of the natural concept. (It needs to be distinguished from a revisionary objectivist account.)

In this chapter I propose to examine these two rivals to the Descartes-Locke tradition, arguing that neither is adequate as providing an account of the natural concept of colour.

1. WHAT IS A THEORY OF COLOUR?

One form the opposition to the Descartes-Locke tradition takes is derived from a rival tradition which favours an objectivist analysis of colour: redness, for example, is that objective physical property which objects have and which, as it happens, causes them to appear in the distinctive way characteristic of red bodies. It is interesting and somewhat paradoxical that each tradition draws much of its appeal from scientific considerations. The subjectivist analysis draws strength from the fact that physics, the most advanced and fundamental science, has increasingly found less place for colour. On the other hand, the objectivists can legitimately point to the fact that colour vision is a biological endowment not only for humans but for many other animal species. It seems plausible that if we possess colour vision and if we have evolved to possess it, then there is some objective feature in the world that colour vision picks up. That is, it is plausible that our colour vision is colour-catching (and not colour-generating).

Not all philosophers on colour appeal to science, however. There has flourished for a long time a defence of the dispositional analysis that appeals to conceptual considerations. That different groups of philosophers appeal to quite different considerations raises some questions about what exactly a theory of colour is, and of how philosophical and scientific accounts of colour are meant to mesh. Before proceeding we ought to pay some attention to considering the kind of question a theory of colour is intended to answer and the kind of answer that will be acceptable. The question is often presented in the form: what kind of property is colour? or: what are colours essentially? or: what is the nature of colour? What is not so clear is what will count as an acceptable answer. Some philosophers, e.g. Gareth Evans, John McDowell and Colin McGinn, defend their thesis that colours are dispositional by claiming that in order for someone to grasp the concept *red*, say, one has to understand that red things are things with the power to be experienced in a certain sort of way.[1] Jonathan Westphal, on the other hand, defends an objectivist account of colour by arguing that to give the proper answer to the question requires giving the real definition of, say, white, i.e. providing an account of what the essential properties of white are, in the way that scientists have provided an account of the essential characteristics of gold and water.[2]

On the face of it, it looks as if these different groups of philosophers are engaged on different projects: one seeking the kind of understanding a person must have who possesses the concept *red*; the other seeking the real essence of redness – that which makes red things red. Perhaps these projects can be brought together without paradox. Perhaps they cannot. There is an important issue at stake here about the nature of meaning.

As a first approximation, these two projects can be brought into harmony if we see them in terms of the Fregean sense-reference distinction. Evans's project involves delineating the sense of colour terms, i.e. describing the concept of colour informing standard competent linguistic usage. Westphal's project can be understood as that of identifying the reference for each colour predicate, i.e. the property that competent

---

1 G. Evans (1980); McDowell (1985); McGinn (1983).   2 Westphal (1991).

linguistic speakers/hearers conceptualise, in the way described by Evans and similar philosophers. That is, just as in the case of singular terms where we can distinguish between an object and a person's conceptualisation of that object by means of the singular term, so we can distinguish between the property objects have and language-users' conceptualisation of that property.

That, at least, is a first approximation. To do better we can modify Westphal's attempt by remedying his fault of *assuming* that colours are natural kinds and hence that the real definitions of colour terms need to be given in terms of the relevant natural kinds. For there are some linguistic expressions for which the essential definition and sense are identical (or at least intimately related). Examples are those terms that are defined functionally: poison, ship, golf-ball, novel, marriage, king, fashionable, envy, malice and so on.

To give an account of what colour is essentially requires first locating the concept of colour that one is trying to give an account of. One can of course stipulate that what I mean by 'colour' is an objective physical property, or one can stipulate that by 'colour' I mean that physical concept that physicists have worked with. But to do that is to give up the attempt to give an account of what colour vision involves and of the role colour and colour concepts play in the lives of ordinary colour-perceivers and users of colour language.

I take it that debates about what colour is essentially are debates about what properties or features are essential to that kind of colour that ordinary colour concepts pick out. We all agree that tomatoes are red, ripe bananas are yellow and brilliant sunsets are golden or reddish golden, and we want to know in what these colours – red, yellow, reddish golden and so on – consist. The relevant concept of colour is one expressed in the practices and language use of ordinary people. To say this, however, is to leave it open that scientists may be the ones to tell us what colour is essentially, just as, so Kripke and Putnam suggest, scientists have told us what water and gold are essentially.[3] In the case of water and gold it is held that our ordinary concepts of water and gold contain an implicit reference to the relevant natural kinds: that the ordinary concept contains a place to be filled in by discoveries by the relevant experts. This account seems to be a coherent one, even though it is not clear that it fits colour. Another possibility is that the ordinary concept

3 S. Kripke (1980), *Naming and Necessity*, 2nd ed., Cambridge: Harvard U.P.; H. Putnam (1977), 'Meaning and Reference', in Stephen Schwartz (ed.), *Naming, Necessity and Natural Kinds*, London: Cornell U.P.

of colour is confused or, if not confused, contains some kind of serious mistake. It seems to me that this is the view of philosophers such as Descartes and Locke, and more recently John Mackie.[4] Again I find this also a possible account. It seems to me to be an open question whether the right account is along the lines of the Putnam-Kripke model or the error theory or some other. At least prior to further important considerations, it is open. I should add that, just as Descartes emphasised, to hold that colour perception involves some kind of mistake does not mean that on that score it is useless. Descartes's claim is that the mistakes are systematic ones and that, for most human purposes (and likewise for those of nonhumans), the systematic mistakes do not undermine those purposes: indeed, they may well serve to make things work better.

If I am right, then this means that the sort of project engaged in by Evans (and others) may also need modifying. His aim is to delineate the kind of understanding a person must have who possesses the concept *red*. It could be, however, that the way a particular term operates within a language involves a complex interplay between levels of concept and levels of understanding. Just possibly, the meaning of a term could be given by its role within a network of intercommunicating speakers, a role that individual speakers/hearers can contribute to without understanding the role (at least without understanding it fully). To illustrate, take the term 'pain'. Let us suppose that pain is defined essentially by its occupying a certain causal role. Even if this is true, we could well have a community of language-users who communicated about pains, both their own and others', without understanding that this was what pain was. They could be a community of Cartesians who thought of pains as inner mental states for which good arguments by analogy could be provided. These Cartesians offer and accept public criteria for ascribing pains, but they misdescribe and misconceive (let us suppose) the role of these criteria. (They suffer from false consciousness about pains.) Similarly, if Berkeley is right we could say the same thing about physical-object terms such as 'apple', 'mountain', 'chair'. Similarly about 'God' if Feuerbach is right; similarly about moral terms if MacIntyre[5] is right or if Hume (in a different way) is right. Obviously there are limits to how thoroughgoing such misconceptions can be, but it does seem possible that for many properties, there can be (degrees of) false consciousness. Whatever is true for political properties, colour is just such a case.

4 J. Mackie (1976), *Problems from Locke,* Oxford: O.U.P., pp. 10–36.
5 A. MacIntyre (1984), *After Virtue,* 2nd ed., Notre Dame: U. of Notre Dame Press, esp. chs. 1 and 2.

2. COLOURS AS NATURAL KINDS

Many philosophers who argue for the objectivist account argue that we should aim to do for colour what scientists have done for such natural kinds as gold and water. As far as gold is concerned, science has been used to tell us what the nature of gold is, what gold essentially is – namely, what its atomic structure is. Of course, prior to making this discovery people used gold, recognised gold, referred to gold, lusted after gold and killed for it. The concept of gold that informed their thought and their practices was something like this:

> Gold is that substance or natural kind, whichever it is, that is the causal basis for the characteristics by which we recognise gold.

Some of the characteristics are its colour, its density, its metallic feel and so on. In a similar spirit, objectivists about colour have urged that we should regard colour in the same way as we have regarded gold. The colour red, for example, should be regarded as

> that feature of physical bodies that is the causal basis for the way those bodies appear – e.g. for the ways characteristic of red objects.

On this account, what the colour red essentially is, i.e. the nature of redness, is given by an account of a certain physical feature that physical objects – tomatoes, robins, wines, blushing faces, rubies – have, and that we use our visual experiences to pick out.

One philosopher who argues in this way is Jonathan Westphal, in his book *Colour*. Whiteness, he argues, is essentially high diffuse reflectance: it is the ability of surfaces to reflect a high proportion of incident illumination. Greyness and blackness, he maintains, can be given similar essential definitions. So too, eventually, might the chromatic colours.[6]

I agree that we should aim to provide an account of the nature of colours, i.e. of what colours are essentially – but we should be alert to the possibility that there is more than one model for giving accounts of what a property is essentially. More positively, I want to argue that the model used for gold and other natural kinds is not appropriate for colour.

That the natural-kind model is not the only possible model is a point familiar both in the philosophy of mind and in thinking about social contexts. What makes certain things the things they are is the functional role they play. *What a table* is essentially is given *by its aptness for serving*

6 Westphal (1991), ch. 2, esp. pp. 15–28.

certain purposes (what, for Aristotle, was its form). The functional role can be defined in two ways: either in terms of the object's causal powers, i.e. it is a causal function, or alternatively in terms of the purposes or uses it standardly has. What a poison is essentially, what makes something count as a poison, is its aptness for causing damage to an organism. What counts as a traffic light or a traffic signal, on the other hand, is determined by the use to which it is put.

The difference between the two ways of saying what a thing is essentially can be illustrated by the two concepts 'temperature' and 'thermometer'. Being in a certain temperature state (say, 60 °C) is being in that state which we normally identify by use of thermometers and which, in the case of gases, happens to be the average kinetic energy of the constituent molecules. Temperature is essentially the kinetic-energy state.

What a thermometer is essentially is something quite different. In order to be a thermometer, a device must have two sorts of features:

(i) It must be capable of acquiring states that are causally correlated with temperature states of other bodies, at least in certain ranges;
(ii) It must be such that it is convenient to be used by humans.

What governs the second kind of feature is, first, the types of objects whose temperature people wish to discover, e.g., human blood, daytime ambience, and second, people's capacities for reading the thermometer.

What makes something count as a thermometer is its having those features that make it apt for a certain use: being used to measure temperature. What it is essentially is determined by its aptness for measuring temperature, and although it would not be apt unless it had certain features which resulted in certain of its states' being correlated with appropriate temperature states, its being apt is a different property from its having those features. For one thing, different thermometers can have very different sets of relevant features.

The reason why we treat the concepts 'temperature' and 'thermometer' differently rests on our having different interests and purposes. In both cases, certain features provide the underlying causal basis appropriate for a correct application of the terms 'temperature' and 'thermometer': it is because of our interest in the causal powers of temperature that we regard temperature as essentially that causal basis; it is because of our interest in *discovering* the temperature of bodies that we regard the aptness for measuring temperature as essential in the case of thermometers.

Our social life depends heavily on the use of concepts like that of 'thermometer': table, chair, fashionable, polite, warning, traffic signal, golf stick, policeman, lawyer, bus and square-leg umpire. Take a term such as 'fashionable'. Articles of clothing, hairstyles, ideas, singers and politicians become fashionable and then decidedly not. What makes something count as fashionable is obviously complex, but it is tied up with attitudes toward and the social roles of clothing, hairstyles, ideas etc. Certainly to be fashionable a thing must have some feature in virtue of which it is fashionable, but what this means is that that thing has some feature which makes it apt, in the circumstances, for inspiring a certain social attitude. Wearing purple flared trousers made me very fashionable in the seventies but would incite quite different attitudes now.

My account of terms that express social concepts such as being fashionable, being a thermometer and being a table is that these are not pure dispositional terms but rather are to be thought of as follows:

For X to be fashionable is for X to have some feature which makes X apt for serving such-and-such a role (purpose, use etc.).

In other words, X must have both intrinsic and relational features, but what is essential to its being fashionable is its aptness for the relevant role.

It is therefore a mistake to assume, as Westphal does, that the Kripke-Putnam model applies generally and therefore to colours. He does claim to argue that whiteness is essentially high diffuse reflectance, but he assumes without argument that some version of the Putnam-Kripke theory must be right.

How do we determine the success of a reference in a possible world? Let us consider in outline Putnam's well-known proposal for determining the referent of a term like 'water' in possible worlds. Take this – we point at a good sample of water in the actual world, and call it w^1. Now there is something which *explains* the typical properties or stereotype that a sample such as w^1 has – that it is clear, drinkable, freezes at a certain temperature under such and such conditions, and so forth. Call this something N for nature. Putnam's proposal is that w^2, a sample of something in a possible world called W_2, is water if it has N, whether or not w^2 has the same stereotype as w^1 does in W_1, the actual world.[7]

He argues that since in this world high diffuse reflectance of white objects explains all the typical properties of white, then it is the real essence of whiteness.

To argue this way, however, is to assume that the Putnam-Kripke theory is the *only* theory of real essences; in short, that whiteness is a

7 Ibid., p. 41.

natural kind. The point is, however, that whether or not terms such as 'water', 'poison', 'table', 'whiteness', 'solubility', and 'conductivity' refer to that which explains the properties of the stereotype or 'typical properties' is determined by the *intentions* of the relevant linguistic community – even if the intentions are 'intentions', i.e. specified in something like Locke's myth about Adam[8] or W. Sellars' myth about Jones[9] or Putnam-Kripke's about dubbing ceremonies or baptisms.[10] The intention may be that 'gold' refers to that which explains the stereotypical properties, or it could be that the term essentially picks out dispositional or functional properties. There is without doubt a causal explanation for why, say, toadstools are poisonous for humans and mushrooms are not, but being poisonous is not constituted by having that property that explains why toadstools are poisonous. It is easy to imagine a world in which toadstools are not poisonous for humans and mushrooms are – i.e. the stereotype fits mushrooms in that world and not toadstools. In that world, toadstools have ceased to be poisonous.

What form our intentions take depends on our interests and purposes. This can be brought out even by considering science, which provides the best examples fitting the Putnam-Kripke model. There are many important terms even in the most fundamental sciences where what the term picks out is not the basis for a disposition but the power or disposition itself. Examples are expressions such as 'electrical resistance', 'electrical conductor' and 'electrical insulator': to be an electrical conductor is to be something that has the power to conduct electricity. Other cases are 'force' and 'potential'. Perhaps the best example, however, is 'impenetrability': it seems to be a fact about material objects that they hinder the approach of other material objects. This may even be one of the essential marks of a material object. (See Frank Jackson for a good discussion.)[11] Whether or not there is a causal basis for this power, and whether or not there is only one kind of basis (which is unlikely), impenetrability is an important characteristic that we want to know about. Examples such as these show that we should not assume without argument that colours are natural kinds and not dispositions. In some cases the power or disposition is of far greater significance than the basis for the power (if any or if several).

---

8 Locke (1961), Book III, ch. 6, paragraphs 44–51.
9 Sellars (1963), pp. 177–80.
10 Kripke (1980), p. 96.
11 F. Jackson (1977), *Perception: A Representative Theory*, Cambridge: CUP, pp. 130–3.

3. ESSENTIAL DEFINITIONS OF COLOUR

Westphal's account of colour is based on the assumptions that colours form natural kinds and that an account of the nature of colours is one that provides a real definition of colour. Unlike other objectivists with whom he would seem to have much in common, such as D. M. Armstrong,[12] he sees the best candidates for real definitions, at least for colours of surfaces, to lie in the light-modifying powers of objects rather than in intrinsic features of the surfaces.

Gareth Evans, in company with many others, offers what seems to be a very different account of colour:

We allow and seem obliged to allow that a knowledge of what it is for something to be red consists in, or at least requires the capacity to tell, by looking at it, whether or not it is red.

He says of someone who has learned a colour word in the standard way that he will have a capacity to recognise the colour when presented with it, although he will have many other ways of identifying it.

But it is to the colour he is disposed to identify on sight that we attach dominant weight in considering which colour he has in mind.[13]

One important difference between these two accounts (Westphal's and Evans's) is that, according to the former, the colour objects appear to have merely serves to fix the reference for such colour terms as 'yellow', 'blue,' etc., and does not define the colours essentially, whereas on Evans's account the way an object appears does define the term essentially. For Westphal it is possible to have a distinction between fool's red and real red; for Evans no such possibility is allowed.

Westphal assumes that colour predicates fit the Kripke-Putnam model for natural-kind terms such as 'gold', 'water', 'tiger' etc. On the face of it, Evans seems to be presupposing a different role for colour predicates. In this section I want to explore some areas in the topic of meaning in order to clarify the role of colour predicates in the language.

The difference, at least in aim, between Evans and Westphal may be more apparent than real. Evans also subscribes to something resembling the Kripke-Putnam model of meaning for natural-kind terms and, like Kripke and Putnam, draws a parallel between the role of proper names

---

12 D. M. Armstrong (1969), 'Colour-Realism and the Argument from Microscopes' in R. Brown and C. D. Rollins (eds.), *Contemporary Philosophy in Australia*, London: Allen and Unwin, pp. 119–31.
13 Evans (1980), p. 272, p. 270.

and the role of natural-kind terms such as 'elm', 'leopard', etc. Evans's account, however, has an important advantage. He makes explicit the role of sense in both name-using practices and natural-kind-term-using practices, and provides a theoretical account of its role. The role of sense is present in both Kripke's and Putnam's account, but it is less theoretically developed. In the appendix to this chapter I provide a more detailed account of the differences between Evans's account and that of Putnam and Kripke. In so doing I discuss how the accounts apply to the case of 'yellowness'. Very briefly whereas Kripke argues that predicates such as 'yellow' have a referential component, Evans's account provides a mechanism for how sense helps secure reference.

That acknowledging the importance of sense can make a difference can be seen if we examine the passage in which Westphal introduces Putnam's proposal for determining the referent of the term 'water':

It is that set of properties that 'explains the typical properties or stereotype that a sample of water has: it is clear, drinkable, freezes at a certain temperature under such and such conditions and so forth'.[14]

As it stands, this proposal has an important ambiguity: either the explanatory basis is the referent of 'water' because it is the *intention* of language-users that the referent be the explanatory basis for the stereotype, or the explanatory basis is the referent of water, *irrespective of the intentions* of language-users.

The account provided by Evans is one in which the intention is important. The explanatory basis is the referent, all right, but its being the referent works, as it were, only via the intentions of language-users. Some support for this position can be found in Kripke. In his discussion of tigers and whether animals having the normal characteristics of tigers but lacking their internal structure would be tigers, he argues that they would not. The reason, he says, is not because the old concept of tiger has been replaced by a new scientific definition:

I think this is true of the concept of tiger *before* the internal structure of tigers has been investigated. Even though we don't *know* the internal structure of tigers, we suppose – and let us suppose that we are right – that tigers form a certain species or natural kind.[15]

The point is that what will make something count as the referent of a term will only work against the backdrop of a framework of intentions,

14 Westphal (1991), p. 41.   15 Kripke (1980), pp. 120–1.

beliefs and thoughts. On the causal theory of reference for a name, either of an individual or of a natural kind, the referent is determined as 'that . . . which stands in a causal relation to appropriate uses of the name'. Setting aside definite descriptions, there seem to be two principal ways, normally, that we have for fixing the reference for a name: (i) the referent is named in a dubbing or baptism ceremony; (ii) the individual or natural kind is known to a privileged group of participants in the practice in a certain way, one in which the individual or kind plays a causal role vis-à-vis the uses of the name. In both of these ways the intentions of the community of speakers/hearers are important.

In thinking of the initial (hypothetical) act of dubbing samples of 'gold', say, we think of the initial language-user intending, and importantly *being taken as intending,* that 'gold' name a certain natural kind. It is only if language-users believe that there are natural kinds and also believe that in that situation they have samples of a natural kind (and not a sample of a mixture) and intend 'gold' to name that natural kind, can the dubbing ceremony fix the reference. It may be that other participants in the 'gold'-using practice don't have to confront the same samples as the dubbers, or to have the same stereotype of gold, but one thing they must share with the dubbers (if they are to have understanding) is the assumption that gold is a natural kind.

As things stand, it is plausible that 'gold', 'water', 'oxygen', 'leopard' etc. name natural kinds, but this reflects beliefs and practices of language-users which might very well have been different. As Putnam himself pointed out in a later variation on his twin-earth example, water might in fact be a mixture of alcohol and H_2O (20%/80%), and the term 'water' might be used to refer to that mixture rather than to any natural kind. Likewise the term 'air' in common usage surely refers to a certain mixture of gases O_2, N and CO_2 (of varying proportions). Among phlogiston chemists 'air' was not the name of a natural kind; rather it was something of which there could be different kinds (it was similar to 'gas', 'solid', 'liquid', 'metal', 'vapour' and so on).

As for names of natural kinds, so for ordinary proper names. At the baptism of a child, when someone says 'I dub thee "Moses"', she intends to name a certain individual belonging to a certain kind of individuals, and not any of a whole string of other possible name-bearers: child-while-in-the-basket, child-for-this-day, child-until-puberty, the body of the child (rather than the child person) and so on.

Turning from dubbing or baptismal ceremonies to the other important way in which the reference of a name is fixed, it would appear again that intentions are important. One of the ways is described by Evans: the referent of *NN* in a name-using practice is that person known to a special group of participants in the practice – producers – as *NN*. What this means is that the producers recognise a certain person as the same person as *NN*. Here the referent plays a causal role vis-à-vis the uses of the name on behalf of the privileged sub-group of the community. It is necessary that there be a place for such uses and such causal roles, since baptismal ceremonies are in many cases nonexistent; and secondly, the practice over a period of time may change in such a way that a different referent comes to be named. Not all participants in the name-using practice are producers; some are consumers, but what consumers must understand is that there are or have been producers to whom the individual is known. The important point is that the producers must know or recognise, and be so understood by those who understand their name-using utterances, a given individual as the *same person* or the *same natural kind,* or whatever, as encountered previously.

Thinking about how Evans's model is applied to the use of names for singular objects reveals how the model could be extended to cover colour predicates and colour properties. In a name-using practice, a certain name can be understood to refer to a certain individual or natural kind which the producers in the practice *recognise* as the same individual or natural kind. Likewise a certain predicate, say, 'yellow', can be understood to express a certain property: one which producers *recognise* as being the same property.

The property (or instances of it) plays a causal role in the person's recognition, but there are two aspects to the practice: (a) the causal role and (b) the recognition of the same property. Redness according to this account is essentially a kind of property that can be recognised as red and plays a causal role in its being recognised.

On this view, redness is not just a property that, as it happens, appears a certain way. The appearance has an essential role to play. There are certain linguistic practices using colour terms. Using such colour terms with full understanding requires knowing which properties redness, yellowness, etc., are. Knowing which property redness is involves having the ability to recognise objects as red. Redness is a property which plays a causal role via this recognition in the application of the colour concepts.

If I am right, then a contrast drawn by Westphal in his book on colours is misplaced. Westphal sets out to solve a set of puzzles proposed by Wittgenstein by giving real definitions of colours, definitions which state what the colour is or what being coloured is, and 'not definitions of the words which are their names'.[16] By contrast Bernard Harrison in his *Form and Content*, though he attempts to answer the question 'what are colours?', is said by Westphal to address a different topic: what he asks is a question about colour concepts or categories, i.e. what we do with words.[17]

This, however, is a false contrast. Even with a natural kind such as gold, giving an essential definition of gold is not something completely divorced from the question of what our concept of gold is. Drawing a contrast between the essential definition of 'gold' and the essential definition for 'adultery' (or 'fashionable') is drawing a contrast that can be made within a framework in which the concept of gold is a very different kind of concept from that of adultery. The chemist can only come up with an essential definition for gold if she has the appropriate concept of gold that allows a place for a suitable essential definition – even if it should turn out eventually that the chemist has to replace current concepts with new ones.

4. ARE APPEARANCES ESSENTIAL TO COLOUR?

The theory of meaning developed by Evans requires the appreciation of a delicate interplay between Fregean sense and reference. One of the things it allows for is that the way colours appear is crucial to colour names naming the properties that they do. However, for all that I have argued, it is possible that an alternative way works for colour predicates. It could be, that is, that for these predicates, as for others, the appearance can be used to secure the reference, but only in an accidental way. The model for how this can be done is exhibited by "gold". The way gold appears is usually taken as picking out a natural kind, one that constitutes gold, but in a nonessential way. It is possible to show, however, that this is not a good model for understanding colour predicates.

Traditionally colour is defined by the way it appears. Putting it another way, colours are recognised by the way things appear. One tells that something is red or yellow or green by looking. There are no colour thermometers or colour sticks to help one measure the colour of bodies. It is true that certain conditions are better for identifying colours than others – daylight is better than dusk, and (usually) sunlight better than shade – and some people are better than others. In vague terms we can

16 L. Wittgenstein (1977), *Remarks on Colour*, ed. G. E. M. Anscombe, trans. L. L. McAlister and M. Schattle, Oxford: Blackwell, esp. pp. 3–6; Westphal (1991), pp. 2–3.
17 Harrison (1973); Westphal (1991), p. 6.

pick out standard conditions and normal observers, although these may vary from one context to another. The best conditions for evaluating the colour of the stars or of fireflies occur at nighttime, and of coral-sea fish, below the sea surface.

This in itself doesn't tell us anything special about colours. After all, temperature thermometers are relatively recent inventions. Not so long ago people told how hot it was by how it felt (although against this, they could also tell by how the flowers drooped or the haze shimmered or the eggs frizzled). We need to answer the question whether for colour we could find a property analogous to temperature such that we could devise a colour thermometer. If so, we would expect to find, just as we have for feelings of warmth, that there are some objects which *appear* to be the same colour (even to standard observers) but *really* are not.

One would not expect the colour thermometer to disagree wildly with the judgements of standard, nondefective observers. If that happened it would indicate that what the thermometer was measuring was some other property than colour. Still, so the story would run, the colour thermometers would be the more accurate devices, and the colour perceptions of, say, humans just rough-and-ready guides to be overruled on occasions of conflict by the standardised international colour thermometer.

It is almost universally recognised that this story is a fantasy. There is no hope of doing for colour what has been done for temperature and for length. This is because of the fact that, apart from a very specialised domain, colours have no significant causal powers. There are no significant causal laws governing colour. There are no causal powers that things which are blue have in common, and which moreover enable us to distinguish them from things which are yellow or are green and so on. There are, it is true, some causal truths which include colour terms, such as that ripening pears (or wheat-sheaves) go from green to yellow, spiders with red stripes are venomous and so on, but these either describe colours as effects or alternatively are cases where both the colour and the causal effect are effects of some other causal factor.

Still, I have admitted that there is a specialised domain in which colours do seem to exercise causal powers, namely the domain where coloured things have causal effects on colour perceivers: human beings and a range of other organisms. This has led some philosophers, e.g. D. R. Hilbert, to espouse anthropocentric realism, according to which colour is an objective property of objects, albeit a complex and rather strange property, which has few systematic causal effects except on

63

human perceivers and hence is of very little interest except insofar as it has those effects. Given that there is such an objective, albeit idiosyncratic, property, we might reasonably expect to be able to construct colour thermometers that could mimic the responses of human perceivers and provide measurements of the colours of these objects.

What this account overlooks, however, are certain facts about the role colours play, facts which mark colours out as rather special. To appreciate the significance of these facts, we need to pay attention to some of the central features of the Putnam-Kripke account of real definitions.[18]

Kripke and Putnam developed their theories of meaning for such terms as 'gold and 'water'. The idea is that the use of these terms is such that they are intended to refer to natural kinds and to be able to do so in contexts in which none of the language-users know which natural kinds they are. Typically language-users are able to identify an object as gold by means of its appearance, or possibly by some way it has of behaving, but these identifying characteristics are not taken to be essential properties. Those that are essential are those required to define the substance as a natural kind, e.g. atomic number (as it turns out).

One implication of this account is that it is possible for there to be something which counts as fool's gold, i.e., that has the appearance of gold but is not. Likewise if we gave the same kind of account for colours as for gold, then it would be possible for us to discover that there is something such as fool's yellow, fool's blue and so on: something that appeared yellow but was not. (This may sound innocuous enough. It is not. The suggestion is that something should pass all the tests we currently have for deciding it is yellow but that it should turn out not to be yellow.) Indeed, all the objects in the world might change the colours they appear to be but not change colour at all.

The way the Putnam-Kripke account is set up, the way an object appears does not count as one of its essential properties. That is a reasonable approach to take for certain kinds of objects, e.g. natural kinds, where our interests largely lie with their causal properties and powers. It is certainly the case for molybdenum and lead and sucrose. It may even be the case for gold and water. With respect to the latter, it is true that we are interested in their causal powers, and it is true both that they are natural kinds and that we are interested in them as natural kinds. It is, however, at least possible that we should want to distinguish between water-as-a-natural-kind and water-defined-socially, just as we

18 I also take up Hilbert's proposal in Chapter 6, esp. Section 9.

may want to say that what counts as a man or a woman or as a human being differs for different contexts, depending on whether we are interested in biological facts or social-cultural facts – or to take a less controversial example, just as we may wish to distinguish between a biological father and a social father.

Likewise there might be some kinds, unlike natural kinds such as electron or molybdenum, where appearance is an essential property. Being handsome and ugly are two examples. So too are being dreamlike, being demonic-looking, being panoramic and so on. I suggest that colours such as yellow, brown, olive, turquoise, blue, purple, white, black and so on form just such another set of properties for which appearance is essential. Yellow objects have a characteristic appearance that marks them off from those that are blue, green or white. It is, I claim, essential to something's being yellow that it has just such an appearance. It is moreover by having that appearance and by the fact that red, chartreuse, orange, white, etc. have their respective appearances that we can say that yellow is closer to orange than to red or to blue, that a vivid yellow is closer to white than a vivid blue, that pink is closer both to white and to grey than is a deep, rich red and so on. Or, putting it in brief, it is because colours appear the way they do that we can form three-dimensional colour arrays having the structure and character that they do.

It is true that we can construct three-dimensional colour arrays by physical and psychophysical means, but these arrays have a character and structure different to that of the colour arrays constructed by reference to the way colours appear. The fact that there are these different kinds of colour systems, defined by appearance or by psychophysical means, needs of course to be explained. On my account according to which appearance is essential to colour, there are two ways to explain it. Either we can say that there are different kinds of colour – psychophysical colour, colour-as-it-appears and possibly physical colour – or we can say that colour-as-it-appears is the primary kind of colour and that there are secondary or derivative kinds of colour, e.g. psychophysical colour, physical colour.

Why do I say that the way it appears is essential to something's having the colour that it does? To answer that requires asking ourselves what role colour plays in our lives. Why care about the colours of objects? Oversimplifying, there are two major reasons. First, colours serve as signs or as indicators. They enable us to identify an object, to sort it out from its background and to reidentify something as the same object or of the

65

same kind, as a peach or a ripe banana or as a fox. Second, colours have what we might call a life of their own. There are relationships of contrast and harmonies among colours; they have emotional and aesthetic effects: they can be soothing or disturbing, stimulating or unnerving and so on.

For creatures in the wild, colours have always served these dual roles, but as we have formed complex societies both roles have been magnified. From as mundane a task as their use in traffic lights to their more noble roles in painting, theatre, gardening, indoor decorating, fashion, ceremonial and pageantry, colours have been used in, and have been designed to serve, these roles: to serve as signs and symbols (i.e. as natural and conventional signs) of danger, grandeur, high birth, illness, highly individualistic personality and so on, and to induce emotional and aesthetic effects. From their use in war paint and in eye shadow to the subtle lighting in restaurants, colours have played a role rich in human drama and emotion.

This litany of well-known facts makes it obvious that at least part of what is essential to colour is the way it appears, and that if someone were to argue that it was possible to distinguish real yellow from fool's yellow, where the latter consisted in the yellow appearance and the former might have, say, no particular characteristic appearance, then that would be crazy. If fool's yellow goes with yellow-as-it-appears, then for most purposes it is fool's yellow that we want.

If there were some interesting causal powers that objects had in virtue of being yellow, and others in virtue of being blue, green, etc., then there would be some point to distinguishing between two kinds of colour, e.g. physical colour and colour-as-it-appears, much as we can distinguish between biological fathers and social fathers or between absolute size and angular size. But it is clear that there are very few interesting causal powers shared by objects even with the same surface colour. As one objectivist, the anthropocentric realist, D. R. Hilbert, concedes, the only causal powers shared by objects of the same kind are anthropocentric ones – powers to induce the same response in objects having the peculiar visual apparatus possessed by humans with their idiosyncratic response curves.[19] These are real objective causal powers, ones that objects possess and would continue to possess independently of the existence of humans and similar perceivers. It is just that these causal powers are of no significance apart from their power on human perceivers (and likewise on nonhuman perceivers).

19 Hilbert (1987), pp. 11–19, esp. 15.

It is illuminating, however, to contrast the situations of colour and shape. It is true that just as yellow things have a characteristic appearance, so too do square things: they appear characteristically different from triangles and circles and rectangles, not to say trapeziums. One thing about squares that incites our interest is the way they appear. However, it is only one of the interesting things and not at all the most significant. It is far outweighed by their causal powers, or their modification of causal powers. These causal powers are defined in terms of geometrical relationships, and for most human purposes, including explanatory purposes, these are what we find of predominant interest. Were the atmosphere to become so thick, or our visual systems become so altered, that things that currently appear square no longer had that characteristic appearance, we would still be vitally interested in the geometrical properties of square things. Scientists, land surveyors, architects and home-buyers would still want to distinguish shapes. In such an environment we would want to distinguish real squares from fool's squares.

Finally, one of the most significant features of colour appearances is that they can be systematically ordered into a complex three-dimensional colour array. Although there are different systems, there is a certain structure and character to the colour system which is based on the way colours appear. This character and structure is not exhibited in any specification of physical properties of physical bodies or of the light reflected by bodies. I wrote earlier of colours as having two roles, one as signs of other properties, the other related to having a life of their own. It is this life-of-their-own aspect that enables us to construct the psychological colour systems with their distinctive characters. But of course it is not only through appearances that colours play this role; appearances are also significant in their other role, as signs.

It is not the case that viewing colours as appearances requires thinking of them as some kind of second-class type of property. The way many discussions of colour go, especially those of some philosophers, the only point to distinguishing properties and identifying them is if these properties are natural kinds or are properties with distinctive causal powers. Accordingly, if it should turn out that colour is not causally significant, that for example the only physical property shared by objects with the same colour is some gerrymandered property (P_1 or P_2 or P_3 or P_4 or . . .), then this shows that something is wrong with colour – that it lacks something important.

Not at all. Colour is simply a different kind of property. It is defined essentially by its appearance. Nothing wrong with that. Appearances are properties too. (They have rights.) For some purposes appearances are more important than other properties. Appearances are not everything, but they are not nothing either.

It may be of course that the fact that colours are essentially appearances will come as a surprise to the naive among us whose unreflective view of colour is the natural one: for such people, colour is simply an objective, intrinsic property of bodies. That this should not be a surprise for the naive should not be a surprise for us. If we are not troubled by the thought that colours are essentially reflectance curves or properties related to reflectance curves, why should we be surprised if colours should turn out essentially to be appearances. If the surprise of the naive is no obstacle in the one case, why should it provide a problem in the other?

It may be wondered whether it is consistent for me to say both that appearances are essential to colour and that it would come as a surprise to the naive to learn that the appearances are essential. For the emphasis in my approach is on giving an account of the natural concept of colour. The brief answer to that is that, as far as the naive are concerned, even if the natural concept is their concept, they do not have full explicit knowledge of all elements of the concept. In being aware of an object's colour they are in fact aware of the object's appearance, but not as an appearance. They take the appearance for the reality.

Whatever view naive perceivers (or we in our naive moments) take of colour, it is true that yellow objects appear in a distinctive way to naive perceivers, a way characteristic of yellow objects. When naive perceivers think of what it is for something to be yellow, what they have in mind is the way it appears to them. That is, they recognise something as yellow by looking at an object that is yellow and having it appear yellow to them. It is because this is the case that naive perceivers will sometimes be led to believe that something is yellow when it is not: the object merely appears yellow to them.

5. THE DISPOSITIONAL ANALYSIS

I have argued that the way things appear is essential to their having the colours they do. This may look as if it supports a dispositional analysis of colour. It suggests the following analysis:

(1) x is red iff x has the power to appear red (to a normal observer, under standard conditions)

But this is far too swift. First of all, the following analysis is not ruled out:

(1a) x is red iff x has *some* property by virtue of which it has the power to appear . . .

There is some evidence that Descartes and Locke sometimes at least attributed such a 'mixed' or 'impure' dispositional colour to physical bodies. This analysis fits the passage in which Descartes writes:

When we say we perceive colours in objects, it is really just the same as though we said that we perceive in objects something as to whose nature we are ignorant, but which produces in us a very manifest and obvious sensation, called the sensation of colour.[20]

In addition, as we saw previously, it is possible to take colours as intrinsic properties for which the appearance plays a crucial role, either in fixing the reference for colour names or for thinking about the property. In the latter case, redness is

(1b) That property which is recognisable, by looking, as red.

Analysis (1b) reflects the use of Evans's ideas, against those of Westphal. The difference may be put figuratively. For Westphal the function of one's experience of blue is to latch onto an objective feature of the world. For Evans it is to latch onto an objective feature in *a certain specific way*. Westphal's account emphasises the objective feature; Evans's account emphasises as well the way in which the feature is caught.

Sorting out which of these accounts is right will depend on sorting out a range of other things, e.g., what it is for something to have an appearance or to appear in some way. In particular, analysis (1b) could be supported by appealing to certain theories of perception. It seems possible, for example, to develop a theory of perception that historically has had a strong following, some kind of Direct Realism. According to this, there are some objective features that physical objects have – shape, size, colour – that we are capable of perceiving the objects to have. Moreover the objects have those features in just such ways as they are perceived as having them. They not only appear square; they *are* square, and the squareness they have is the same squareness they appear to have. According to this theory, objects are square – they have this intrinsic property – and they are recognised as having that property. Squareness is a property that perceivers can recognise objects as having. It seems to me that, on this model, there are two aspects to being square: it is an intrinsic property of objects, and it is recognisable as being square. Its appearing a certain way is an essential part of its being square.

20 Descartes (1954), p. 195.

What I have described is a very simple model of perception. I claim that this model is implicit in our conceptual practices. Furthermore, this ought not to be very controversial. It should not be surprising that *some* theory of perception is implicit, and if some is, it should not be surprising that it be simple, natural and obvious – and this model is all these things. Neither should we be too surprised if, despite all these things, it should also turn out to be false.

Although this account of colour fits neatly with the ideas of meaning developed by Evans,[21] it conflicts directly with his explicitly stated position on colour. For Evans a pure dispositional analysis is the only possible account: 'all it can amount to for something to be red is that it be such that if looked at in normal conditions it will appear red'.[22] However, in my earlier discussion of essential definitions, in which I contrasted Evans's theory of meaning with Westphal's use of Putnam's theory of essential definitions, I developed a possible model for colour, one in which colour is thought of as a property of an object satisfying two requirements: (i) it is a property that appears in a certain distinctive way (a colour-distinctive way), and (ii) it is the property of the object that plays the appropriate causal role in the object's appearing that way. If this model were the right one, then yellow is not, contrary to what the objectivists imply, a property that, *as it happens,* merely appears a certain way. Nor would it be, as some anti-realists hold, merely a disposition to appear a certain way. Both requirements are essential.

I think that this model for colour is correct: it is the concept of colour embodied in our ordinary conceptual colour practices. However, although this is the right account of the concept of colour, there is actually no property that satisfies the dual requirements. In other words, colour is a virtual property, just as phlogiston and caloric were virtual natural kinds.

Others besides Evans have explicitly argued that colour is essentially dispositional, e.g., McGinn, McDowell and Dummett.[23] The basis for their thesis is the claim that in order to grasp the concept 'red', say, i.e., to understand what is meant by calling something red, it is necessary that the person understand that what counts as something's having the property *red* is its having a certain disposition, i.e., the disposition to appear to perceivers in certain characteristic ways. Here the emphasis is on what is necessary for an individual to understand in order to be said to have

21 G. Evans (1982), pp. 81–5, and chs. 9 and 11.   22 G. Evans (1980), p. 272.
23 McGinn (1983); McDowell (1985); Dummett (1979), p. 26.

grasped a certain concept. McGinn endorses the following characterisation of secondary qualities:

those whose instantiations in an object consists in a power or disposition of the object to produce sensory experiences in perceivers of a certain phenomenological character.[24]

But can it seriously be suggested that all language-users competent with colour concepts understand colours in this way? Surely it is possible for many language-users to lack the concept of 'sensory experience'. Surely it is possible even for those who do have the concept to deny, as Ryle does, that sensory experiences are involved when one sees coloured bodies.

Surely it is possible for a language-user to be fluent in the use and understanding of colour predicates without thinking of colour as a dispositional property. Wouldn't the test, or at least a test, for a person's understanding what it is for an object to count as being red, be that the person, when asked to provide examples of red objects, can do so, can bring red objects when requested or ordered, can change one object for a better red and so on? Surely one can have facility in the use of sentences that include the term 'red' and can understand those sentences without thinking of redness as a dispositional property. This is not to say that the language-users need deny that it is dispositional. It simply seems to be the case that they could be proficient in the use of the colour terms without asserting or denying that the property is dispositional. The question simply never arises. If so, how can it be argued that it is necessary for understanding what it is for something to be red that one know that having the property red is having a certain disposition?

There is an important principle at issue here. I disagree with the philosophers above not over the claim that at least part of what is essential to colour is the way things appear, but over the reasons behind the claim. I argue that the way things appear can be essential without perceivers' being conceptually aware of ways of looking as 'ways of looking', or of colours as dispositions to look a certain way. What is important, of course, is that the perceivers identify colours, i.e. by recognising them, but that does not require the conceptual awareness at issue. In this I am in agreement with Christoper Peacocke, although our discussions lead in different directions.[25]

24 McGinn (1983), pp. 5–6.
25 Christopher Peacocke (1984), 'Colour-Concepts and Colour Experience', *Synthese*, 58, pp. 365–81.

It is a quite separate question as to how a competent language-user would reply to the question of whether colour is a dispositional quality. I doubt that there is a determinate answer that one could expect from such an inquiry. Moreover it is plausible that there is no determinate reasonable answer to the question.

We might try to determine an answer in the following way. Take an ordinary piece of A4 white paper, one with a sharp edge. If one brings this paper close to the eye, the sharp edge becomes fuzzy. The paper has the fuzziness dispositionally: it has the disposition to appear fuzzy at the edge (or fuzzy-edged) if it is brought close. It is tempting to contrast the dispositional fuzzy-edgedness with the intrinsic sharp-edgedness. The paper has the sharp edge intrinsically (i.e. nondispositionally). We might then ask which property the colour red is like from the point of view of the normal colour-competent language-user: is it like the dispositional fuzzy-edged property or the intrinsic sharp-edged property? Given this question, it strikes me as not implausible to think of red-ness as similar to the intrinsic property of having a sharp edge: a property an object has irrespective of whether it is seen or not.

On the other hand, is it so clear that the property of having a sharp edge is a nondispositional property? Well, it can be but need not be. Or, putting it in a less oracular fashion, we can distinguish both an intrinsic *and* a dispositional property with respect to having a sharp edge.

The point is that there is a whole set of features which can be defined either independently of how objects appear or in terms of how they appear. Some of these features are traditional primary qualities, e.g. shape, size and number: it is simply the case that by virtue of having a certain shape or size objects have characteristic appearances. Other features are more complex: that of being metallic, rusty, polished jarrah, mahogany and so on – but they too are related to a characteristic appearance. Given that with respect to these features we can distinguish between the way things are and the way things appear or look, we can distinguish between two concepts for each quality – one a concept of an intrinsic property, one a concept of a dispositional property. The dispositional property is defined essentially by the way things with a certain quality characteristically appear: what is essential is the special distinctive appearance, *not* the intrinsic quality.

Bodies that are cylindrical in shape have a characteristic cylindrical appearance. Thus we can distinguish between two types of shape property: intrinsic shape and dispositional shape (visual shape). It is absurd to attempt to identify the dispositional property with the intrinsic property.

It is perfectly possible to have both of these concepts. They are not different ways of thinking about the same property. They are different concepts having to do with different, though, as it happens, related, properties.

Nevertheless, though it is possible to distinguish these concepts and possible for the same person to have both concepts, it is also possible for a person to have just one of those concepts. A blind person may have the intrinsic-shape concept but lack the visual dispositional-shape concept. A Berkeleyan idealist may have the dispositional-shape concept but lack the intrinsic-shape concept.

Finally, it is possible that one's concept of shape is indeterminate with respect to those two concepts. The concept one possesses combines both concepts without the person's distinguishing them – for the very good reason that there is no need to distinguish them and little to be gained from doing it. The concept of circularity, for example, can be constituted in the following way:

> x's being circular consists in having that property by virtue of which it has the power to appear circular, i.e. in the characteristically circular way.

According to this account, being circular consists in having two properties: a dispositional property – the power to appear in a characteristic way – and an intrinsic property that is the causal basis for the disposition. Circularity is neither essentially intrinsic (solely) nor essentially dispositional (solely); it is essentially both. There may be no need conceptually to distinguish the two kinds of property. For many ordinary purposes there is no need to make this kind of distinction, and we can easily imagine language-users functioning happily and profitably without the need arising to make the distinction. If and when the need does arise, then there will be motivation to separate out two concepts. The original concept will be replaced by two concepts, each serving different purposes which were formerly served by a single concept.

If I am right, we can with respect to, say, 'square-ness' distinguish three different, albeit related, concepts of square-ness. Two are as follows:

(i) Intrinsic squareness: that property of objects which, as it happens, is the causal basis for the characteristically square visual appearances.
(ii) Dispositional-squareness (dispositional visual squareness): that disposition which objects have to appear visually in the square-characteristic way.

The first concept allows for the possibility that objects that are currently square might come to lose that dispositional power (e.g. were the characteristics of light and of visual systems to change). Indeed, it allows for the possibility that there might be square objects that currently lack that power, e.g. subatomic particles, black holes etc. The second concept allows for the possibility that two objects that share the same dispositional power may yet not share the same causal basis. There is, however, a third concept that somehow unites the other two (or is best thought of as the historical ancestor of the other two):

(iii) Square-ness$_H$: that property of objects which is the causal basis for the visual appearances characteristically square

The important difference is that the two distinct possibilities that the other concepts allow for are not open, given this concept. This concept is a concept of a complex property: it combines essentially the intrinsic feature and the disposition.

My thesis is that historically the concept of squareness begins in this complex form. At first there is no need to recognise or point in recognising the two kinds of possibility that the more refined, specific concepts allow. However, the more complex concept splits into the two distinct concepts as and when there arises a point to recognising those possibilities.

Colour can be thought of by analogy with this example of squareness. Besides the pure objectivist view and the pure dispositional view there is a third account. Any given colour, yellow, say, is an intrinsic property objects have, commonly a property of surfaces. It is a property which we recognise and have learned to recognise bodies as having. On this view, objects that are yellow are objects which have a characteristic appearance – at least under 'standard' conditions (however loosely and variably those are understood).[26] What this means, in part, is that yellow objects can be recognised as yellow by looking at them, at least under the right conditions.

On the view that we are now considering, something's appearing yellow is not a property different from its being yellow, or not entirely different. One knows what it is for something to appear yellow if one

26 C. L. Hardin (1988), *Color for Philosophers,* Indianapolis: Hackett, has described the problems with identifying standard conditions for colour judgements, pp. 67–91. These problems do not apply here. For most circumstances, especially in the early historical development of colour concepts, there is presupposed a loose set of standard conditions which do apply in those circumstances. The problems arise when we try to be precise or when we try to apply colour concepts in scientific contexts.

knows what it is like for something to be yellow and if one knows what it is like to be in a position to decide by looking that something is yellow: that is what it is to know what it is like for something to look yellow. Once we know this we are also in a position to know of certain things which are not yellow that they look yellow, at least in certain circumstances.

On this account we are simply trained to recognise some things as yellow and others as blue, white, green, etc. One can only be trained if yellow things have a characteristic appearance; but colour perceivers do not, initially at least, acquire a concept of 'appears yellow'. They are trained to acquire a concept of yellow, and this is applied in colour perception. At a later, more sophisticated stage, language-users acquire the distinction between *is* yellow and *looks* yellow.

What is this initial concept of being yellow? I maintain that it is a concept of a virtual property. What this means is that it is a concept of a property which in actual fact no physical object has. It is an intensional property: a property of a physical surface, objective in the sense that the surface has it independently of whether anyone is looking. It is a property that stands in a set of relationships to associated properties: yellow, blue, green and red. We can construct a systematic colour array with the dimensions of hue, relative chromaticness and relative whiteness/blackness.

What I am supposing is that just as we can have concepts of individual objects that do not exist – Banquo's ghost, the man in the moon, the philosopher's stone – and of substances that do not exist – caloric, phlogiston – so we can have concepts of properties that do not exist. These I am calling concepts of virtual properties. Colour, thought of as a property of physical surface, is just such a one. Colour as a physical property is a virtual property. There are no instances of physical objects that have such a physical property. The reason for this is that there is no property such that

(i) It is an intrinsic property of physical surfaces

and

(ii) It forms a set of interrelated physical properties that mirrors the relationships set down in the colour array.

This raises the question of how we can come to have the concept of colour that we do if there are no physical instances. Locke and Descartes have an answer to that. We form sensory representations of the world.

These representations represent objects in the physical world as having these virtual colours, and they do so because the representations have the character implicit in the three-dimensional colour array. The representations do not have the virtual colour – they have the right kind of structure, but they are not physical. To have the colour in the virtual sense they would have to be physical. But they represent physical objects as having the colour.

To say this, however, invites another objection. I began by saying that we all agree that tomatoes are red, bananas yellow and some sunsets golden red, and that what we want is an account of what those colours consist in. I conclude by giving an account of what colour is essentially that has the consequence that nothing is ever red or yellow or golden red. Accordingly, I have produced a reductio ad absurdum of my own position.

Not surprisingly, I think that the force of this objection is superficial. First, let us note that I did not begin by saying that tomatoes are red and bananas yellow etc. but rather by saying that we all *agree* that tomatoes are red, etc. I have also arrived at the conclusion that tomatoes are not red – in the sense that we naively and naturally think of them as red. What I am required to do is to explain our agreement on colours, given that objects do not have them.

I do have an explanation for why we all *agree* that tomatoes are red and bananas are not. Tomatoes are represented by our visual system as red and bananas are represented as yellow. Moreover it is highly valuable and useful that they are so represented. And finally, for all of the purposes that colour serves in our lives, all we need is that some objects are represented as yellow and some as red and others as pink and so on. It is not necessary that, in addition, they be yellow and be red and be pink. So although I say that objects are not red and yellow and blue, I have an explanation for why we think they are.

Moreover, having given this account, I can also explain that there is a dispositional sense of colour in which objects are red and yellow and blue:

> For x to be yellow$_D$ is to have a disposition to cause, in the right kind of way, x to be represented as yellow$_I$.

We should also note that if the visual system can represent objects as having intrinsic qualities yellow$_I$, blue$_I$ etc., it can also represent objects as having the corresponding dispositional qualities. One has only to think of the case of simple shapes. Both cubes and cylinders, for example, have

76

characteristic appearances that are distinctive of each. A cylinder has certain causal powers independent of how it appears, powers that distinguish it as a cylinder, but it also has a characteristic appearance that is distinctive of it and different from that of cubes, spheres, egg shapes and so on. When I see a cylinder as a cylinder, then it seems to me clear that my visual system represents, or is apt to represent, something that is cylindrical and also something disposed to look cylindrical (and indeed something that is looking cylindrical). Perhaps naive perceivers do not make the distinction between being cylindrical and looking cylindrical, but with some degree of sophistication one can. For those of us capable of making that distinction the same perception (or perceptual experience) can either make us aware of (or represent) something that is cylindrical, or something that looks cylindrical, or both.

I hold that the same is true for colour. We can distinguish between intrinsic colour (colour$_I$) and dispositional colour (colour$_D$), and it is possible for our colour perceptions to represent either property or both. However, unlike the case of being cylindrical, there are no physical instances of intrinsic colour, only instances of dispositional colour.

7. CONCLUSION

For many terms, e.g. 'gold', 'molybdenum', 'elm', it is clear that for many language-users their understanding varies widely and that some have much shallower understanding than others. It is plausible that many language-users function with a stereotype for 'gold', 'elm', etc.: a stereotype that may not hold true for the substance or property in question, one that may not be sufficient to distinguish between different substances, and one which may be different from that stereotype possessed by other language-users.

According to the theories of Putnam and Evans, the way language operates requires a division of labour: for Putnam between experts and nonexperts, for Evans between producers and consumers. According to each, it is implicit in the linguistic practice to which both parties contribute (experts and nonexperts; producers and consumers) that one party plays a leading or central role. If one has a stereotype of 'gold', then 'gold' is taken to refer to that natural kind which occupies a certain causal role vis-à-vis the stereotype in question. More particularly, 'gold' refers to that natural kind which occupies a particular causal role in the linguistic practice in which various stereotypes of 'gold' play their limited role.

The advantage of Evans's theory is that it allows for those cases in which a natural kind or quality can be conceptualised. It seems to me that many terms fall under just such cases. That is, terms such as 'square', 'yellow', 'fashionable', 'adulterous' apply to (or express) properties conceptualised-in-a-certain-way. The conceptualisation is essential in a way the stereotype is not. Moreover, once we allow a role for such conceptualisations, we can then allow that in some cases the conceptualisation refers to the causal role played by the property or quality in question, and in some cases it does not. I suggest that 'square' and 'hardedged' illustrate the first kind of case and 'fashionable' and 'adultery' the second. Finally, it seems to me that we need to acknowledge that such conceptualisations may evolve and may split and that several different conceptualisations may occur. The term 'king' is one such example. (When the members of the early U.S. congresses feared that George Washington might want to become king or even that he would become king, the kind of king they had in mind was different from the kind of king that the British George VI was.)

But most important of all, once we have admitted the role of such conceptualisations, we need to be aware of the possibility that built into at least some of them will be assumptions that are false. In the case of social concepts, e.g., king, fashionable, justice, legal, etc., it has long been the charge of some social theorists that at least some of these concepts have false assumptions built in. Marxists and feminists of course have made many such claims. Whether or not, and to what extent, such theorists are right in these claims are questions into which I do not propose to enter. All I need is to point out that it is possible that they are right, at least in some cases.

Likewise, when we turn to less controversial cases in which some of the assumptions involve causal roles and properties, we should acknowledge that it is not unlikely that some of our conceptualisations will employ causal assumptions that are false. Natural-kind terms such as 'caloric', 'phlogiston' and 'élan vital' are some examples. Likewise, I suggest, we can have predicates which apply to properties which should be recognised as virtual properties: the conceptualisations employ false causal assumptions. Colour terms such as yellow, magenta, red, orange and blue are, I maintain, just such terms. The fact, however, that these assumptions are false, let me insist, does not mean that the predicates for the virtual properties do not have valuable roles to play. Unlike those social concepts whose function, it is alleged, is to maintain class and gender barriers, the colour concepts enable us to deal perceptually with the world with more efficiency and more enjoyment.

APPENDIX: THE REFERENTIAL COMPONENT OF PROPERTIES: EVANS AND KRIPKE

Kripke and Putnam have separately developed a causal theory of reference, a theory applicable to names both of individuals and of natural kinds. Though they have a special interest in such names, their theory seems capable of being extended to cover properties – at least certain of them – as well. Not only does Kripke explicitly allow for such a possibility, but he uses the model in a brief discussion of yellowness, which is, of course, apposite in this context. After expressing dissatisfaction with the commonly held belief that 'yellow' expresses a dispositional property, he goes on to endorse the view that the reference of 'yellow' is fixed by the description

that (manifest) property of objects which causes them, under normal circumstances, to be seen as yellow (i.e. to be sensed by certain visual impressions).[27]

The point, as Kripke pointed out earlier, is that the term 'yellowness' contains a referential element, which implies that the term rigidly designates, i.e. applies to the same property in every possible world.[28]

In assimilating such predicates to the names of natural kinds and individuals, Kripke wishes to stress the referential element in such terms and to argue that, just as the descriptive theory of names is almost never appropriate, neither is it here. However, we might wish to allow that a general term contains a referential element without adopting either his model, at least as it stands, or the descriptive theory that he opposes. For we could adopt the model presented by Gareth Evans, a model which, though sharing certain crucial features with that of Kripke and Putnam, makes a significant advance.[29]

The crucial difference between Evans's account and that of Kripke (and that of Putnam) turns on the role of Fregean sense. On Kripke's model, such a sense, for many names, plays no role in the explicit account of how the reference for the name is secured and preserved. For some names, however, and indeed for some names for natural kinds and

27 Kripke (1980), pp. 127–8, 140.　　28 Ibid., p. 128.　　29 G. Evans (1982).

79

properties, Fregean sense can play a role. It is said to do so, however, in two very different ways.[30] First, a definite description is used to fix the reference for a name. In this case the name rigidly designates the object in question, and the sense effectively drops out: it plays no vital role in the understanding of what the term refers to. Kripke's example is that of the term 'one metre' whose reference is fixed by some such description as 'the length of rod S at time t_0'.[31] Alternatively the name can be thought of as synonymous with a definite description (or set of definite descriptions), in which case it designates nonrigidly. Such a name is taken by Kripke to be a descriptive name. (This is disputed by Evans. See below.) According to Evans's account, however, a name can operate in a third way. Not only does it rigidly designate, but the Fregean sense plays an important role.

Evans provides a far more detailed account than Kripke does of the mechanisms whereby reference is both secured and preserved in name-using practices.[32] Crucially, much more emphasis is placed on the role of Fregean sense in such mechanisms. The explanation for this rests on the stress that is placed on what is said by the use of a term. What is *said* is a matter of what it is to understand a sentence containing the term. In the case of names and other singular terms, this normally means having individuating knowledge of which object (or natural kind) is being referred to. For some terms this means having some individuating knowledge but not necessarily any particular piece of knowledge. For other terms it may be that it requires having, in a broad sense, the right kind of knowledge. It seems clear enough that if we do wish to hold that terms such as 'yellow' (when applicable to physical objects) have referential components, it is open to us to treat 'yellow' as belonging to the second kind. The crucial piece of knowledge in this case is contained in the ability to recognise and distinguish objects as yellow.

For our purposes, Evans opens us to two relevant possibilities, ones which are introduced by his different accounts of descriptive names and ordinary proper names. First, there are certain descriptive names which need to be distinguished from abbreviations for definite descriptions. An example Evans uses is this: we introduce the name 'Julius' by saying, 'let Julius be the person who invented the bifocals.' The name 'Julius' is a referring expression whose reference is fixed, by stipulation, by description. Other examples are Deep Throat, Mr Big, Jack the Ripper and

---

30 Kripke (1980), p. 59.   31 Ibid., p. 55.
32 G. Evans (1982), ch. 11, 'Proper Names'.

Homer. One of the features of such names is that understanding sentences containing them, which means knowing which object is referred to, requires understanding how the reference is fixed. That is, one understands which description is used to fix the reference. Such a description is understood even when considering a counterfactual situation in which Homer did not bother to write the *Iliad*, or in which Deep Throat kept quiet about Watergate.

In having this feature, such referring expressions differ from the kind illustrated by Kripke's example of 'one metre', whose reference is fixed by 'the length of rod S at time t_0'. Here it is stated that the stipulator picks out an accidental property of a certain length – she might have picked out some other – and uses it to fix the reference for 'one metre'.

The second class of name discussed by Evans is that of ordinary proper names. The account of how these names function requires reference to the relevant naming practices in which the relevant language-users participate. Two elements in such practices are essential: (i) the existence of individuating knowledge of the object named and (ii) the fact that this object plays a causal role in participants' having the individuating knowledge. Typically participants have information that is derived, causally, from X or have the ability to recognise X and to distinguish it from others. A further feature of this account is the key role in the practice ascribed to 'producers'.

Evans provides an account of ordinary proper name-using practices which involve 'producers' and 'consumers', a view which represents a variation on the division-of-labour theme discussed by Putnam.[33] The producers comprise a core group of speakers who are central to the practice. They are those who have been introduced to the practice via their acquaintance with x (the object named) and know which thing that is – usually by having the ability to recognise x. Consumers are people who need not have such knowledge but know that there are some people, producers, who do (or did). No matter how reference is originally fixed for a name, whether e.g. by dubbing ceremonies or by definite descriptions, the continuing existence of the practice requires the existence of a core group who have the individuating knowledge, typically the ability to recognise and distinguish the object concerned.

The necessity for a core group of producers and the fact that typically their individuating knowledge of which thing (kind) is involved consists in their having certain recognitional abilities allow us to see how this

33 Ibid., ch. 11, esp. pp. 376–91.

account of names can be extended to cover properties such as yellowness. In the case of yellow, it is that property for which there is a core group of speakers (most of us) who have the ability to recognise instances of yellow, and to distinguish it from other colours. On this model, yellowness is not a property fixed by a definite description, e.g. the property which as it happens appears in such-and-such a way. It is that property which competent language-users recognise! Of course it is because yellow things appear that way that people recognise yellow. This means that it is central to the yellow-naming practice that yellow refer to that property which appears in the distinctive way. Its appearance is not accidental.

To summarise: we can see that there are two ways provided by Evans' account of using names for colour which enable us to hold on to the view that the way colours appear is essential, and not some accidental feature. One is to treat colour names as descriptive names, ones whose reference is fixed by the way they appear but where understanding that this is so is necessary to knowing which colour is involved. The second, which is more plausible, is to hold that colour names are similar to ordinary proper names: (i) understanding their use requires individuating knowledge; (ii) the colour property plays a causal role in having that individuating knowledge. Whatever the case for other proper names, it is a crucial element in colour-naming practices that the way they appear provides not only individuating knowledge but knowledge that is central to the practice.

According to this account, colour is not a dispositional property. It is a property of objects, one recognisable as yellow. On the face of it, this seems to leave it open that science or philosophy or both should provide arguments that there is no such property. If so, then on the Evans account the term 'yellowness' refers to nothing, and sentences using 'yellow' fail to express a thought. If this is a consequence, it does not seem to me to be a devastating objection, despite appearances. There are various ways of escape open to us. One is to say that the colour-naming practices aim at certain targets which they fail to capture. Given this, we should try to work out what properties best satisfy the purposes of such practices, given a charitable interpretation of the overall projects in which the participants are engaged. Alternatively we treat the property that is being aimed at as a virtual property or intensional property: we construct a view of what that property would be like if it existed. To do this is likely to require employing a certain counterfactual but superficially plausible theory of perception. There is a natural candidate for such a theory: the direct realist account of perception beloved of generations of philosophers, and the view of most ordinary perceivers.

We need also to explain why perceivers appear to recognise this 'physical' property and how they readily and consistently group objects together which they call 'yellow', and do likewise with those they call 'red' and so on. Again a natural explanation is readily available. It is the one favoured by generations of other philosophers and scientists. Ordinary perceivers are grouping 'yellow' objects together and distinguishing them from others that are 'red', 'blue' etc., but they are doing so because what they are recognising is a phenomenal quality. For most purposes, luckily for us, this does not matter. For one thing, even if objects are not yellow, it is with them 'as if they were yellow'. For another, what the phenomenal colour allows us to recognise is dispositional colour, the power to appear in the way that allows us to group objects as 'yellow', 'red', 'blue' and so on, respectively.

4

The natural concept of colour

In his objectivist analysis of colour, Westphal claimed not to be providing an account of 'the' concept of colour or the ordinary concept of colour. Rather his aim was to give an account of what colour is essentially, on the model of scientific accounts of what gold and water are essentially. To adopt such an approach is to say that the way a colour appears is not part of what that colour is essentially. Rather the way it appears provides a technique for picking out the colour, a technique that theoretically at least could be replaced by some other.

As we saw, this is a misguided approach to colour. First of all, it won't do to contrast, as Westphal does, an account of what colour is essentially with an account of the concept of colour. It only makes sense to look for 'the essence' of a property or substance within a framework in which there is a concept of a property or substance which has a certain essence. In itself this does not count against the claim that colour really is, say, spectral reflectance, any more than it counts against the claim that water is H_2O. However, as I have argued, the appearance is actually essential to colour. In the case of gold (and of water) a certain natural kind is conceptualised as the natural kind which *as it happens* appears a certain way, whereas in the case of blue and colours in general, a certain property is conceptualised as a physical property that does appear a certain distinctive way. The only thing is, it turns out that there simply is no physical property that appears that way. Colour is, I argue, a virtual property. Our colour experience represents objects as having properties they do not have, viz. colours. In other words, I am defending an 'error thesis' of colour perception, although I differ from fellow error-theorists such as Descartes and Locke about the nature of the colour as it is represented.

There is a problem, however, with the position that I have formulated. Against Westphal, I said that in the case of colours a certain property is 'conceptualised as a physical property that does appear a distinctive way', but against Evans and others, I argued that among the unsophisticated (i.e. most of us most of the time) appearances are not noticed as such. It needs to be stressed that by 'conceptualised' I mean to refer to the conceptual practices people engage in. According to this view, the concept of 'appearance' may be implicit rather than explicit in these practices. I need to defend this notion of implicit concepts. I also need to develop and argue for a specific account of what the concept is and to show what the exact role of appearances is.

In providing this argument I am developing and expanding the thesis set out in Chapter 2. There I presented my version of the 'error theory' without explicitly arguing for it. However, in describing it and displaying how it avoids the obvious problems for the Descartes-Locke position while exploiting its advantages, an implicit argument has been presented. For many, this will be sufficient. One of the aims of this chapter is to make that argument explicit.

1. THE NATURAL CONCEPT OF COLOUR

In presenting an error theory, it is necessary to identify a 'natural concept' of colour, one which incorporates what might be called a 'natural view' of colour, i.e. a view of what kind of property it is. That is, it is vital to make explicit what the natural concept or view is. It is important not just for an error theory but for giving any adequate theory of colour. One reason for requiring such an account is provided by the fact that we are biological creatures with colour vision and that colour vision has an important role to play in our lives. A second major reason is the fact that in our cultural and social life there are a wealth of uses for colour, giving rise to a flourishing colour vocabulary. In the normal lives of people, both of everyday people and of the 'over-man', there are enormous uses for colour: lighting, pictures, films, signs, fashion, food, make-up, theatre, clothes, traffic lights, cars, etc. A theory of colour may end up modifying or rejecting the natural view, but if so it had better have some good reasons.

Unfortunately, there is a subtle ambiguity here, as elsewhere, when we speak of a 'natural concept' or 'natural view'. Descartes and Locke were figures in a long tradition of thinkers who held that we are naturally prone to make a certain kind of mistake: we are subject to a natural tendency to think that physical objects have colours that they do not have. We can, however, take this remark in two quite different ways.

One way is to say that the error is intellectual. There is a mistaken belief that we have a tendency to acquire. On this view, there is nothing wrong with our concept of colour or the way our experiences represent colour, i.e. with the concept of colour or the kind of colour which objects are represented as having. It is simply the case that we are naturally prone to make a certain mistake, to form, understandably but mistakenly, a certain belief about what kind of property colour is and where instances of it are situated, e.g. on the physical surface of bodies.

The second way to take the remark is to say that the error is not an intellectual one, or at least not an explicit one. There is a false belief presupposed by the natural concept of colour. The natural concept is one that is built into the way our experiences represent things. For example, in learning to use our visual experiences to make or to express colour judgements, we naturally acquire a certain concept of colour, just as we acquire concepts of shapes and sizes.

I think it is possible to find in Descartes and Locke passages to support either interpretation. Irrespective of the accuracy of that historical thesis, I claim that it is the second interpretation that provides the most plausible and defensible construal of the error theory.

To some extent, the ambiguity is harmless. Either way, it is possible to describe a natural view about colour and, having done so, to determine whether it is false or not. Even if the natural view simply expressed a mistaken intellectual view that we are prone to make, although not inevitably, it would still be an interesting thesis, one that is persuasive and influential. Even if it is wrong, it would be important to show why it is wrong, and to explain its appeal. However, if the natural view is taken in the other, the implicit, sense, it is even more vital that we provide some account of it. If it is wrong, we need to be able to make it explicit and to show why it is wrong, but, more important, we need to explain why it is successful, especially if it is wrong.

Descartes and Locke contrast the natural, naive view of colour with a more sophisticated view, one which takes colour to be a power or disposition to induce appropriate sensations. This distinction between naive and sophisticated views is neutral with respect to the distinction between implicit and explicit views. In the explicit case we treat the sophisticated view as one that we can attain after reflecting on, and correcting, the naive, or natural, view. As far as the implicit view is concerned, the position would be as follows. Normally the naive concept expresses the way we naturally and naively think of colours, that is, when we make colour judgements and have colour thoughts. However, at a later stage we may develop a new sophisticated concept of colour.

In considering the implicit view, we would need to answer the question about which colour the visual experiences represent objects as having. The right answer is that we need to contrast earlier and later stages in the development of each perceiver, or to contrast different moods or attitudes which a perceiver can be in at different times, i.e. a naive or sophisticated mood or attitude. The same visual experiences can represent different things, either at different stages or in different moods or attitudes. At any given time the experiences represent one thing but are apt to represent another.

There is no reason why the same visual experiences cannot represent different things at different times, or even different things at the same time. If I go to the theatre or a film and see Berkoff playing Herod or Branagh playing Henry V, the actor's performing on a given occasion can be thought of in two ways: 'Herod was charming, is now cross' or 'Berkoff is astounding the way he switches.' Some people claim that one cannot think of both things at the same time. That is, one cannot both think of the character and what he is supposed to be doing and also think of the actor and what the actor is doing in portraying the character. That strikes me not only as prejudice but as false prejudice. Perhaps one loses something if one ceases to be lost in the character, but it seems simply false that one cannot both be shocked at what Herod is doing and at the same time admiring of how Berkoff manages it. Indeed, in watching a pot-boiler, one can be shocked at oneself when one notices that one's emotions are being manipulated – at falling for it so easily.

There is another problem that arises when, in relation to colour as it is represented, we think of 'naive' and 'sophisticated' concepts. A naive attitude is not normally regarded as desirable. It is something, once recognised for what it is, to be replaced by the more sophisticated attitude. In referring to the naive concept of colour I do not wish it to have this implication. Above all, we should not think of the naive concept as restricted to use by naive people, i.e. those ignorant of much science, philosophy and many facts of common knowledge. It is appropriate to all of us in our naive moments, moments which recur even when all shades of innocence have departed. 'Naive' is probably not the right word. The attitude is more akin to the one we adopt when we go to the theatre or to the cinema. We suspend certain beliefs and certain responses. If we are watching a portrayal of King Herod, we put

87

aside our knowledge that the actor is neither a king nor a Hebrew, but rather is a nonroyal Englishman.

There are contexts in which it is appropriate to adopt the 'naive' attitude to colour, just as in the theatre it is appropriate to regard the actor as if he is King Herod or Henry V. Moreover the sophisticated concept of colour presupposes, I argue, the naive concept. The dispositional property of green that lettuce has is a disposition to appear a certain way. Which way? It is a disposition to produce experiences that represent the lettuce as green, as green in the naive way. Such terms as 'naive', 'pre-analytical', 'pre-critical', 'unreflective', 'primitive', etc., are unfortunate in having misleading connotations. Perhaps, borrowing from the theatrical context, the right word to describe the attitude I have in mind is 'engaged'.

2. A QUESTION OF METHODOLOGY

The ambiguity that I raised in the last section arises often in philosophical discussions. We are presented with accounts of the natural view of X, or with the naive view or the pre-theoretical view or the commonsense view of X. In assessing such accounts there are certain problems that need to be addressed but seldom are.

Sometimes the term is meant to refer to a certain theory, one we are naturally inclined to believe. As such, certain problems should inevitably arise in discussing what the 'natural view' is. Do we have in mind the view that an unsophisticated, unreflective person would give if asked? Or should it be the view of the rational educated layperson? It seems to be one of these views, for example, that Michael Dummett referred to as 'the plain man's view of colours'. (See the brief discussion of Dummett's views in Chapter 2.)[1]

If it is the commonsense view, is it the theory that enlightened common sense would deliver, or is it the commonsense view untouched by theoretical considerations or specialised knowledge? Various philosophers at different times have claimed to present, or have been thought of as presenting, a commonsense theory on various matters: Aristotle, Reid, Berkeley, G. E. Moore and so on. Whatever else these theories are, they are generally not the same as the view that everyday people would give if asked their view.

There is, however, quite another way of thinking of the natural view.

1 Dummett (1979), pp. 27–9. See also my Chapter 2, p. 53.

With respect to colour, for example, we may be thinking of that concept, or theory about colour, that is implicit in the colour-conceptual practices of those who think about and talk about colour and behave with respect to colour. People make colour judgements and use colour language to talk about colours. We are asking about the concepts and theoretical principles presupposed by those judgements and language use, especially having in mind the social use of language. Without wishing to downplay the interest and importance of the other questions, it is the last question that interests me.

It may well be that commonsense philosophical views are best construed as answers to this kind of question. Whether they are or not, this type of question is important. An illustration of the approach I have in mind is provided by P. F. Strawson in the following remarks on perception:

Our perceptual judgements . . . embody or reflect a certain view of the world: as containing objects, variously propertied, located in a common space, and continuing in their existence independently of our interrupted and relatively fleeting perceptions of them;

and in further remarks when he goes on to argue against Mackie's (and Hume's) characterisation of 'naive realism', according to which the percipient is said to fail to draw any distinction between sensible experiences ('perceptions') and independently existing things:

It seems to me as certain as anything can be that, as an integral part of that scheme, we distinguish naturally and unreflectively, between . . . our perceivings of objects and the objects we can see and hear and feel.[2]

Of course it is commonplace, in the post-positivist world we inhabit, to accept that theory is normally embodied in our concepts, but we need to distinguish two ways in which this may happen. First, a person's personal beliefs and theories may affect that person's observations, judgements and thoughts. Second, the set of concepts embodied in a set of conceptual practices may incorporate a 'theory' or certain theoretical principles or assumptions. It is plausible to believe, for example, that the principle of causality or the assumption that people and things occupy a three-dimensional space in time are such principles, underlying at least many conceptual frameworks (which of course does not in itself mean that they are true or cannot be rejected). It is the second sense of theory-dependence that seems to be the most important.

2 P. F. Strawson (1979), 'Perception and Its Objects', in G. Macdonald (ed.), *Perception and Identity*, London: Macmillan, pp. 41–60; these quotations, pp. 44, 48.

There has been much discussion of late in the philosophy of mind about folk psychology. Much of this presents folk psychology in disparaging terms as on a par with folk physics and folk medicine. This attitude strikes me as seriously misconceived. First, much folk medicine for at least two thousand years did a lot better than much professional medicine, and in certain respects still does. The traditional Chinese remedy for malaria, for example, is vastly superior to current scientific treatment, which in most African countries today is useless. Folk physics, likewise, still has an important role to play. Secondly, we need to distinguish between an explicitly held theory of physics, psychology or whatever and one contained implicitly within a body of language. The latter kind of theory may not be very exciting, but if the language has survived for a length of time, it is possible that the theory has something valuable. Of course it may still be false, but that does not mean that it is not beneficial, nor that it should be dismissed. Above all, it does not mean that it should be quickly dismissed.

In any case, I take the interesting 'natural view', at least with respect to colour, to be the view that is implicit in our conceptual practices. People make colour judgements; they have colour thoughts. What concept of colour are people employing when they make these judgements and have these thoughts? This is the sensible question to ask, not the question of what theory they would give if asked their views about colour.

Of course, having said this, it does not follow that what we explicitly think about colour has nothing to do with what the natural concept is. It is perfectly consistent with my position to say that it is partly through language-users' explicit beliefs about colour that the natural concept gets embedded in colour-conceptual practices. It simply depends on the details of the particular concept in question. Moreover, as we saw in the discussion of Descartes's and Locke's views, it may be that there is an explicitly held theory that is so influential or beguiling that it is important to deal with it, even if it is not the 'natural view'.

3. THOMAS REID AND COMMON SENSE ON COLOUR

Thomas Reid was one of the strongest critics of the Cartesian-Lockean view of colour. In particular he rejected the claim that physical objects do not have the colours that the 'vulgar' claim they have. For, he writes, all people who have not been tutored by modern philosophy understand

90

by colour 'not a sensation of the mind, which can have no existence when it is not perceived, but a quality or modification of bodies, which continues to be the same whether it is seen or not'.[3]

There seem to be clear parallels between Reid's view, and the way he argues for it, and that favoured by more modern philosophers. Examination of his reasoning, however, reveals the problems confronting defenders of such views. He speaks of the common language of mankind showing evidently that

we ought to distinguish between the colour of a body, which is conceived to be a fixed and permanent quality in the body, and the appearance of that colour to the eye, which may be varied a thousand ways, by a variation of the light, of the medium, or of the light itself.[4]

The permanent colour of the body is said to be the cause which, by the modification of light or of the intervening medium, produces all this variety of appearances. These appearances, Reid claims, are what Locke calls ideas. What is distinctive in Reid's view is that the appearances (ideas) of colour suggest the conception or belief of some unknown quality in the body which occasions the idea, and 'it is to this quality and not the idea, that we give the name of colour'.[5]

There is, however, a problem in attributing to the 'vulgar' this conception of colour as an unknown quality, a problem addressed by Reid himself. How is it that the vulgar can distinguish, or even think of, red and blue if both terms name unknown qualities? Reid's answer is that

when we think or speak of any particular colour . . . it is really in some sort compounded. It involves an unknown cause, and a known effect. The name of colour belongs indeed to the cause only, and not to the effect. But as the cause is unknown, we can form no distinct conception of it, but by its relation to the known effect.[6]

Accordingly, when 'I would conceive those colours of bodies which we call scarlet and blue', I must join together in the imagination the unknown quality and some effect or some relation that is similar. The most obvious basis for the distinction between scarlet and blue is the appearance.

Hence the appearance is, in the imagination, so closely united with the quality called a scarlet colour, that they are apt to be mistaken for one and the same

3 T. Reid (1970), *An Inquiry into the Human Mind,* ed. T. Duggan, Chicago: Chicago U.P., p. 99.
4 Ibid., pp. 99–100.   5 Ibid., p. 100.   6 Ibid., pp. 100–1.

thing, although they are in reality so different and so unlike that one is an idea in the mind, the other is a quality of the body.[7]

But to give this answer to the problem facing him is to put Reid in a position that scarcely differs from that of Descartes and Locke. He seems to agree that we are naturally apt to mistake the colour appearance for the quality, even though they are so different. Descartes and Locke also distinguish between colour as a quality of physical bodies and colour as idea, and say that we know the former only through its effects and crucially that we have the tendency to (mis)take the appearance for an objective quality.

What Descartes and Locke insist upon (at least when they are being careful) is the systematic ambiguity of colour terms: that 'red' can be used with either of two related meanings, as qualities of objects and as qualities of appearances, with the former making reference to the latter. Reid holds instead that the colour term applies only to the unknown quality and that the latter is identified only by its effects (the appearances), which are known but not named. One might reply on behalf of Descartes and Locke that if the effects are knowable then they ought to be nameable, and what better name than the colour term for the corresponding quality, albeit that the term is used ambiguously? The point here is that the ambiguity is systematic; and indeed perhaps because of that, not very obvious.

To adopt this approach to colours would be to say of them what Reid says of smells and of tastes, sounds, heat and cold. The term for the smell of a rose, he writes, signifies two things:

1) A sensation which can have no existence but when it is perceived and can only be in a sentient being or mind;
2) Some power, quality or virtue in the rose, or in effluvia proceeding from it, and which has a permanent existence, independent of the mind, and which by the constitution of nature, produces the sensation in us.[8]

Reid argues that the vulgar give no name to the idea or appearance of colour because they never make it an object of thought or reflection. This puts Reid in the odd position of saying that the appearances must be known as effects of unknown qualities (colours) in order for the colours to be thought of, but are not themselves the objects of thought.

He does hold that the appearances are signs for which our natural

7 Ibid., p. 101.   8 Ibid., p. 45.

constitution is so framed that they are naturally taken as signs for objective qualities. One might understand how signs can suggest objects and qualities without one's noticing the signs. But Reid ought not say this if one's thoughts about those qualities require thinking about the signs (which are the known effects). In other words, Reid wants to say that the signs are not noticed (the objective qualities are), and yet he needs to say that the content of thought about the objective qualities requires reference to these signs, that is, to the known effects.

The problem with Reid's account is surely that he is wrong in claiming that for those untutored in philosophy (and science), their conception of colour is of it as an unknown quality. First, even to think of colour as an unknown quality requires something like the appreciation of an atomic theory of matter, or of the point underlying such theories. Secondly, surely the untutored would be puzzled indeed to be told that they did not know what such qualities as red, yellow and black were. Surely they would find that just as puzzling as the claim that objects do not have colours: the claim that Reid says the vulgar would justifiably reject. Thirdly, if for colours we distinguish, as Reid says we do, between the effects (appearances) and their unknown causes (the colours), it is not true that the effects are never the objects of thought or reflection. When I look at my peach bedroom wall and say how faded it is and how nice the wall would be in mauve, how it would lift, I do think of how the wall appears now and how it would appear were I to change it. When I try today to paint last night's sunset, surely it is the appearance of the sunset that I reflect on and try to capture. Moreover, suppose we do distinguish between effect and unknown quality, as suggested by Reid. We ought to be able to suppose there to be different unknown qualities which have the same appearance (i.e. to be metamers). Would we (the vulgar) think of the objects as having the same colours, or different ones? I suggest that we would regard them as having the same colour.

In opposition to Reid, I hold that the untutored would claim to know what colour qualities are, and that moreover they say such things as that pink is closer to red than to green or to blue, that yellow is lighter than green, that orange is between red and yellow, and so on. Secondly, they do not customarily distinguish between objective quality and appearance. Nevertheless there is a difference between the quality in a rose and its appearance to a typical person, and it is also true that that person takes the appearance to be the quality. The percipient does not think of the appearance (sensation) as an appearance and identify that with an objective quality. Rather, that which she takes to be an objective quality, one that has a range of causal powers, is in fact an appearance.[9]

The mistake we make in our 'vulgar' mood is a mistake, but a perfectly understandable one. No disgrace in that. The mistake serves a very useful purpose. It is no less a mistake, for all that, but not all mistakes are bad, or to be regretted, or even necessarily to be eliminated.

It takes some sophistication to distinguish between (a) an objective quality and (b) an appearance of that quality taken as an effect of that quality. I do not think that the untutored make such a distinction. Moreover it is perfectly reasonable that they do not.

An alternative to Reid's view, one that is suggested by some of his remarks, is to say that the view of the untutored is not that colour is an unknown quality but that colour is a power or disposition to induce effects (appearances). This has the advantage of allowing the effect to be part of the thought involved in colour thoughts. It has the disadvantage of fitting neither what they say nor what they do in their colour practices. There is in addition the problem of saying what the appearances and effects are. That is, what terms do we use to identify these appearances? If we say that red objects are those that have the disposition to look red, then what is the sense of 'red' in which they look red?

The virtual-colour concept overcomes these problems. It has two major virtues: it makes the most sense of the vulgar's colour thoughts and colour-conceptual practices; it shows the way to how thought about colour should proceed.

4. THE MEANING OF COLOUR TERMS: THE LINGUISTIC AND PERCEPTUAL ASPECTS

In trying to describe the natural concept or the natural view of colour, we need to cover two aspects. First, we need to take into account that, for a colour perceiver, the visual experiences represent objects as having colour. Thus if I see the cricket ball as red, if I experience it as red, if my visual experiences represent the cricket ball as red, then there is a certain property, that of being red, that is involved. We need to say what this property is.

Second, we need to take into account the fact that there is a colour language. People use colour language to make colour judgements and to express colour thoughts. We describe that sunset as golden red, that sky

9 I expand on this point later in this chapter; see Section 9.

as light blue, this rose as pink, and so on. We suppose that the bedroom wall might 'lift' if it were peach or alternatively be softer if it were cream. Moreover we can express more complex colour thoughts: *that* is a deeper (darker, paler, . . .) red; *that* is more of a green than a blue; there is a sharp contrast between *that* black and *that* pink; and so on. It is also a characteristic feature of colour practice that colours can be ordered systematically. The colours merge with each other: red to yellow to green to blue to red. Likewise each colour merges to white and black and to grey. I am not claiming that everyone is familiar with the Munsell system of colour classification, or the Swedish Natural Colour System, or any other. What I am saying is that such colour systems broadly capture certain principles implicit in colour-using and colour-naming practices.[10] We need to ask what concept of colour people are employing when they make these colour judgements and have such colour thoughts.

Let us describe these two aspects of colour as the perceptual (sensible) aspect and the social aspect respectively. The point about the latter aspect is that each of us has a colour language in common with others, and the question about what the natural concept is, is a question about what the shared concept is. That is, it is a question about what is the concept or view that is implicit in the colour-conceptual practices in which the various members of the linguistic community participate.

I am not in this context appealing to Wittgensteinian arguments against private languages. (In my view these arguments rule out certain 'private' languages and allow others, and it is far from clear that any important philosophical position depends on a private language in the unacceptable sense.) I am simply asserting what seems to me obvious, that, as it happens, our colour language is social: one's descriptions of perceptual experiences draw upon the public language which one shares with others. This fact, it should be added, does not rule out the existence of a private component. Indeed, as I shall argue in the final part of this book, reference to phenomenal aspects of colour experience is vital.

There is a connection between the social-linguistic aspect and the perceptual aspect. The former incorporates or absorbs the latter. It does so in two ways. First, the right account of the meaning of colour terms must make reference to the way colour is perceived. Secondly, and more specifically, it must make reference to the way things appear.

10 Of course these systems are devised for a range of different purposes, and hence some systems are more 'natural' than others, but this does not affect anything I have just said.

The importance of these aspects may be brought out as follows. In trying to give an account of what colour terms mean, we need to do a number of things. We need to be able to explain the following:

(1) How language-users apply the terms correctly, i.e., under what circumstances they judge that 'lettuce is green' or that 'that sunset is golden' or that 'the moon tonight is yellow';
(2) How they learn to apply the terms, i.e., how they acquire competency in colour language;
(3) How communication takes place.

At least we need to show how it is possible to explain such things. Any adequate account of the mechanisms involved in such tasks is clearly going to require an account of the perception of colour. More specifically, once we get down to the details of the socially based colour terms, we need to make reference to the way things appear. The description of the way things appear is a janus-type description: it presupposes knowledge of what it is for something to appear to one.

We describe the way things appear in the following terms: *that* looks yellow, *this* looks rusty, Brian looks thin, Martha looks pale and so on. I claim that the way such descriptions function in the language requires the existence of a core group of language-users who judge that something looks yellow, thin, rusty and so on, on the basis of its looking so to that person. In other words, it requires the existence of a core group of 'looks' experts. If I am one of those experts, it is because *x* looks rusty to me that I judge that it does look rusty. For many examples of 'looks . . .', the core-group of experts is so wide that it may include almost everyone. Almost all, except the blind, are experts for colour, at least for very broad ranges of colour. In other cases the core group is very narrow. For example, in reading an X-ray photo some experts can say 'That looks threatening', 'The other looks harmless' and so on, but most of us are in no such position. We need to be clear here. The X-ray expert does not just say that 'that looks harmless to *me*'. What she says is that it looks harmless. This last judgement could be challenged by another expert. It is because the spot looks harmless to her that the first expert is in a position to say that it does look harmless, i.e., that it looks harmless to someone in a position to know.

5. A ROLE FOR EXPLICIT BELIEFS

In identifying what the natural concept of colour is, what is important is that we determine which concept it is that is implicit in colour-conceptual practices. It need not express the explicitly held belief of language-users about colour. Nevertheless, once we set out what is required in giving an account of what colour terms mean, we have allowed a place for the explicit belief, or at least for certain explicit beliefs. For although the explicit belief has no privileged status with respect to the truth about colour, nor to what is the implicit natural view, it may play a causal role in the mechanisms involved whereby people learn to apply colour terms and communicate with others about colours.

It is a description of such mechanisms that Gareth Evans has furnished.[11] It is contained in the theory of meaning he has provided for names, both of individuals and of natural kinds. His theory is opposed to the two major theories of how names secure reference: the causal theory and the descriptive theory. Or, more accurately, it incorporates and excludes elements from each. According to Evans's theory, the name refers to a certain individual, one which plays an appropriate causal role in the use of the name but where one of the factors involved in the causal mechanism is a certain kind of knowledge possessed by language-users. The description, or a certain description, is important not simply because it refers to that which satisfies the description. Its importance lies in the fact that it provides part of the causal mechanism whereby the individual (or natural kind) plays its causal role.

Given this fragment of a theory of meaning, we can understand how it is *possible,* at least in the case of ordinary language-users, that their beliefs about colour should play an analogous causal role in the appropriate causal mechanism. Indeed, as I shall argue, one can apply just such a theory to colour terms. I acknowledge that Evans writes of *knowledge* where I am writing of beliefs, but this modification, I argue, is acceptable. First, I do not claim that all the explicit beliefs are false, so there is some knowledge contained. Insofar as knowledge is necessary in order for the causal mechanism to function properly, this will be sufficient. Secondly, I argue with respect to the beliefs that although they are false, it is for many purposes just as *if they were true.* This means that, in the right circumstances, it is as *if they amounted to knowledge.*

6. AN IMPLICIT THEORY OF PERCEPTION

For some terms, particularly colour terms, an account of what these terms means requires giving an account of the way things appear. That

---

11 G. Evans (1982), esp. chs. 9 and 11.

is, colour terms such as 'yellow', 'blue', 'pink' etc., refer to the properties that they do because things appear yellow, appear blue, appear pink and so on. For us to give an account of how these appearances play a role in the conceptual practices, we need to provide a basic theory of perception.

I maintain that in order for appearances to play a role in conceptual practices, some theory of perception, however basic, must be implicit in these practices. The appearances, I maintain, need not be recognised as such. Indeed many language-users take the appearances for the reality. The theory is not very complex. It is that theory that is often termed direct realism. Its core features are these:

(a) The physical qualities perceived exist independently of their being perceived;
(b) They can be perceived exactly as they are, i.e., without distortion and not through another medium, and they often are;
(c) The physical qualities play a causal role in the perception of those qualities.

This theory of perception not only has a role in underpinning the sensible-quality feature of colour, but is also involved in the colour-language feature. For the plausible account of what colour terms name and how the names get secured in colour-naming practices requires an account of the role colours play in the perception of colour and in colour-naming practices.

It is important to realise that though this theory carries some epistemological weight, it is relatively mild. It is not equivalent to the 'window model of perception' which I discussed earlier, following Burnyeat, as a possible theory of perception.[12] The window model is one form of direct realism. It can be thought of as offering the crudest of mechanisms for perception, the window being the model for the senses. Direct realism, by contrast, offers a set of theses without being committed to any particular mechanism. Of course it may be argued that the theory is false because no acceptable mechanism can be found, but my use of the direct realism theory does not rely on its being true. What I claim is that it is implicit in conceptual practices characteristic of ordinary natural language, not only for colour but for many other properties, e.g. shapes, sizes, distance, motion or rest and so on. Clearly it makes sense to say that the theses are implicit in the practice, without there being any conception of the mechanism involved. We might usefully consider another case for which parallel claims might be made. It is also possible that ordinary language involves certain theses about souls and spirits

12 M. Burnyeat (1979).

being distinct from but causally interacting with physical objects, without containing any conception of the mechanism for interaction.

7. COLOURS AS SENSIBLE QUALITIES

It is a fundamental feature of the perceptual aspect that colour is a sensible quality. An object's colour can be, and normally is, identified by looking at it. More than this, colours are properties for which there are distinctive and characteristic sensible appearances. In other words, there are sensible appearances captured by expressions such as 'looks red', 'looks blue' and so on. It is also implicit in ordinary colour practices that physical objects are red and look red, and that the sense of 'red' in which they are red is the same as in 'looks red'. In addition the criterion for something's being yellow normally is that it appears yellow, at least to the right kind of person in the right circumstances.

It is part of the task of a theory of colour to provide an account of how colour is a sensible quality. This in turn requires that we provide a further account of 'looks . . .', as in 'looks yellow'. And further, to do that requires showing how 'looks yellow to me' relates to 'looks yellow to her (you)'.

Part of the colour conceptual-practice is this: perceivers recognise and discriminate objects on the basis of colour. That is, they recognise colours and discriminate among them. Someone who has become a member of colour-using practice is someone who can recognise an object's colour. Of course blind people can use colour terms, but these people are secondary members of the practice. It is essential to the practice's being what it is that there be people who discriminate on the basis of colour, who recognise an object's colour. (Newspaper polls and exit polls may predict a winner, but they are secondary, being derivative of election polls.)

My recognition of red and yellow consists in this: it is on the basis that x looks red to me that I am in a position to declare that it is red. Though there are times when x looks red but isn't, my justification for the claim that it is red, when I know that it is, is its looking red.

One feature of our colour concepts is that we make judgements that objects have colours: that sunset is golden, your trousers are purple and so on. Another is that we compare colours, or objects on the basis of colour: that is a deeper blue than this; that is a darker red, that a paler green; this is closer to red than that. In other words, our colour thoughts take the form not only of 'x is yellow', but 'y is more yellow than z'; 'y

is a deeper yellow than r'; 'x and y are closer in yellowness than are y and z' and so on. These judgements are not just judgements about objects x and y, but are judgements about universals. For y to be more yellow than z, what is involved are two universals: y and z are instances of two universals (shades of yellow) that stand in a certain relation to each other.

Our analysis of that part of colour-conceptual practices which is expressed by the claim that colour is a sensible quality reveals the existence of a number of interrelated features. Together they underpin the colour-conceptual practices that are so much a part of our lives:

(a) There is a set of colour truths both simple and complex: physical objects are yellow, red, green . . . ; some are a paler red than others.
(b) There is a structure or order to the set of relationships holding between colours: they can be ordered systematically.
(c) Colours are sensible qualities: they are properties for which there are distinctive appearances.

Together they enable us to draw certain conclusions about colours and their appearances, i.e. between colours and the way they are perceived. Summarising, a typical colour red is a feature such that:

(i) It is a property of physical objects.
(ii) It occupies a role in the three-dimensional colour array.
(iii) For each competent colour-discriminator it is true that 'I recognise by its looking red to me that it is red; I see the object and see that it is red'.
(iv) It plays a causal role in that recognition.

I directly see the redness. The same redness that I see plays the appropriate causal role. It is the same property that satisfies the roles in (iii) and (iv) that occupies the role in (ii).

We can combine the last two conditions by specifying that colours are properties which play a special dual role in colour perception: a causal role and a presentational role. That is, colour is both a property which plays a causal role in the perception of colour and the feature with which each of us is presented in perception.

8. KNOWLEDGE OF COLOUR APPEARANCES

This specification of the natural concept of colour has to be understood in a certain way. It does not provide a definition in the sense that anyone who understands colour terms must at the same time know of the separate clauses in the specification and know whether or not they apply. Nor does it provide a set of necessary and sufficient conditions which we could substitute, with appropriate grammatical modifications, in sentences employing colour terms.

What I am claiming is that the specification provides an account of the colour properties which the set of social colour-conceptual practices pick out. The way they do that depends on the kinds of causal mechanisms that Evans has described and that I made use of above and in the last chapter. One part of these causal mechanisms involves knowledge on the part of the participants in the conceptual practices. Crucially, not all of this knowledge is knowledge *that* so-and-so is the case. Some of it involves knowing *how* and knowing *which*.

The point about colour concepts being perceptual concepts, and more strictly being sensible concepts, is that they involve this kind of knowing how and knowing which. In particular, they involve knowing what red looks like, knowing how to recognise red, knowing how to distinguish red from pink and from orange, and so on. Grasping such colour concepts requires acquiring this kind of knowledge. That is, it requires the possession of intuitive knowledge and not just abstract knowledge.[13]

One major advantage of this account is that it enables us to understand how colour appearances can play an important role without the participants being aware of them as such. I have previously argued that appearances are essential to colour, even though it is sophisticated for people to be able to distinguish between a quality as it is and as it appears. This apparent paradox is shown to be only that: apparent. Our knowledge of appearances, of the way the colours look, is typically intuitive knowledge. It is not abstract knowledge. A perceiver can know what red things look like without ever knowing *that* anything looks red. The perceiver may never know that anything looks red, because she has not yet acquired explicit knowledge of the distinction between 'is red' and 'looks red' (nor of the distinction for any colour).

9. QUALIA

It is, I have claimed, implicit in the natural concept of colour that colours are the sorts of properties that together have the kind of structure characteristic of the three-dimensional colour arrays. This point can be expressed by saying that colours are qualia in the open sense; that is, they are open-qualia. The notion of open-qualia was introduced in Chapter 2, by taking the notion of (phenomenal) qualia and widening it to allow

13 See Chapter 9, Section 5, for a further discussion of these two kinds of knowledge.

that features standing in relationships of similarity and difference might be physical features. That is, we can take phenomenal qualia to be defined in the following way:

> Phenomenal qualia = the qualitative or phenomenal features of sense-experience in virtue of having which the sense-experiences resemble and differ from each other, qualitatively, in the ways that they do.

I argued that, given this notion of phenomenal qualia, it was possible to go on and define a notion of open-qualia: qualitative features which stand in just those relationships without necessarily being phenomenal qualities of sense-experiences. That is, it is left open whether the features are phenomenal or physical. Of course making such a definition provides no guarantee that there are any such qualia.

Saying that a property is an open-quale involves three elements:

(a) It is a feature by virtue of which it stands in the appropriate relations with other qualia;
(b) It is the property each person recognises as being the colour that it is;
(c) It is an intrinsic, nonrelational feature.

As far as (b) is concerned, it connects with clause (iii) in the specification of the natural concept of colour, but something needs to be added. For a person who recognises colour, a person who is central to the practice, it is crucial that that person is aware of the colour as something that 'I recognise', i.e., something that he or she recognises. That is, for people who understand the use of colour terms, not only is yellow a feature which plays a causal role in the recognition by any competent person, but it is a feature that that person knows by recognition.

10. THE RIGHT ACCOUNT OF THE NATURAL CONCEPT

By a close study of our colour-conceptual practices, as provided in the last three sections, it is possible to describe a set of interrelated features which together play a role in the colour-conceptual practices that are so much a part of our lives. From reflection on these features it is possible to extract an account of the 'natural concept' of colour. This need not be the same thing as the view of colour that unreflective people would give if asked.

The natural concept is the concept of colour described in Chapter 2, Section 7, where it was referred to as 'the right view of colour'. A typical colour term, say, 'golden' which functions in a sentence such as 'that sunset is golden', expresses a concept of the following kind. The property of being coloured golden is a property satisfying the requirements:

(a) It is an intrinsic, nonrelational property possessed by publicly accessible objects such as sunsets, hair, rings . . .
(b) It is an open-quale of objects;
(c) It plays a special causal and presentational role in perceivers' perception, i.e., in their recognition and identification of the colour.

This is the concept of 'golden' that is contained in the representational content of colour thoughts or colour judgements. That is, for sentences using 'golden' (red, yellow, blue . . .) it expresses what is understood by someone who has full understanding of the sentences.

However, it turns out that nothing exemplifies this concept. There is no property of physical objects which satisfies the three requirements set out above. In particular, there are no physical properties of objects that are qualia and that play the causal role. Nothing, that is, has the colour property, so defined. This kind of colour is a virtual property, just as caloric and phlogiston are virtual natural kinds. There is nevertheless a major difference. For colour, unlike caloric and phlogiston, there is a significant dispositional property: the power to induce perceptual representations of an interesting kind. Which kind? They represent objects as having those colours which they do not have, those virtual properties.

It is a consequence of the natural concept of colour having both causal and phenomenological features that, the world being what it is, colours are virtual. This aspect of the account developed here distinguishes it sharply from the theory of colour provided by Charles Landesman. He too emphasises the insights of those in the Descartes-Locke tradition, but he argues for what he terms 'colour skepticism'. This thesis is an epistemological one, expressive of doubt that we have knowledge that any object has colour. It is distinguished by Landesman from 'colour nihilism', the view that denies that any object has colour.[14] The theory of virtual colours would be a form of colour nihilism. It is my reliance on Gareth Evans's account of reference that is crucial in establishing my own thesis, which is much stronger than colour skepticism.

14 See Landesman (1989), Ch. 8, 'Colour Skepticism'.

11. REVIEW

This account of the natural concept of colour is the account of that concept which is implicit in our ordinary conceptual practices. Indeed, it would be close to the explicitly held belief of many people (suitably prompted). It turns out, however, that the natural concept of colour contains certain false claims. There are in fact no objects which have the colours as normally conceived. Virtual colours are intrinsic, nonrelational properties of physical objects; they play a special role in the perception of colour, and collectively they form a set of interrelated physical properties that mirrors the relationships expressed in the well-known colour arrays. We can see therefore that Descartes and Locke were correct in their 'error thesis' of colour perception, although they were wrong in what they took the natural concept to be.

Notwithstanding the error thesis, it does not follow that the natural concept does not have a valuable role to play. What we need to do, if we support an error theory, is to explain how the error-laden concept developed and how, given the circumstances, it could be as valuable as it is. Not surprisingly, the answers to these two questions, as we have seen, are related. They both depend on the fact that even if objects do not have colours, it does not matter in many contexts. For many purposes, it is as if the objects had such colours. The point is that even if colour is a virtual property, there is a significant and important dispositional property: the power to induce sensory representations which represent objects as having (virtual) colours.

This leaves us with a further question, one that was raised in the preceding chapter but set aside. This is the question of how we should proceed once we have recognised that colours, as naturally conceived, are virtual. The answer to this question is contained, I submit, in the answers to the other two questions. It depends on recognising that we developed the natural concepts we did because they served certain purposes of significance, and that we still have those purposes. What is perhaps different now is that we have developed some additional interests.

Part II

The colours objects have: the pluralist framework

Our visual experiences normally represent objects as having colours, colours which they do not have. These colours are 'objective' properties but virtual ones. Virtual colours are intrinsic, nonrelational properties of physical objects; they are features which have certain causal roles to play and are properties which, as a group, are endowed with a distinctive (phenomenological) character.

The explanation for why we have developed such a concept of colour is, first, that objects have the disposition to appear in certain distinctive ways, that is they have the disposition to cause in us sensory representations of the world; and second, that these representations have the character they do. These representations represent objects in the physical world as having the virtual colours, and they do so because they have the character implicit in the three-dimensional colour array. Thus we can explain both why we developed the virtual-colour concepts and why they have been so valuable.

This means that although Descartes and Locke were wrong in their formulation of the error thesis and in their formulation of the natural concept of colour, nevertheless their instincts were right. Phenomenal colour does have a role in explaining why we have the colour concept that we do, why it has the form that it takes and how our experiences represent objects as having colours. Moreover Descartes and Locke are also right to argue that there is a viable perceiver-dependent dispositional property, a disposition to appear in characteristic ways to perceivers (of the appropriate kind).

Having said that, we still need to develop an account that prescribes how we should proceed to think about colour, at least in general terms. For a comprehensive theory of colour, so I argue, we need to develop a pluralist account. This pluralist view allows for the possibility of an objectivist concept but requires both dispositional and phenomenal concepts of colour.

105

Certain objectivist claims, e.g. those of Thomas Reid and Jonathan Westphal, have been considered and found wanting. Their view is that the way colour terms currently function is that they name objective qualities that for the moment may be unknown but that one day will be revealed by science. There are, however, other strategies that the objectivist might follow. One is to deny the assumption implicit in my account: that there is in fact no objective property of physical bodies that satisfies the requirements presupposed by use of the natural concept of colour. This denial can take either of two forms: that colour is an irreducible objective property of objects, or alternatively that colour can be treated as reducible to some objective property of physical bodies. The other strategy for the objectivist to follow is to accept that the natural concept of colour essentially involves appearances but argue that it ought to be replaced. That is, the objectivist is presenting a revisionary analysis of colour, proposing that there is no place for the natural concept and that it should make way for an objectivist concept.

In the second part of this book, both strategies are explored and rejected. The pluralist account of colour is defended, an account which has the consequence that, whatever valid claim the objectivist can mount, there is a need for a dispositional concept of colour. The significance of this is that the dispositional concept not only plays a part in explaining why we formed the virtual-colour concept and in explaining why that concept was valuable, but also in prescribing how we should continue to think of colour.

5

The pluralist framework

To develop an adequate theory of colour (or an adequate philosophical framework for such a theory), we need to do two things. First, we need to be able to give an account of the role that colour plays in the lives of colour-perceivers and in the many flourishing colour discourses that there are. Second, we need to develop an account to prescribe how we ought to think about colour, at least in principle. The Descartes-Locke tradition, in essence, solves the first problem by proposing a dispositional account of colour. This is done largely by arguing that although objects do not have the virtual colours, for many purposes this does not matter: it is as if objects did have the colours. They appear to have the qualities. The beauty of this solution, as we shall see, is that it also paves the way for the resolution of the second problem.

1. THE CRUCIAL STEP IN THINKING ABOUT COLOUR

The natural concepts of colour developed the way they did because they serve important purposes. Very broadly, these purposes are epistemological and aesthetic/emotional. Colour is important, first, as a sign of the presence of, and for the identification of, fruits, flowers, friends, enemies, helpful conditions and so on. Secondly, colours have a life of their own, i.e. they serve aesthetic and emotional purposes.

This being so, we can understand why colour might equally well serve these purposes if it were a dispositional property, and in particular if it were a disposition to appear a certain way. This is particularly so if we remember that historically the epistemological interest in colours is largely bound up with colours' being the signs of the presence of things that fit human purposes, e.g., ripe/poisonous fruit, venomous insects, and so on. Nevertheless, although it is the way colours appear that makes them significant, that in itself does not favour a dispositional analysis over an intrinsic-quality analysis. For the intrinsic quality could appear in the right way. It is just that there is good reason to reject the claim that there is such an (irreducible) intrinsic quality. Moreover, although the purposes for the colour concept are largely epistemological and aesthetic/emotional, they are not exclusively so. There is a certain range of general truths about coloured bodies:

Ripening pears (wheat, bananas . . .) go from green to yellow
Ripening apples (of a certain kind) go from green to red
Acids turn blue litmus red; bases turn red litmus blue
Spiders with red stripes on the back are venomous
Black hair tends to grow grey with age

And so on. At least with respect to *this* body of truths there is some plausibility in identifying colour with some physical structure. Likewise with respect to colour-matching experiments such as some Maxwell and Helmholtz performed, there is some plausibility in picking out a colour concept that makes colour a disposition to induce certain physiological responses.

It is possible to bring some order into this apparent disunity. For there is no reason why we should not have more than one concept of colour. The natural concept of colour is intended to serve a range of purposes. We find, however, that nothing exists that satisfies all the requirements. However, all is not lost. It is possible to develop a new set of colour concepts that as a whole serves all or most of the previous purposes. None of them taken singly serves all, but each serves some. Very roughly, there are two major roles for colour: one comprises the epistemological, aesthetic and emotional roles, the other the causal. The first set of roles is served by the colour appearance; the second could be served by whatever causal basis (or bases) there is (are) for the appearance.

Once it is recognised that colours, as specified by the traditional concept, are virtual properties and that there is no property that serves all the functions relevant to that concept, the way is open to recognise two new concepts of colour: dispositional colour, to take over and consolidate the role served by the appearance, and physical colour, to take over the causal role.

The crucial step in our thinking about colour is to take this step. Further complications arise as we try to discover what physical colour is. First of all, we have good reason to distinguish between different kinds of physical colour: surface colour, volume colour, light colour and so on. Second, it may well be that physical colour is not in fact an intrinsic feature of physical surfaces but instead a relational feature, e.g. of a surface-in-a-particular-illumination. What physical colour is is an interesting question, but the crucial philosophical step is to distinguish between physical colour, whatever it is, and dispositional colour (and with the latter, phenomenal colour). Taking that step is quite independent of finding an answer to the question about the nature of physical colour.

2. CONCEPTUAL SPLITTING

What I have described is a process of conceptual splitting. Concepts, like many another thing, have histories, and for some of them their history involves a splitting or a 'fission' into two new concepts related to the first.[1] This process, I have argued, applies to colour. An illuminating example of conceptual splitting that may help to clarify this thesis about colour is given in the history of the concept of size. There is obviously a sense of size such that men are larger than rabbits and rabbits larger than beetles. This property is an absolute, intrinsic property that all men, rabbits and beetles have independent of the conditions they are in and how they are perceived and by whom. A man standing on a mountain-top is bigger than a rabbit, sitting or standing, at either the top of the mountain or at the bottom. There is, however, a different property of size, angular size, that does vary according to position. If I am at the bottom of a mountain, then a man at the top is a smaller angular size than a rabbit at my foot. The angular size of a man is defined in terms of the angle subtended at any given point. Accordingly a man or any object has as many angular sizes as there are points from which to observe him. Notwithstanding that, there are certain positions or distances from which it is usual or customary to observe men. They do not include two inches or ten miles.

Once we make a clear distinction between these two kinds of size, we have no difficulty in thinking of a man as having a larger intrinsic size than a rabbit but a smaller angular size than the same rabbit, relative to a particular point of view. Our being able to make that distinction depends, however, on our having the capacity to think of viewing the rabbit and the man in terms of geometrical lines joining the observer and either the man or the rabbit. Those geometrical lines we can now think of as defined by light rays. Once we have the ability to construct such lines in thought, then we can understand angular size and how it depends on the viewing position.

1 This account of conceptual splitting, or 'fission', was developed originally in J. B. Maund (1981), 'Colour: A Case for Conceptual Fission', *Australas. J. Phil.*, 59, pp. 308–22.

But it wasn't always so. The representation of perception in terms of geometrical lines is a relatively late phenomenon. It was in fact a sophisticated conceptual advance, as was that contained in thinking of the atmosphere as having weight and as a fluid, or in thinking of light as being something that travelled. Prior to that, people did not have, and could not have had, a concept of angular size. Of course people would have been aware that as objects receded into the distance they appeared different, although even this piece of knowledge may not have been all that obvious. The phenomenon of size constancy, in addition to the other constancy effects, would have had a tendency to make it easier for such knowledge to be ignored.

Even after the development of geometrical lines to represent the way in which objects at a distance were perceived, it took time before a clear concept of angular size developed. Even then, as well as before, people drew a distinction not between absolute intrinsic size and angular size but between size and apparent size. In other words, the contrast was drawn between the real size of an object and the 'apparent' size – the size it appeared to be. An interesting illustration of this point can be found in the treatment by Descartes, in the *Dioptrics*, of the perception of size.[2] His discussion is in terms of real (absolute) size and apparent size. Significantly, he cites the axiom of ancient optics, which he says is not always true: the apparent size of objects is proportional to the angle of vision. Both this axiom and Descartes's discussion are in terms of apparent size rather than angular size. People who remember learning their optics at school may recall having been taught the distinction between real depth and apparent depth of an object in a water tank, real shape and apparent shape, real size and apparent size.

The contrast between 'real' size and 'apparent' size suggests that the latter is nonexistent or imaginary. However, once we have made the distinction in terms of intrinsic size and angular size, this impression should disappear. It illustrates what J. C. Austin pointed out about the distinction between a real duck and a decoy duck: it is not a distinction between something that exists and something that does not but between two existing things.[3]

Originally people, including scientists and philosophers, had one concept of size, and with that single concept drew a distinction between real size and apparent size. Now we have two concepts of size, and with

2 Descartes (1954), pp. 254–6.
3 J. C. Austin (1962), *Sense and Sensibilia*, ed. G. Warnock, Oxford: Clarendon, pp. 62–77, esp. 70.

respect to each we can draw a distinction between real and apparent size. For example, with respect to angular size, the effect of size constancy (or size regression) means that the angular size of a man often appears larger than it is. Not only do we have two concepts of size, we have three. For with respect to angular size it can be important to distinguish between geometrical angular size and optical angular size. The one is defined in terms of an angle bound by geometrical lines, and the other by optical lines. If light rays pass through a heavy atmosphere, then by refraction the optical angle subtended at the eye will be different from that of the geometrical angle. Accordingly we can define two kinds of angular size: geometrical and optical.

Analogously, when we turn to colour and endeavour to provide an account of physical colour, we can distinguish between different kinds of candidates for physical colour. Concentrating on the colour of physical surfaces, we can distinguish among four kinds of physical feature:

(a) Intrinsic physical features of the body's surface
(b) The light affected at the object's surface
(c) The effect of the surface on the reflected light at a given distant point
(d) The contribution of the surface to the light received at a given distant point, relative to the overall distribution of light surfaces

All of these are physical features. All of them are properties of the surface in question. Someone intent on giving an objectivist analysis of colour should regard these as eligible candidates. The curious thing is that objectivists seem to think that there can be only one genuine candidate. However, there is no reason why we should not develop a 'pluralist' account of colour, which allows all of these cases to be regarded as physical colours. Just as there are different kinds of physical size, so there might be different kinds of physical colour. What the pluralist insists on is that, in addition to these kinds of physical colour, there is a viable dispositional property tied essentially to the way objects *appear*.

Likewise, when we turn from surface colours to film colours, source colours, volume colours and so on, it is possible to draw similar distinctions. The abundance of such distinctions makes things complex; but whoever thought the theory of colour would be simple? The fields that make up colour science and interact with the fields of engineering, industry, fashion and design have developed in such a way that these distinctions have been drawn. Not that it is always easy to recognise that this is so.

As with concepts of size, we have come to make these distinctions because of the historical development of our concepts. As a result of our

111

gaining knowledge – about the chemistry and physics of surfaces (and volumes) of objects, about the properties of light and of illumination, about physiology and psychology, about painting and painterly effects – there has emerged the realisation that there is a point to distinguishing between the different concepts. Before we discovered that detailed knowledge, however, we had, and still have, a considerable body of knowledge about colour. This comprises a body of truths of which some account needs to be taken if we are to put forward an adequate comprehensive theory of colour. These 'truths' may come to be revised or rejected, but they provide a starting point. If they are to be rejected, good reasons need to be provided. Among the 'colour truths' we can distinguish different kinds:

(1) There are lots of truths about coloured objects: tomatoes are red, apples green or red, sunsets golden, the cloudless sky blue, and so on.

(2) There are general facts or principles about coloured bodies: e.g., ripening pears and wheat go from green to yellow, acids turn blue litmus paper red, spiders with red stripes on the back are venomous, black hair tends to grow grey with age, and so on.

(3) The way colours are identified and recognised is by the way they appear to perceivers. There are no colour thermometers or other measuring devices. Certain conditions are better than others for identifying colours; certain people are better than others at identifying colours. As a result we can pick out certain conditions as standard conditions and certain observers as standard observers. (What we call 'standard' may itself be relative to context.)

(4) Colours can be ordered systematically so as to make up colour systems, each with a distinctive, complex character.

(5) There are 'phenomenological facts'. Reds merge into blues and also into yellows but not into greens. Blues merge into greens and reds but not into yellows. And so on. Yellow makes a stronger contrast with black than with white.

(6) There are certain aesthetic and emotional facts. For certain people, green is soothing. Soft pastels are suitable in certain contexts; mauves and browns are not. Light colours and dark colours have different effects on mood, and so on. Certain colours are harmonious, and so on.

(7) There are truths comprising the way perceived colours vary with illumination, distance, and so on.

(8) There are truths about how the colour of surfaces is affected by the background against which an object is seen.

The range and extent of the general principles, classified under items (2) and (8), have been emphasised by Justin Broackes.[4] (For further discus-

---

4 Justin Broackes (1992), 'The Autonomy of Colour', in D. Charles and K. Lennon (eds.), *Reduction, Explanation and Realism*, Oxford: Clarendon, pp. 421–66.

sion, see 'The Autonomy of Colour' below in Chapter 6.) These general facts or principles include causal truths, although the nature of the causal powers may be difficult to discern. (I also take this issue up in Chapter 6: (See 'The Causal Role of Colour'.) The principles need not be thought of as natural laws, physical laws, exceptionless regularities, uniform universal generalisations and so on. Like many another principle, they are general principles which are subject to qualification, saving clauses, exceptions and so on. Moreover, particularly with respect to the social and aesthetic facts, they do not need to hold for all people at all times and in all contexts. That they do not does not mean that they are not useful and important.

An adequate theory of colour will need to handle such truths as these. This is not to say that the truths are holy writ or eternal verities, irrefutable and immutable. They may be reinterpreted or qualified or even rejected – but an adequate theory will make sense of them. One possibility is that there is not a single determinate concept of colour; that instead there is a family of interrelated concepts that in our ordinary pretheoretical practices are not clearly distinguished – for the very practical reason that for many purposes there is little point to distinguishing them.

If so, there may still arise situations in which it is necessary, or at least beneficial, to distinguish them: either for the scientific study of colour or for the practical pursuit of certain colour-related activities, e.g. in art and theatre, in painting, lighting etc.; or in art and design, in fashion, lighting and so on; or finally for philosophical purposes: in providing a theory that interrelates, even if in very schematic form, those different activities and studies.

It is interesting to compare colour with the other secondary qualities. As it turns out, the causal truths concerning colour comprise a limited and very peculiar range. Things are quite different for warmth and sound. In the case of warmth we have concepts of heat and temperature which are of enormous causal interest, i.e. in a body of causal laws, quite apart from any immediate human concern. Likewise for sound – although sound is of greater importance than warmth, as far as human interests are concerned. This could be phrased better. Of course warmth and cold are important, but there is nothing here to compare with music or with the wealth of uses for colour. It is pleasant to feel warm and not nice to be hot, but it is hardly the stuff of poetry or something to stir the soul.

Although there are these various differences among the various secondary qualities, nothing stops us from making, in all cases, the threefold distinction among physical, dispositional and phenomenal properties, i.e. for colours, sounds, odours and so on.

3. THE PLURALIST VIEW OF COLOUR

It is useful at this stage to refer again to the views of Hering, which I discussed in Chapter 3. Hering's proposal was that colour, primarily, is a subjective phenomenon and that surfaces, bodies, radiation, light, retinal outputs etc. are coloured only in a secondary or derivative sense.[5] Where he differs from such theorists as Locke and Helmholtz is on the nature of the subjectivity. Many philosophers, particularly modern-day ones, offer a directly contrasting proposal: that colour primarily is an objective property where, depending on the opponent, the property is either a physical quality possessed by the physical body or a disposition to modify light or some anthropocentric property – some obscure feature picked out by reference to its ability to excite an appropriate physiological state in observers with retinas having certain visual responses.

There is, however, a third possibility, one which in spirit has more in common with the older tradition than with its rivals. This embodies the claim that there is not just one viable concept of colour but several. Just as for size we can distinguish between different kinds of size – absolute size, geometrical angular size and optical angular size – so too for colour we can distinguish between different kinds of colour, e.g. physical colour, optical colour, psychophysical colour and so on. Each is viable in its own right. Each serves its own purposes and functions. Although they are different, they are nevertheless still related, just as absolute size and angular size are related. What gives point to calling them all colour is (i) that certain characteristic causal relationships hold between them and (ii) certain formal parallels hold between them. Included among the various kinds of colour is dispositional colour: the disposition to appear in (or look) a characteristically coloured way. The colour that objects appear to have is a virtual property, an intrinsic property that objects do not in fact have.

These considerations point to the possibility of a pluralist view of colour. Such a view, I suggest, is worth our attention. Part of what it requires is the recognition that the pluralist matrix of colour concepts comprises a stage that has emerged, or is in the process of emerging, from a historical conceptual development. The natural, primitive concept of

5 Hering (1964), p. 3.

colour was a single concept that is identical with none of the concepts that now make up the pluralist scheme. This primitive concept is what I have called the virtual-property concept. That concept contained different elements and served a range of functions. These elements and functions have been divided among the separate concepts that now make up the pluralist scheme. Our concepts of colour have evolved and have done so by a process of splitting. This suggests another reason for calling the different members of the pluralist set-up 'colours': it records, just as do other evolutionary schemes, their conceptual ancestry.

I hope it will emerge as we proceed that the functions of the virtual-colour concept can be taken over by the dispositional concept, the phenomenal concept and the objective concept. Objects with virtual colours are allegedly (a) objects with certain causal powers, (b) objects which appear a certain way and (c) objects whose appearances have a certain qualitative character. Very roughly, physical colour takes over the causal role, dispositional colour takes over the appearance role and phenomenal colour takes over the qualitative character.

Although the pluralist account makes room for an objectivist concept of colour, it does not make it mandatory. In the remainder of this second part of the book, I examine claims to provide objectivist accounts of colour, especially of reductionist or revisionary types. I argue that there is no successful account of colour which dispenses with the need for a dispositional concept, one which in turn requires both virtual colours and phenomenal colour.

6

Objectivist accounts of colour

The simplest objectivist view of colour is that it is a simple intrinsic property of bodies, one not reducible to any other property. Blue is blue and not anything else. Few modern objectivists defend such a view. It was once hoped instead that different colours would be identified with different microstructures of objects, but the most plausible candidate these days is some light-related quality, e.g. some aspect of an object's spectral reflectance curve. Those who defend such a view normally do so by arguing that colour is reducible to the appropriate light-related quality.

These objectivist accounts are to be understood in realist terms: for each colour predicate there is a physical property that physical objects have and that one can directly see these objects as having. In certain circumstances an object will look to have the colour it (really) has. However, as Keith Campbell and others have argued, there seem to be overwhelming objections to the direct realist view, whether we interpret the latter in the naive form or the critical (reductionist) form.[1]

Crucial premises in arguments expressing these objections are the claims (i) that there is no distinctive causal effect that each and only each colour has and (ii) that there is no single property which *things* which are yellow (and only things which are yellow) have in common. Both of these claims, it should be noted, are held to be true whether colour is taken as transitory colour, the colour of an object in whatever illumination it is placed, or as standing colour, the colour of an object in standard illumination.[2]

---

1 Keith Campbell (1969), 'Colours', in R. Brown and C. D. Rollins (eds.), *Contemporary Philosophy in Australia*, London: Allen and Unwin, pp. 132–57; C.W.K. Mundle (1971), *Perception: Facts and Theories*, Oxford: OUP, esp. chs. 9–11; Jackson (1977), ch. 5; W. Sellars (1971), 'Science, Sense-Impressions and Sensa', *Rev. Metaphysics*, 23, pp. 391–447.

2 This distinction is made in Campbell (1969), p. 134.

In this chapter I consider these arguments and whether the objectivist can meet them.[3] In particular, one attempt to circumvent these objections will be examined: the defence of Anthropocentric Realism by D. R. Hilbert.

1. BLUE IS BLUE AND NOTHING ELSE

The simplest objectivist view is that colour is an objective, intrinsic property of objects, typically of surfaces but sometimes of light sources, of volumes (glasses of wine, icecubes . . .) and so on. On this view, colour is an irreducible property: blue is blue and not anything else. The colour is objective in the sense that the object has it whether or not anyone is looking at it.

This view of colour is a very simple one, whose details have been fleshed out in my account of the 'natural concept' of colour. Even if it were not the natural view, however, it would still be worth discussing. It is a view that has been widely held, and it has been defended by philosophers of some significance. If it is wrong, it is worth showing why it is wrong.

The fundamental reason why the natural concept can be taken to embody an error theory is that there are no physical features of objects which both have the right qualitative structure *and* have the right causal powers, e.g. to affect perceivers. I have assumed this to be true and have not explicitly argued for it. There are, however, arguments that address the point, e.g. those by Keith Campbell and Frank Jackson. Central to those arguments are certain assumptions about colour, causal explanation and objectivity. Since these assumptions are open to challenge, it will be necessary to examine the arguments.

It was in an influential paper entitled 'Colours' (1969) that Campbell presented one of the strongest attacks on objectivist views of colour, whether of nonreductive or reductive varieties. Campbell argued that there is reason to hold each of three propositions:

(1) Colours are properties of what is seen;
(2) What is seen is a physical object;
(3) Colour properties have no place in the most detailed scientific accounts of what physically exists.

On the face of it, these propositions are mutually inconsistent. In his paper Campbell examines attempts to deny proposition (3), by trying to

3 The first half of the chapter reconstructs material originally presented in Maund (1981).

117

reduce colour to some complex physical property. First of all, however, the idea of colours' being intrinsic, irreducible physical qualities of such surfaces is considered, only to be quickly dismissed:

Such a non-reductive realism about colours would be acceptable only if there were associated with all and only red, blue, orange, green things respectively distinctive patterns of effect upon other physical objects.[4]

The emphasis in this passage is on 'all and only'. If colour is a physical property, then we would expect *all* red things to have characteristic causal effects, and the same effects. If colour is irreducible, we would expect that *only* red things would have those distinctive effects. This last expectation has failed to be realised. For it to be true, Campbell says, physics would require 'colour terms as primitives in some branch of explanation'. No such branch has been forthcoming. Nor are the prospects good for its developing.

Thus if colour is thought of as a primitive, unreduced property, it plays no role in the most advanced physical theories and hence seems to have no causal role to play. Consequently, we are faced with two options: either we must reduce colour to some other physical property, either a property of an object's surface or a power to modify light in a distinctive way, or we must give up the claim that colours play any causal role. Neither option is appealing.

The first option, which allows us to maintain that colour is a physical, observer-independent property, means that colour must be reducible to a complex and derivative set of physical qualities. But it is just not true, Campbell argues, that all objects blue under a given illumination have a distinctive light-modifying feature in common. There are many different qualities of objects which enable two objects to so act on a given incident light as to match in colour. Faced with this, one might be tempted to identify (transitory) colour either with an exercised disposition of that body to modify the composition of light in a distinctive way or with the effect of the power's exercise upon the incident light. But this attempt would be no more successful: surfaces with indefinitely many different relative reflectance curves can be the same colour, e.g. turquoise, in a given illumination. Campbell has been rightly criticised for overstating the extent of the difference in relative reflectance curves for each colour.[5] The variety of curves is more appropriate if we are considering aperture colours – the colour the object appears to be when viewed through an aperture. Things are quite different, however, in viewing physical objects

4 Campbell (1969), pp. 135–6.   5 See Hilbert (1987), pp. 51–60.

where it is clear that the colour one is seeing is surface colour. Despite this, it is still true that there exist metamers for surface colours: objects with widely differing reflectance curves will in standard illumination appear indistinguishable in colour. Thus Campbell's point remains.

The second option is that colours do not have any causal role to play at all. The problem with this, as Frank Jackson has pointed out, is that it would land us with the unwelcome consequence that we could never know that a particular object is coloured.[6] For, so he argues, it is a necessary condition of a perceiver's acquiring knowledge about some physical state of the world that he or she be causally affected by that state or by some other state which is itself causally affected by it.[7] As Jackson emphasises, colour does not enter into causal relations with other physical processes, e.g. with light waves, eyeballs, retinas, brain cells, etc. Hence, if coming to know that an object has a certain property depends upon one's being causally affected by that property, then it follows that if physical objects are coloured we cannot know them to be so.

In principle, of course, colours could operate in virtue of an action-at-a-distance force, but the difficulty is that there are detailed physical processes involved in the perception of colour. These physical processes involve electronic states, light waves, retinas, neural cells and so on, but have no place for colours thought of as primitive, irreducible qualities. Given the validity of the physical causal laws, such colours, if they exist, are causally superfluous. Hence, if such colours exist we cannot know them to exist.

The only way to salvage the reality of such colours is to say that objects have the colours and that, even though they play no causal role in the process involving light rays, retinal cells, brain processes and so on, the result of this complex physical process is to reveal for the perceiver the true colours possessed by physical bodies distant from the perceiver. In other words, the end result of the process is that one simply perceives the really existing colours: one sees the colours as they really are.

Such a suggestion gets around the problem posed by Jackson's objections. Unfortunately it faces even greater ones. These were posed with devastating force by C. W. K. Mundle in *Perception: Facts and Theories*, and prior to that by C. D. Broad. Typical is the problem of simultaneous contrast. For any physical object that we see, the colour we see it as having depends on the background. The same object can appear to have any of a wide variety of different colours, depending on the nature of

6 Jackson (1977), pp. 130–8.   7 As we shall see, this claim needs to be qualified.

119

the background. It is not clear what nonarbitrary criterion can pick out the 'real' colour. Secondly, there is the problem of what status the illusory colours have. Thirdly, there is the problem of understanding what the brain is supposed to be doing. It would presumably be both revealing true colours at a place in space and projecting illusory colours to other places in space. This problem is magnified in those cases which combine real and illusory qualities. In a mirror, for example, the brain would be required to reveal real colours and real shapes at illusory places. Or would it be projecting illusory colours and illusory shapes?

It should be pointed out that a sense-datum theorist is not faced with the same problem. First, she is not committed to the view that the brain projects seen colours (or any other qualities) to places in space. Secondly, even if there is a mystery about how the brain produces sense-data, things are not helped by multiplying the mysteries. (Even mysteries have an order.)

2. THE CAUSAL ROLE OF COLOUR

These arguments, by both Jackson and Campbell, depend upon the fact that colour concepts do not play a role as primitive terms in theories of physics. Science, however, does not consist exclusively of physics. There are other branches of science in which there are causal laws involving colour terms, e.g. chemistry, zoology and botany. Moreover there seem to be a host of straightforward causal truths about colour which we can readily recognise. An illustration is a set of remarks by an eighteenth-century tailor:

It is not the black clothes that are trying to the sight – black is the steadiest of all colours to work at; white and all bright colours make the eyes water after looking at 'em for any long time, but of all colours scarlet, such as used for regimentals, is the most blinding, it seems to burn the eyeballs, and makes them ache dreadful . . . everything seems all of a twitter, and keeps changing its tint. There's more military tailors blind than any others.[8]

Furthermore, contrary to what Campbell claims, it does not follow from the fact that all things which are yellow do not have the same distinctive causal effects that the yellowness of an object never has causal effects.[9] Take predicates like 'two' (or 'double') and 'round': it is not true that

8 Robert Hughes (1988), *The Fatal Shore*, London: Pan, p. 21, quoting Henry Mayhew, *London Labour and the London Poor*.
9 Campbell (1969), pp. 134–5.

everything that is double or everything that is circular has the same distinctive causal effects. There are, for example, circular coins, clouds, after-images, gardens . . . whose causal powers differ appreciably; there are also two coins, apples, after-images, theories, laws, Queen Elizabeths. Accordingly it may be that there is a certain causal effect attributable to the colour of certain kinds of things and not others, e.g. birds and not metals or liquids. And certainly we do seem to be able to form true sentences about the causal powers of insects with red marks, birds with red chests and so on.

Indeed there is both at a commonsense level and in some parts of science, e.g. in chemistry, zoology, botany and psychology, a wide range of sentences which seem to imply that colour predicates enter into causal relationships: 'red sky at night, shepherd's delight', 'the wavelength of light at the red end of the spectrum is longer than at the blue end', 'acids turn blue litmus paper red', and sentences about the camouflage properties of cheetahs, tigers, zebras, lizards etc.

It is misleading, however, to take these statements as implying that colours are causally effective. Many of these causal statements fall into two groups: either (a) they state or imply a causal relationship in which colours or changes of colour are the *signs for,* or the causal *effects of,* some other physical state or condition, e.g. 'the change in colour of the ermine's coat seems to be dependent partly upon temperature and partly upon day length' or (b) they state or imply a causal relationship in which colours or changes in colour serve as the cause, but the effect is an effect on some organism which can perceive, i.e. which can recognise and be aware of colours. It seems that with respect to (merely) physical bodies and processes, colours are always the effects, never the causes; that colours are causes only with respect to organisms that can perceive.

But if colours have such peculiar causal properties, a further problem is generated. It seems that a coloured object exercises causal effects in percipients through the latter's recognising or becoming aware of the object's colour. And if the colour causes the percipient to acquire knowledge in this way, surely it must do so by affecting the body in some way, e.g. by affecting the eyes or the retinas in the kind of way that it is necessary for acquiring perceptual knowledge about other features of an object, e.g. its location, its mobility, its shape and size, and so on. But the problem is, of course, that colour and changes of colour seem to have no causal effects on physical processes and properties and in particular no causal effect on light, eyes, retinas or brain cells. Accordingly, if colour is a property (of physical bodies) that has no such physical effects, it is

121

difficult to see how any percipient could ever know that bodies are coloured.

The peculiarity of colour would largely be explained, however, if the colour of a body is the causal effect of some physical property of the body, even if it is a different physical property in different circumstances. For we can then understand why sentences attributing to coloured objects causal powers on perceivers are regarded as true. They are true. Only the appropriate cause acting on the perceiver is not the colour of the object but the property which causes the colour. Take a sentence such as

(1) Any bird that, in circumstances C, is G, will cause E

Then suppose that instead of property G's being the cause of E, there is some other property P which in those circumstances causes both G and E. Then given that any bird that is G in those circumstance is also P, sentence (1) is still true, even though G is not the causally effective property. Accordingly we can consider as true those sentences which speak of the causal effects on perceivers of distinctively coloured creatures such as peacocks, cheetahs, lizard, moths etc., for these sentences will have the form of (1) above, with colour predicates substituted for G. The different causal effects, for example, of white-coloured moths and dark-coloured moths on soot-covered bark are due not to the different colours of the moths as such but to the different physical properties of the moths' coats correlated with the colours. In the case of the tailors whose eyes tended to be blinded by the regimental scarlet, it would be physical properties of the light that had the damaging effect.

Thus we can see that the fact that there are in both scientific and nonscientific contexts true sentences ascribing causal powers and effects to coloured objects is in no way incompatible with the claim that colour has no characteristic causal effects vis-à-vis other physical processes and properties.[10] Hence these truths give no grounds for rejecting the Campbell-Jackson claim that if physical objects have colours, in the unreduced, intrinsic sense, we cannot know that they do.

There is, however, a different reason for thinking that it is irrelevant whether or not colour predicates enter into physical causal laws. Besides concepts that largely serve explanatory purposes, there are concepts whose roles primarily place them within social contexts, e.g. being *fashionable*, being a *chair*, being a *yorker*. Now, it could be argued that

10 What is relevant here is not so much that colour plays no part in physics, but rather that it has no role in optics.

122

colour predicates are akin to such social predicates and therefore that it does not matter that there are no (physical) causal laws in which any colour predicate plays a part. After all, there are no causal laws in which 'fashionable' plays a part either. There is nothing that all fashionable things have in common, and there is no specific fashionable way of modifying light or affecting retinas, and yet, for all that, there are fashionable things and fashionable persons as well.

Social predicates such as 'fashionable' do provide a possible model for understanding colour. Nevertheless it is not true that there are no causal implications in calling something 'fashionable'. Secondly, and even more crucially, to adopt that model would mean that one had given up the simple objectivist account.

To use colour predicates in a social role will still require us to develop some view about the causal power of coloured objects and how it is we come to know, i.e. perceive, that an object has a certain colour. In the case of the predicate 'fashionable', let us note, there is no single appearance that all and only fashionable things have in common. But what counts in one set of circumstances as being fashionable is having e.g. clothes a certain shape, in another set of circumstances having them a certain length or a certain style or a certain colour or a certain cut and so on. In each different set of circumstances, the fashionable thing has some property which in those circumstances counts as being fashionable. And it is that property which does have causal powers and in particular has causal powers vis-à-vis the composition of light, patterns of retinal stimulation and so on that are relevant (though not conclusive) for the perception that something is fashionable.

Accordingly, if we are to model colour concepts on the role of social concepts like that of being fashionable we should expect that for each colour, e.g. being yellow, there is in each set of relevant circumstances some property such that an object's having that property in those circumstances counts as the object's being yellow, where that property plays an appropriate causal role vis-à-vis appropriate perceptual processes and mechanisms.

Suppose, moreover, that we try to answer the question of what it is to *be* fashionable? There seem to be three options: (i) it is to have some one of the disjunctive set of features each of which, in the right circumstances, counts as being fashionable; (ii) it is to be a different property in each different set of circumstances, i.e., being fashionable is a relative property, defined relative to each set of circumstances; (iii) it is to have *some* property such that in the given circumstances it meets the socially defined conventions for being fashionable. To model what it is to be yellow on any of these three views is ipso facto to abandon the simple objectivist view of colour. More positively, the most plausible account of social predicates is account (iii) above, which is analogous to treating colour as a perceiver-dependent dispositional property (or mixed dispositional property).

3. THE AUTONOMY OF COLOUR

There is, however, a more subtle response to the claims made by Campbell and Jackson. This is raised by Justin Broackes who in a recent paper addresses the issues discussed here.[11] By taking up the point made by Putnam and Garfinkel[12] that there are different levels of autonomous explanation, Broackes defends the claim that colours can be used to explain effects, even though the colour predicates do not occur in the explanations of physics and chemistry. Broackes expresses this claim in terms of causal explanation. This is crucial, since his opponent could well admit that there are different levels of autonomous explanation, without the explanations at each level being causal. Van Frassen has shown in general terms how this can be so.[13] More specifically, as Dennett and Dawkins have argued, one can explain many things about computers and biological organisms by adopting 'the intentional stance', that is, by treating an object 'as if it possessed certain powers'. Indeed, the theory of virtual colours can provide innumerable such explanations. Why does Tim see the apple as red? The apple is such that 'it is as if it is red'.

One way in which, for colours, there might be different autonomous causal explanations would be if colour properties are supervenient upon physical properties. For example, it may be that the class of surfaces that are blue may be divisible into sub-classes, each of which has a distinctive physical constitution. Colour explanations might then be autonomous in the sense that they are indifferent to the particular physical realisation of the colour property. This would be true if there were causal principles employing, say, 'blue' and other colour terms which hold irrespective of the individual realisations. There are other ways in which we might think of colour as supervenient and hence of the causal laws as autono-

11 Broackes (1992).
12 Hilary Putnam (1978), *Meaning and the Moral Sciences*, Boston: Routledge and Kegan Paul, pp. 41–2; Alan Garfinkel (1981), *Forms of Explanation*, New Haven: Yale U.P., ch. 1.
13 Bas Van Frassen (1980), *The Scientific Image*, Oxford: OUP, pp. 103–34.

mous, but these parallel the options discussed with respect to such social predicates as 'fashionable'.

Two immediate questions flow from this discussion. One is whether in fact there are at any level any autonomous causal laws involving colours. Broackes argues persuasively that there are some. The second is whether we can specify how colours are supervenient. There is an important point of principle here. Appealing to a notion of supervenience can never be a solution to a problem. It is part of the problem. Putting it another way, it may mark some initial progress in finding a solution, but the notion of supervenience raises a new set of problems which have to be dealt with. We need to explain the way in which the property, e.g. colour, could be supervenient, and we need to specify the criteria that are used to mark what counts as *the same property,* e.g. what are the criteria for something's being blue.

One way in which colour could be supervenient on physical properties would be for it to be a dispositional property, e.g. the power to look blue. Moreover there is a variation of the dispositionalist account which allows colours to be supervenient in this way, and for them to be causally relevant. As we saw previously, the disposition can be treated as 'mixed' or 'impure': to say that x is red is to say that x has some feature in virtue of which it appears red. For those 'causal truths' about colours, we can take the causal power as attributed to the feature in question, whichever it is.

The mixed dispositionalist account, as a recommendation or proposal as to how we should revise our thought about the colours physical objects have, has much to recommend it. Indeed, it is as a proposal that we should take the dispositionalist account which Locke and Descartes bequeathed to us. This account does not, however, provide an adequate descriptive account of what the natural concept of colour is. Nevertheless, this account of colour provides one way in which colour is supervenient. Does the supervenient-theorist subscribe to this account, or does he have another one? If he has another, he needs to explain what it is.

We need therefore to be able to spell out the criteria for something's being blue, another's being yellow and so on, and the criteria must be such that they fit the autonomous causal laws. In the light of this, much hinges on what the autonomous laws are. It turns out that the group of principles described by Broackes is a very special one. The principles are those that involve perceivers or sentient organisms. That is, the principles or laws connect colours with other colours, or directly with appearances, but in all cases it is through the appearances of colour. Moreover the criteria for something's having a colour are in those cases the way the colour appears. Hence taking colours to be supervenient is most easily adapted to a theory in which the way colours appear is essential. Either a dispositional account or a virtual-colour account would be appropriate.

Could the colour that is supervenient be the simple, irreducible, intrinsic property which Campbell so readily dismissed? No. The reason is that if we say that there are two levels of causal explanation, where physical features such as electronic structure operate at one level and the supervenient property at a different level, some account has to be given of how the two features are connected and how the two causal explanations are related. The dispositionalist theory provides such an account. So does the virtual-colour theory. So in biology do those theories which appeal to functions in explanatory contexts provide analogous accounts.

To hold that the colour blue is an irreducible quality able to cause perceivers to have perceptual states on the same occasions as there are physical structures also causing the same states, and to give no account of the relationship between either the features or the styles of causal explanation, surely requires ascending to the mystical. In addition we should note that other features that an object is perceived as having, e.g. its shape, its hard-edgedness, do play a part in the physical processes that cause an object to appear in its distinctive way. A theory which holds that colour does not engage with those processes but still is causally relevant requires a good deal of explaining.

I do not suggest that Broackes defends the view that colours are simple, irreducible qualities with causal powers. What needs to be shown, from my point of view, is that the simple objectivist, in order to defend that position, cannot appeal to the considerations which Broackes employs. If we think of colours as such simple qualities, then it follows that they are virtual colours, for they have no causal powers. This is not to say that they cannot be used to explain, since, as we saw, we can provide explanations of the form 'it is as if x has such-and-such a feature'. Not all explanations are causal explanations.

4. COLOUR AS A DISJUNCTIVE SET OF PROPERTIES

At one time J. J. C. Smart put forward a 'quasi-Lockean' account of colours: red things were those which had the power to cause a standard observer's red-discriminatory behaviour (where 'red-discriminatory' could be defined in a noncircular fashion).[14] Partly, however, in response to the difficulties raised by C. B. Martin and M. C. Bradley, and cited by K. Campbell,[15] Smart then proposed a new theory.[16] He proposed to identify each colour with a set of highly disjunctive and idiosyncratic physical properties. That is, he embraced the account briefly considered and rejected by Campbell that the property of blue is the property of having a special reflectance or a special selective scatterance or . . .[17] This account is rejected by Campbell because it conflicts with the principle that all things which are blue have the same property in common, and clearly the highly disjunctive predicate could not be construed as expressing a single property. Campbell is right, to my mind, that the disjunctive predicate does not express a single property, but what this means is that Smart's account of colour is incompatible with the pre-analytic concept of colour, and accordingly fails as either an analytic account of this concept or as a reductive account of colour. On the other hand, it could be construed as providing a revision of the pre-analytic concept; and given that this concept is in trouble anyway, given that there is nothing that is coloured in that sense, then further argument is needed before Smart's account, as a revisionary proposal, can be ruled out.

It is easy to suppose that the disjunctiveness and idiosyncrasy of the physical properties in the set corresponding to each colour shade, e.g. yellow, reflect a defect of a visual system. But such a fact constitutes a positive merit of the system. If one were to design an organism, or, if you like, a perceptual machine, to acquire information or knowledge of the physical world, then of course it would be essential to design it so that certain physical states would, in certain conditions, characteristically cause distinctive states in the organism or machine. In order that the organism should acquire the knowledge that physical state P_1 is instantiated in the physical world, it would be necessary that P_1 should, typically, cause some distinctive state S_1 in the organism or machine. But it is not necessary that for each distinctive physical state there should correspond uniquely some distinctive organism state. Instead of a one-to-one relation between P-states and S-states, there could be a many-to-one rela-

14 J. J. C. Smart (1961), 'Colours', *Philosophy*, 36, pp. 128–42.
15 Martin's objection is discussed by Smart in (1963), *Philosophy and Scientific Realism*, London: Routledge and Kegan Paul, pp. 81–2. See also M. C. Bradley (1964), review of Smart, *Philosophy and Scientific Realism, Australas. J. Phil*, 42, pp. 262–83; Campbell (1969), pp. 137–8.
16 J. J. C. Smart (1971), 'Reports of Immediate Experiences', *Synthese*, 22, pp. 346–59.
17 Campbell (1969), pp. 137–8.

tion. The reason for this is that the organism's interest in acquiring knowledge of state P_1 will very often be not an interest in P_1 itself but in purposes such as identifying and reidentifying objects and making predictions about their behaviour. And these purposes will be served just as well if on some occasions S_1 is caused by P_1 and on others by P_2 (or $P_3 \ldots$). No confusion is likely to arise if the kinds of objects that have P_1 are quite different from those that have P_2 and, very crucially, normally occur in different situations or environments. The state S_1 will serve to inform the organism, via whatever causal process, that it is confronted by something that has P_1 or P_2 or P_3, but other information about the environment will inform it which of these states is the right one.

There would be little danger of confusion if a given colour, say, red, should correspond to one physical property in the case of a liquid that is red, say, blood; another property when it is a metallic surface like a letter-box, yet a third property when it is a plant; and still different properties when it is a sunset or a light projected on a wall that is red. There is no confusion because there is a division of labour involved. Corresponding to the same colour are different physical properties from different ranges of objects. Colour alone won't enable the percipient to distinguish an object in one range from an object in another (if they both look the same colour), but other environmental features will do that. What colour enables one to do is to distinguish within each range one object from another.

Not only is it not disadvantageous for colour to work in this way, it is positively beneficial. It results in a design advantage for the organism. It is a far more economical use of an organism's perceptual resources for it to use the same type of state S_1 to indicate the presence of any one of a set of different physical property types $(P_1, P_2 \ldots P_n)$ than for it to use a different state S_j for each of the physical properties. From a design point of view, this is the mark of superiority; from an evolutionist point of view, such a system has an obvious advantage.

If these remarks are sound, we cannot dismiss Smart's account simply on the ground that it is revisionary. So too is a Lockean or quasi-Lockean account, and so too will be any adequate account of colour, given the defects of the naive concept. The Lockean account of colour-as-it-is-in-physical-objects is that the colour of physical objects is nothing but a power to appear in a certain way. Smart's account is a possible rival to that part of the Lockean account, or it provides an additional concept if the pluralist theory of colours holds. On the other hand, if we are

128

considering Smart's account as a reductive analysis, then it is deeply flawed.

However, if showing that the account is revisionary does not refute it, neither does claiming that it is revisionary save it. The merits of the Lockean revisionary proposal are that it (a) explains why we have the natural concept and why it has been successful and (b) can be used to serve many of the purposes that we required the natural concept to serve. Given that these purposes are important and that they have not been undermined, which they have not, there is good reason to accept the revisionary proposal.

Thus, even if we could find some reason to adopt the Smartian revisionary proposal, we would have reason to adopt it *in addition* to the Lockean proposal for a dispositional concept. Even more important, the Smart proposal itself seems to require the dispositional concept. For there is one crucial respect in which the two accounts are identical. Each needs to acknowledge a different kind of colour: the colour objects *appear* to be. The disjunctive view is an open disjunction. The only reason for deciding whether a given property P_j should or should not be admitted to the open set is whether the objects that have that property are objects which appear red.

It is important to note that Campbell places what seems to be a very reasonable restraint on the task in hand: any successful candidate for reduction must satisfy a set of principles called the Axioms of Unity, which in schematic form are:

For any colour C_n, physical objects of that colour have something in common not shared by physical objects of colours $C_1 \ldots C_{n-1}$, $C_{n-1} \ldots$ [18]

In less formal terms, there must be something common and peculiar to all things having the same colour. What makes this a reasonable restraint is the character of the colour objects *appear* to have. If someone were to distinguish colour-as-it-is-in-physical-objects and the colour objects appear to have, it would be less reasonable to apply the restraint to the former.

There is another problem for the disjunctive view. For the disjunction to be effective, there would need to be a single specifiable set of standard conditions and normal observers such that under those conditions, if x has any one of the set of properties (P_1 or P_2 or $P_3 \ldots$), then x appears

18 Ibid., p. 133.

red. As it happens, there is no such single set. (See Hardin.)[19] What we have is a variety of different sets of conditions, which in different contexts and under different purposes count as standard. The justification for this claim is left to the next two sections, in which its wider implications are traced.

5. THE PROSPECTS FOR REDUCTIVE REALISM

Campbell argued that there is no single physical property shared by all red things, nor is there any common property in the resultant light from the surface. Nor, he argues, can we hope that the composition of light produced by red objects satisfies some unknown mathematical formula, for light of any given composition can in different conditions make the surface from which it comes appear any one of a large range of colours. In particular the colour seen depends upon the adaptive state of the observer's retinas.

The fact that under a given illumination the same composition of light may cause an object to be seen as having any one of a different range of colours, depending on the observer's physiological condition, does not in itself show that colour cannot be a physical observer-independent property of a physical object. For one could hope to make a distinction between real and apparent colour in the same way that one can distinguish real and apparent size, real and apparent shape and so on. For it may be that there are certain privileged (physiological) conditions such that an observer in those conditions will perceive an object to have its real colour, whereas in other conditions the colour the object appears to have will be an apparent colour.

But, as Campbell argues, when we distinguish real from apparent shape, size, roughness etc. we do so nonarbitrarily in terms of the characteristic mode of interaction of bodies which are (really) square etc., with other bodies thereby specifying a property possessed by the body quite irrespective of what looks like what to whom:

The shape determined by mode of interaction with other bodies has two clear titles to the superiority implied in calling it the real shape: it belongs to the object quite irrespective of the way the object affects any perceiver and it plays a central role in our explanations of how the object comes to have the various apparent shapes which under various conditions it seems to have.[20]

19 Hardin (1988), pp. 67–82.   20 Campbell (1969), p. 144.

Since colours have no characteristic mode of interaction, we must have some other way of fixing the real colour. Normally we fix certain conditions as standard, but the problem in the case of colour is that there seems to be no nonarbitrary way to select any specific set of conditions as standard. Any standard conditions would have to include a specification of the observer's adaptive state, but then, Campbell argues, the so-called real colour could not be accorded any ontological preeminence over its rivals. Objects are 'really blue' only because human observers have a certain adaptive state. Had they evolved some different adaptive state, or were (very improbably) some widespread chemical process to occur to change the adaptive state of human observers, objects that were once 'really blue' would become 'really red (or green . . .)'. Whatever adaptive state we choose as fixing the 'real colour' of an object, it seems arbitrary that we should select that one.

However, it seems to me that Campbell's criticism levels the objection to the account above at the wrong place. It is true that if this account defines colour by reference to a specified adaptive state of the human nervous system, then it will be confronted by the problems raised by Campbell. But to hope to work, the view must require not that real colour is to be defined by reference to the adaptive state but rather that when the observer is in that adaptive state she is in a position to see the real colour of an object. Campbell's objection to that line of approach was that there is no characteristic mode of interaction that objects of the same colour have. But if the problem is that in the same illumination different physical properties will look the same colour, depending on the adaptive state, then selecting one adaptive state as standard will serve to select one of these physical properties, and that physical property will have a characteristic mode of interaction, and for that property there will be independent criteria for determining whether an object has it.

Campbell's objection would need to be reframed. It might for example be argued that although adopting any one of the set of possible adaptive states does allow us to pick out one property as the 'real colour' and that for each such property there will be independent criteria for its application and as well a characteristic mode of causal interaction, it is arbitrary which one property is selected. There is no special reason why one property rather than another should be regarded as the real colour.

Suppose for example that physicists did discover a complex formula which could be used to describe the composition C_1 of light produced by all things that appeared blue to observers in a given adaptive state A_1. (Campbell argued that even if such a formula were found, objects

131

producing that kind of light would be seen by observers in different adaptive states as having different colours.) A_1, let us assume, is the adaptive state in which humans are most commonly situated. For some other less common adaptive state A_2 there will be some other complex mathematical formula to help describe C_2, the composition of light produced by things which look blue to observers in adaptive state A_2. The question now is why should not real blue be identified with the power to produce light of composition C_1? It cannot be argued that there are no independent criteria for determining whether light is of composition C_1. Nor can it be argued that light of that composition has no characteristic mode of causal interaction. It does have a characteristic mode, though apart from its interaction with the nervous systems of humans (and other colour percipients) its causal interactions are not very interesting. And that is the rub. In the case of shapes and sizes there are all sorts of important geometrical and causal relationships between these properties and other physical and geometrical properties. But in the case of these hypothetical light compositions there are likely to be no important or interesting relationships – other than their connections with the perceptual systems of observers! Accordingly, neither C_1 nor C_2 is of any special significance, and it is for this reason that it is arbitrary that real 'blue' be associated with C_1 rather than with C_2 (or C_3 or C_4 . . .).

However, there could be ways in which C_1 might be more significant than C_2 or any of the other compositions. For it might be that for C_1 there is a range of illuminations in which light of composition C_1 is the causal effect of a range of different physical properties, which in turn are physical properties useful for identifying and reidentifying physical objects and for predicting the behaviour of physical objects. (There are interesting causal laws in which those physical properties have a role.) Assuredly there would be some illuminations in which other light compositions C_2 or C_3 will be the distinctive causal effects of physical properties, but there may be two ways in which C_1 is more significant:

(1) The power and scope of C_1 is much greater than of any of the other possible candidates.
(2) For the range of illuminations encountered in this world, C_1 has far greater power and scope than the other candidates.

The greater power and scope will be in C_1's role as an indicator of the presence of the physical properties. The fact that C_1 is superior to other light compositions in the illuminations which, as it happens, are more frequent in this world does not make it arbitrary that real colour be linked with C_1. In other words, the fact that the criteria used to pick out the 'real' colours of objects are human-oriented or socially based is consistent with the claim that properties so selected are objective physical features of objects.

6. 'REAL' BY CONVENTION

The crucial point about the distinction between real and apparent (or between 'is F' and 'appears F') is that this distinction applies only against a background of standard or normal conditions. There are, however, two ways in which such conditions can be picked out. Standard conditions are those under which the way a thing appears reveals the way that it is – and the thing is that way (is square, rough, red . . .) independently of whether it appears to anyone. Alternatively, one set of conditions is picked out as special or privileged in some way: they are the conditions most commonly encountered, or the conditions under which optimal discriminations can be made, or they are the conditions in which for each object, or range of objects, the object is most commonly found. Now, this way of specifying the conditions as standard suggests that what we are calling the 'real' colour of an object is fixed by convention and not by nature. That is, it is not what is commonly thought of as a realist view at all. On the view in question, the real colour is simply defined by reference to the way things appear with certain conditions fixed as standard, by convention (which, as we have seen, does not mean that it is arbitrary).

Here, however, we need to be careful. What counts as the real colour may be fixed by convention, but there are two ways in which the convention may operate. Let us say that the real colour is fixed by the appearance an object has under those certain conditions that are in turn fixed by convention as standard. There are two ways in which the convention might be understood. First being *really* red may be understood as simply having that appearance under those conditions which have been designated as standard. To be red is nothing more than to have that appearance. On the other hand, the convention may operate quite differently. The convention could be that real redness consists in that physical feature of objects by virtue of which, under standard conditions, they appear red. Which conditions are standard is defined by convention, but to be red is not to appear red: it is to have a certain feature where the feature is identified by the appearance. In a certain card game, the dealer is decided by convention, but there are two aspects to the convention: (i) the convention is that the highest card provides the means for selecting the dealer and (ii) the convention is that the dealer is the person selected by the drawing procedure. Drawing the top card is the means of selecting the dealer, but it is not constitutive of what it is to be the dealer.

In other words, when it is said that it is by convention that the appearance fixes what the real colour is, this may mean either of two things: (i) the appearance is, by convention, constitutive of the 'real colour' or (ii) the appearance is used to pick out which physical feature is the real colour, but it is not constitutive of the real colour.

Two things emerge from this discussion. First, either the red appearance is constitutive of the 'real colour' a physical object has, or alternatively the red appearance is used to identify real redness that physical objects have. On the first option, there is no physical redness possessed by objects independently of the way they appear. On the second there is, but there are two kinds of redness, physical redness and the redness that is constituted by having the power to appear in a distinctive way. Thus, even if in such circumstances there is a point to identifying physical redness, it will not eliminate the point of having a different kind of red, either virtual red or phenomenal red, which serves as providing the content for the disposition objects have to appear red. Indeed, far from this sense being eliminated, it is necessary in order to have a viable concept of physical redress.

The second thing to flow from the discussion is that, given the conventional way in which conditions are fixed as standard, and thereby colours fixed as real, it is possible that the conventions could operate as follows: in different contexts and for different purposes, different conditions are designated as standard. This means that in different contexts what counts as a real red is a different physical feature. Given this situation, we can say e.g. that red is under conditions C_1 to be identified with P_1, under conditions C_2 with P_2, under conditions C_3 with P_3 and so on. By contrast with the previous open Disjunctive View, we might term this the Variable Disjunct View.

It needs also to be recognised what is not shown by this discussion. I have not provided any support for an objectivist account. What I argued was that Campbell goes too far in claiming that under no circumstances could scientists come up with anything that would count as a successful candidate for reduction. This is not to say, however, that the scientists will do that, nor to deny that there might be other arguments against the possibility of reduction. In the next section we will look at some other reasons.

7. THE VARIETY OF STANDARD CONDITIONS

Campbell's argument, it is important to note, is framed in terms of a hypothetical possibility: were scientists to discover some mathematical formulas applicable to the light distribution from a surface such that all red things had a unique characteristic formula, this would not provide a successful candidate for reduction. Jonathan Westphal and D. R. Hilbert claim that there is such a formula, although they do not claim to be able to specify it, except in a very broad qualitative way.[21] They think that there is good reason to think that there is some formula and reason to think that someday scientists will be in a position to specify it. ('We have reason to think that the victim was murdered by person or persons unknown.')

Campbell, I have argued, goes too far in claiming in effect that under no circumstances could scientists come up with a successful candidate for reduction. This, however, is not to say that Hilbert and Westphal are right in claiming that there is some successful candidate currently unknown. There is strong evidence to think that they are wrong. Any anthropocentric formula that scientists give us will depend on a characterisation of standard conditions and normal observers, and there is good reason to think that the only possible characterisations are context-relative and purpose-relative. This indeed is the argument so persuasively presented by C. L. Hardin in *Color for Philosophers*. He points out that colour scientists do employ the notions of standard conditions and normal observers, but the way they characterise these conditions and normality is heavily dependent on our needs and interests. There is no single set of standard conditions:

Standard conditions are chosen by color scientists with three considerations in mind: (1) the nature of the object or property to be observed or measured, (2) the capabilities and limitations of the observer or measuring instrument and (3) the purposes for which the observation or measurement is to be taken.[22]

Different conditions apply, depending on whether we are concentrating on surface colour or aperture colour. And as far as aperture colour is

21 Westphal (1987); Hilbert (1987).
22 Hardin (1988), pp. 67–82; this quotation, p. 67.

concerned, a wide range of choice is allowed: whether to look at the colour in an aperture or through a dark tube, what colour the surround should be, whether the angular subtense of the sample at the eye should be $2°, 4°, 10°$ etc. and so on.

The variety of standard conditions makes it more attractive for the objectivist to adopt the view of colour sketched at the end of the last section: to say that red, for example, should be identified in one set of conditions C_1 with P_1, in a different set of conditions C_2 with P_2, in another set of conditions C_3 with yet another property P_3, and so on.

It is instructive to compare this account with Smart's open-disjunctive view discussed in a previous section. There were two major problems with the disjunctive view. First, given that it employs an open disjunction, the only reason for deciding whether a given property P_j should or should not be admitted to the open set is whether objects that have that property are objects which appear red. Secondly, for the disjunction to be effective, there would need to be a single specifiable set of standard conditions and normal observers such that under those conditions, if x has any one of the set of properties (P_1 or P_2 or P_3 . . .), then x appears red.

Given these problems, the move to the variable disjunct view looks more appealing. It is, however, no more successful. Once again we need to ask what makes us say that it is *red* (and not blue, yellow etc.) that, under C_1, is identified with P_1 and also, under C_2, with P_2. What makes it red in both cases? Surely the only viable answer is in terms of objects with both features appearing red. In other words, what our attempt does is to identify a kind of redness, call it physical redness, a physical feature that physical objects possess, which is defined by reference to a power or disposition to *appear* red, where the latter red is a different primary sense. Either that primary sense is of phenomenal red, i.e. red-as-it-is-in-experience, or alternatively it is virtual-red, i.e. red in the intensional sense.

A further problem is presented by the notion of 'normal observer'. To a large extent one can contrast observers suffering from a visual defect with respect to colour from the class of normal observers, those capable of making and agreeing on a large range of colour discriminations. Those with the colour defects are not able to make as many colour discriminations and in particular fail to make crucial discriminations, e.g., between red and green. As Leon Hurvich pointed out in *Colour Vision*, there are some persons in whom colour vision is anomalous even though on the whole it is very much like that of normals:

These individuals tend to use the same colour names that the normal does for the many objects they both see in their common environments. On rare occasions however these individuals do not agree with the colour name that a normal applies to a given coloured object (and vice versa).[23]

These people tend to make the same number of colour discriminations as do the normal observers. And they 'stubbornly' resist the charge that they are defective. Where they differ from the normal is on which precise sample they identify as the unique primary hue. The sample identified by normal people as 'pure yellow' will be seen by these anomalous people as greenish yellow (or in some cases as reddish yellow). Likewise what the anomalous identify as pure yellow will be shifted slightly along the green-yellow-red portion of the colour circle.

It would seem that, relative to normal people, these anomalous observers suffer from a small but detectable shift in their colour judgements along the colour circle. Indeed, the notion of 'normal observer', here as elsewhere, is a statistical notion; many people are more or less anomalous. The anomalous people, it should be noted, agree with normal people about colour matches. In addition, they tend to agree on colour-naming, since most colours will be identified by anomalous and normal alike as greenish yellow, reddish yellow and so on. This means that the anomaly will, for most ordinary purposes, be hard to detect. Hence it will not usually matter. On occasion, however, it will.

For our purposes what is significant is that it looks very arbitrary to call one group of people 'normal' and another 'anomalous'. What it indicates is that colour should be given a Protagorean analysis: to be yellow is to be yellow-relative-to-a-person (or group of persons).

8. ANTHROPOCENTRIC REALISM

It seems to be a hopeless task to seek among the physical properties of surfaces for the candidate that will identify physical colour. The causes of the way colours appear are many and varied.

The best candidate for objectivist identification would seem to be some property related to the object's effect on light. Spectral reflectance seems the most likely candidate. Recent attempts to defend just such a position have been provided by Westphal and D. R. Hilbert. Reflectance is a dispositional property. Chromatically coloured bodies have the power to absorb and reflect differentially light of different wave-

23 Hurvich (1981), ch. 16; this quotation, p. 223.

137

lengths. Spectral reflectance curves describe this differential set of powers for visible light between 400 nm and 700 nm.

Hilbert's position is described as anthropocentric realism.[24] He concedes that making the distinctions between different reflectance curves that colour vision enables us to do gives us the ability to identify and distinguish properties that are both objective and of interest primarily to colour-perceivers. His point is that the fact that these properties have little interest other than for the use colour-perceivers can make of them does not stop them from being objective properties.

Hilbert allows that in order for the identification to be successful the physical properties that are to be identified with the colours must have the essential properties of colours, and as a system must stand together in relationships that are essential to the system in which the colours are interrelated. Hilbert claims to be able, with his account, to provide just such a set of physical properties. Despite this claim, it is difficult to see how he has provided any such account. He certainly does not show how the reflectance curves stand together in the right kind of relationship. At one stage he seems to be suggesting that the relevant properties are those that have appropriate effects on systems that mimic human observers' receptor cells. This represents a possible candidate for reduction (or identification), but this would be a psychophysical reduction, not the physical reduction that was promised. The psychophysical reduction is no more successful than the physical, but it is instructive to look at the attempted physical reduction and see why it fails.

A simple discussion by D. Judd and G. Wyszecki illustrates the problem faced by the physical reduction. Someone in business is trying to specify the difference between a desirable deep red and an unwanted brownish red so that standardised products can be manufactured. This person could do quite well using a spectrophotometer to construct spectral reflectance curves. By so doing one can show, first, that a white surface has the highest reflectance and a black the lowest, and secondly, that the whites, blacks and greys – the achromatic, or neutral, colours – reflect roughly equal proportions of light at all wavelengths, whereas chromatically coloured surfaces reflect (and absorb) differentially different wavelengths.

Even more significant, however, a tan whose colour is lighter than either of the two reds reflects more at every part of the spectrum than either red specimen. Moreover the tan, brownish red and deep red

24 See Hilbert (1987), esp. ch. 7, for a statement of this position.

produce progressively more saturated colours which correspond to the steepness of the reflectance curves.

However, there is a problem in applying the rule for lightness to try to explain why the brownish red appears lighter than the deep red. On the face of it, the curves indicate that the reverse should occur. The explanation of course is that

the spectral region between 550 nm and 600 nm where the brownish red reflects more strongly than the deep red counts for more than the longwave end of the spectrum where the reverse is true.[25]

As Judd and Wyszecki point out, for objective specification one needs to take account, for spectral reflectance, of a set of weights for various parts of the spectrum. Another way of putting this point is as follows. To explain why objects appear the colour they do, not only with respect to hue but to lightness and saturation (or their near equivalents), we need to take into account the differential responses of the three cones in the retina. These responses are characterised not only by reference to different sensitivities to different wavelengths but also by having differently shaped curves (e.g. with different heights for the maximum sensitivity).

Now, of course, one could simply respond to this point by claiming that, where the results turn out to be unexpected, the results are simply illusions. That is, the brownish red only looks lighter than the deep red; it is really darker. That it looks lighter is simply an illusion wrought by the colour system we have. After all, we know that hard-edged towers can look curved and two equal lines can look unequal (as in the Müller-Lyer illusion), so why should we be troubled that objects that are not lighter should look lighter?

Well, we could say that, but it seems to miss the point. What the businessman is interested in is how the samples will appear. If the sample looks wrong, it will be no consolation to be told that that is only an illusion, that *really* everything is all right. The two samples 'are really the same – they only look different'. Things are quite different for colours than they are for shapes and sizes. A real estate agent who tries to sell houses with Ames distorting rooms in them is likely to have a hard time of it.

Colour really is different from natural kinds such as lead and gold. For the latter, the causal powers are more significant than the appearance, or at least than short-lived appearances. For such natural kinds there is point

25 D. Judd and G. Wyszecki, *Color in Business, Science and Industry,* 2nd ed., New York: Wiley, pp. 37–44; this quotation, p. 42.

to saying that x and y are not really alike – they simply appear to be similar. In the case of colour there is not.

It is also instructive to consider Hilbert's discussion of the problems posed by surface metamers – objects which in daylight have very different reflectance curves but appear to be the same colour.[26] On the face of it, it would seem that such examples count against the attempt to identify surface colour with spectral reflectance and to favour a dispositional analysis. Hilbert, however, argues that the identification of colours with reflectance allows a more satisfactory solution than does the dispositional account.

As Hilbert points out, if we choose the right sort of illumination, a pair of objects that appear identical in colour under normal circumstances will appear to differ in colour:

In the anthropocentric realist account of color this perception of color difference will be a veridical perception. In a dispositional analysis, however, such a perception of color difference will be illusory.[27]

This, says Hilbert, puts the dispositionalist in the odd position of supposing that we can see a real physical difference between objects, i.e. a difference in reflectance, by suffering from an illusion of colour difference. On the other hand, the fact that all differences in reflectance will be perceived as colour differences under some illuminations provides, it is alleged, a substantial if not conclusive argument for individuating colours in the fine-grained manner required by Hilbert's account.

There are a number of things wrong with this argument. First, it can hardly count as an objection to a dispositional account that according to it we can see a real physical difference between objects by suffering from an illusion of colour difference. According to one form of dispositional account, colour perception involves an error theory, i.e. perception of physical differences works by the perceiver's suffering from systematic illusions: objects are represented as having colours which in fact they do not have. So what Hilbert sees as an unwelcome consequence is embraced by his opponents as one of the central features of their account.

Secondly, even for a dispositional analysis that avoids an error theory, it should only be expected that under some conditions real physical differences can be seen by having illusions of colour difference. According to the dispositional analysis, objects will have the same colour if they appear the same under conditions that count as standard. It is only to be expected that there are some physically different objects which

26 Hilbert (1987), ch. 5, pp. 82–100.   27 Ibid., p. 26.

under those conditions do appear the same. Given that possibility, it is not surprising that there should be some nonstandard conditions under which those physically different objects will look different in colour.

Thirdly, if the anthropocentric realist holds that the perception of the colour difference in the unusual illumination is a veridical perception, then he ought to say what the two colours of the two objects are. A typical metameric example is one in which two surfaces in daylight are identical greens. In tungsten illumination, however, one is green and the other brown. Let us agree that the former is green. What colour is the second? It is not green, since it has been revealed to be different. Neither is it brown, for it has a different reflectance curve from surfaces that are brown. If it is neither green nor brown, what is it? I cannot see that there is any sensible answer the anthropocentric realist can give to this question.

Finally – and this is a problem related to the last – metamers are objects which match in all dimensions: hue, saturation and lightness. We also have surfaces of different hue which match with respect to lightness in daylight illumination. At least some of those will not match in lightness under tungsten illumination. If Hilbert's answer is correct for full-blown metameric matches, should he not also say that these two surfaces, of different hue, really do not match in lightness either? The tungsten illumination reveals physical differences that are really there but that we cannot detect under normal illumination. Alternatively, if he says, as most of us would, that under tungsten illumination we suffer from a lightness illusion – objects which are really the same in lightness appear to be different – then he will be saying that in this case an illusion of lightness difference reveals a physical difference (for there are physical differences between the two surfaces and their reflectance curves). Thus he would be committed to the same 'failing' that he finds in the dispositional analysis.

9. THE CHARACTER OF PSYCHOLOGICAL SPACE

The major problem with the attempted identification of colour with spectral reflectance and related properties is that the psychological space has a character in its set of interrelationships holding between the colours that does not match the character of the relationships holding between spectral reflectance curves. Psychological colour space contains four psychologically unique primary hues – yellow, blue, green and red – which contain no element of the other colours. Moreover it contains several

141

series of complex hues, yellows merging one way into reds and the other into greens. Blue merges one way to red and the other to green.

Given certain assumptions about the peculiar way colour vision works, we can understand in broad terms how objects with one kind of spectral reflectance curve should appear different from others. But the assumptions about colour-vision mechanisms are crucial. The spectral reflectance curves by themselves give no clue. That surfaces should have the range of reflectance curves they do gives no indication as to why there should be four primary hues and why all colours should be combinations, but only certain combinations, of those four. There is no indication why there should be four rather than three or five or six primary colours. Nor is there any indication why the four primary chromatic colours should be arranged into a series such that each merges into white or black or grey. Even if it were true that each perceptible colour could be produced by a surface with its own distinctive spectral reflectance characteristics, these surfaces would not constitute a system that reflects the fourfold character of the psychological colour array.

Again we should contrast colours and shapes. A circle is a special form of ellipse. Elliptical curves can be drawn with greater and lesser eccentricities (the ratio of one axis to the other). If the ellipses are viewed perpendicularly, then each ellipse has its characteristic appearance, from that point of view. One can construct the ellipses in a certain order, according to their appearance and also according to their eccentricities. In this case, unlike colour, we can construct a physical series that matches the appearance series. We can of course construct an ordered array of colour chips that, as in the Munsell system, matches the array of psychological colour space. (Indeed, for the Munsell system it is the array.) However, the principle of ordering for those material chips is the way they appear. There are no physical properties and relationships that govern the ordering. (A unique physical specification can be given of each chip, but that is a different thing.)

Here we can see a justification for the Lockean-Cartesian point that for the ideas of secondary qualities, unlike the ideas of primary qualities, there is no pattern of resemblances among physical properties to match the ideas. Colours are different from shapes. It is, I suggest, a similar point that has attracted most colour theorists to the Lockean-Cartesian point of view. (What is not so clear is whether the same point holds for other secondary qualities, e.g. sounds, tastes and feelings of warmth.)

The significance of the character of the colour space is also underscored by the fact, cited before, of the existence of anomalous trichromats. These are the people who are as gifted as the normal in making colour discriminations, but for them the hue colour circle is slightly shifted. Given this, we need to distinguish between red-for-the-normal and red-for-the-anomalous. Given as well that the physical property that is causally responsible for something's appearing red to the normal is different from that causally responsible for something else's appearing red to the anomalous, it is clear that the basis for describing each set of respective colour experiences in terms of 'red' is the way things appear.

10. DIFFICULTIES WITH PSYCHOPHYSICAL COLOUR

Psychophysical colour is the property specified in terms of dominant wavelength, excitation purity and luminant reflectance (in the case of surfaces) or luminant transmittance (in the case of volumes). Of this tripartite specification, the dimension of dominant wavelength best corresponds to that of hue, excitation purity to saturation (or chroma or chromaticness) and reflectance to lightness (or value or whiteness or brightness).

Specification of psychophysical colour in this threefold way presupposes the construction of some tri-stimulus space or chromaticity diagrams on which can be drawn a tongue-shaped area bounded by a curved spectrum line for the wavelengths corresponding to all the spectral hues and a straight line for the nonspectral purples, magentas and so on.

It should be noted that psychophysical colour in itself could not be thought of as the real colour of physical objects but presupposes some complex physical quantity that just might count. Psychophysical colour provides a specification of colour, and it achieves that task by providing a system that enables matches to be made to observers' judgements. However, it may be thought of as also providing an indirect specification of a physical quantity, relative to an objective observer built with a system of light-sensitive cells with appropriate response characteristics.

Even so, psychophysical colour does not give us what colour is essentially, either directly or indirectly. To see why not, suppose someone were to make the claim that it does give us what colour is essentially. That is, we are asked to take as the standard observer an ideal observer, e.g. as specified by the Commission Internationale d'Eclailage (CIE), with idealised spectral responses, and to specify all the colours in terms of characteristic combinations of responses. Accordingly a given physical sample is yellow just insofar as it produces in this standardised observer the combination of responses that constitutes yellow – and it is yellow whatever human perceivers think.

As far as the CIE standard observer is concerned, we do in fact find that at least as far as exact matches are concerned, the judgements of actual living observers do not match those of the ideal observer. Never mind, real colour, we are asked to suppose, is colour defined by reference to the standard observer. What the rest of us are aware of are illusory colours and illusory matches between colours.

It is not surprising that the judgements made with respect to the standard observer differ from judgements made by living observers. The standard observer is constructed by averaging the responses of ordinary actual observers among whom there is considerable variability.

A second but related limitation for psychophysical colour is that equal intervals on a CIE chromaticity chart do not correspond to separate equal steps in perceived values of hue and chroma (for Munsell criteria). Chromaticity loci of Munsell colours of constant chroma, instead of falling on concentric circles, fall on very distorted elliptical curves more closely bunched towards the red-blue part of the chart (for constant lightness). Chromaticity loci for constant line, instead of falling on straight lines, fall on curved lines, some departing considerably from a straight line.[28]

Thirdly and even more important, there are certain defects intrinsic to psychophysical colour. First, the standard system is constructed taking certain conditions as standard – viewing an object through a certain angle of view, e.g. 2°, and viewing the object with a certain surround. Different angles of view and different surrounds will give different results. In addition the dominant wavelength is defined relative to a certain illuminant. The chromaticity points for CIE Ill C, CIE Ill D_{65} and E (equal energy light) are quite different. Hence the same sample will have different dominant wavelengths relative to different illuminants. Yet further, there is a range of colours that have no dominant wavelength: those colours whose loci fall between that of the illuminant and the line for extraspectral bluish reds and purples. In such cases what is done is to specify a complementary dominant wavelength which thereby enables one to specify such colours. This technique enables us to satisfy the major purpose of chromaticity charts – to provide a unique specification

28 Hurvich (1981), pp. 295–6.

144

of a colour sample. But that task is quite different from giving an account of colour.

Finally, there are relationships that hold among colours-as-they-appear that are not captured by the chromaticity charts for psychophysical colour. Hurvich for example points out how the hue appearances of samples change as the lightness levels change:

> We need only remember that every spectral stimulus has fixed chromaticity co-ordinates. Nevertheless . . . changing the lightness level of spectral stimuli (the CIE Y value) changes their appearance. They become bluer or yellower at higher light levels and redder and greener at lower energies . . . The fixed positions of spectral stimuli on the CIE chromaticity chart give no hint of this.[29]

The effect described by Hurvich is the Bezold-Brücke phenomenon. There is, however, an even more important defect of psychophysical colour specifications for representing colour-as-it-appears. The latter can be represented on a three-dimensional colour solid in a variety of ways, two of the most significant being the Munsell Colour System and the Swedish Natural Colour System. Besides the fact that equal steps in perceived hue and chroma (chromaticness) do not correspond to equal steps on the chromaticity charts, the latter do not provide any basis for accounting for one of the central features of colour-appearance systems: the place of the psychological primaries. In the Natural Colour system four primaries – yellow, blue, red and green – are identified. These are four elementary colours containing no part of any other colour. We can, however, arrange each primary in a series of hues which merge with one of the other primaries – for blue, the two series are blue-red and blue-green. On the other hand, there is no blue-yellow series or red-green series.

It is simply a fact about colour-as-it-appears, except for people whose colour vision is defective, that these relationships hold. No explanation is given in the chromaticity charts for these relationships.

The spectral hues on the CIE chromaticity chart fall on a curve representing wavelengths between 400 nm and 700 nm. There is, however, no significant place for the psychologically unitary hues. For the CIE standard observer, yellow, green and blue fall on wavelengths 578, 499 and 477 nm respectively. Among observers with normal colour vision, the wavelengths fall in the following ranges:

29 Ibid., p. 295.

Unitary yellow	568–583 nm
Unitary green	495–535 nm
Unitary blue	467–485 nm

Unitary red is only produced by a mixture of single-wavelength light of 400 nm and 700 nm.[30]

Given the way the CIE coordinate system is constructed, it is not surprising that the uniqueness of these unitary primaries should not be represented. That is only to be expected. However, neither should the fact that we should not be surprised at this prevent us from recognising that the system does not perform this task. The significance of this failure is important in those contexts in which some people, those who forget the purpose of the system, attempt to use psychophysical colour as providing an account of what colours are essentially.

Very briefly, psychophysical colour will not serve as a basis for the reduction of colour or for identification of colour, simply because we can construct a system of psychological colour space in which the different colours stand to each other in a set of relationships of similarities and differences that does not carry over to (is not reflected in) the three-dimensional colour space that can be constructed for psychophysical colour.

Once again, in considering psychophysical colour it is crucial to acknowledge that such a concept simply cannot hope to serve as providing a reductive analysis of colour. This does not mean that there is not a careful or viable psychophysical colour concept. Indeed, and this is one of my major themes, there is room for a variety of colour concepts. The value of a psychophysical colour concept depends on what purpose it is intended to serve. One thing is clear: it does not serve all desirable colour purposes.

11. CONCLUSION

There seem to be three options for the person who wishes to maintain an objectivist view of colour:

(1) The single-property view:
x is red   iff x is P_n
(2) The disjunctive view:
x is red   iff x is P_1 or P_2 or P_3 or . . .

30 See Agoston (1987), pp. 183–4.

146

(3) The variable disjunct view:

x is red if under C_1 x is P_1 or
           if under C_2 x is P_2 or
           if under C_3 x is P_3 or
           if under C_4 x is P_4 or . . .

The first view, the single-property view, seems at best a speculative, highly optimistic view. The balance of evidence is strongly against it: there is little reason to think that there is a single, unitary set of specifiable standard conditions and normal observers. Nor does there seem to be the slightest reason to think that any of the plausible candidates for reduction will have the right character for a genuine reduction.

There are several problems with the disjunctive view. First, it is an open disjunction. The only reason for deciding whether a given property P_j should or should not be admitted to the open set is whether objects that have the property are objects which appear red. Secondly, for the disjunction to be effective there would need to be a single specifiable set of standard conditions and normal observers such that under those conditions, if x has any one of the set of properties (P_1 or P_2 or P_3 or . . .), then x appears red. As it happens, there is no such single set. What we have is a variety of different sets of conditions which in different contexts and for different purposes count as standard.

The variety of standard conditions makes it more attractive for the objectivist to say that red, for example, should be identified in one set of conditions C_1 with P_1, in a different set of conditions C_2 with P_2, in another set of conditions C_3 with yet another property P_3, and so on. This move, however, is no more successful than the previous. Once again we need to ask what makes us say that it is *red* (and not blue, yellow etc.) that under C_1 is identified with P_1 and also under C_2 with P_2. What makes it red in both cases? Surely the only viable answer is in terms of objects with both features appearing red.

In other words, our attempt to identify a range of different physical features, each of which in its characteristic set of circumstances will count as red, presupposes a distinctive appearance, one shared by the different physical features. This means that in addition to the objective concept of colour, we would need the dispositional concept. And the latter concept presupposes the virtual-colour concept, or possibly a phenomenal-colour concept.

The lesson to be learnt is that attempts to provide reductionist objectivist accounts of colour can at best succeed if they are turned into quite different things: attempts to provide a revisionary account of colour. Even so, any resulting objectivist concept of colour requires in addition a dispositional concept. In the pluralist framework of colours, this is only to be expected.

7

Revisionary accounts: objectivist and dispositionalist

Objectivist accounts of colour normally assume that colour is reducible to, or can be identified with, some microstructure or, more plausibly, some light-related quality. The attempts we have so far examined and rejected may be thought of as conservative. They assume that our colour discourse is largely in order: there is a physical feature which colour appearances or our colour concepts pick out, and the important task is to identify it.

There is, however, an alternative strategy: to propose a revisionary account of colour, one in which it is proposed that colour is thought of as an objective, perceiver-independent quality. (The possibility of following such an approach arose in the last chapter.) When we examine this strategy, however, we find that, at best, its success would not eliminate the need for a subjective, dispositionalist account. For all it would provide is a case for a pluralist account of colour: one in which there is an objectivist *and* a dispositionalist concept of colour.

1. REDUCTION, IDENTIFICATION AND REVISION

In arguing for an objectivist view there are a variety of approaches from which to choose. One can be a reductionist, believing that colour can be *reduced* to some more complex physical property. Secondly, one can *identify* colour with some physical property, in a nonreductive manner,[1] or, finally, one can avoid either approach by following a revisionary strategy.

The first two approaches can be contrasted by considering such examples as temperature and light. It is plausible that temperature for gases in equilibrium is average kinetic energy of the constituent molecules and that light is electromagnetic radiation from the visible spectrum. There

1 This was the approach followed by Westphal (see Chapter 3) and by Reid (see Chapter 4).

are, however, two ways of looking at these identifications. The first is the reductionist way. It is plausible to say that temperature has been reduced to this mechanistic property. What this means is that there is a set of laws involving temperature and that those laws are reduced to laws operating at a deeper and wider level, in this case mechanics. At least, if we identify temperature (for gases) with mean kinetic energy, then we can derive the temperature laws from the laws of mechanics (providing we make certain other corresponding identifications).

A second way of looking at the identification is this. Temperature, it is claimed, is a state that occupies a certain role. That is, given the way the concept of temperature functions, temperature is understood to be 'that state which occupies such-and-such a causal role' or 'that state which is the causal basis for such-and-such thermometer measurements'. On this way of looking at things, temperature is understood to be a certain state, *whatever it is,* that has a given causal status. Once we discover that in fact there is a certain mechanical state – average kinetic energy of the constituent molecules – that has this status, then we have discovered what temperature is. There are two ways in which the identification may be supposed to work. They correspond to the ways in which the causal role may be said to function under the Kripke-Putnam and Evans approaches, respectively, as discussed in Chapter 3.

There is, however, a completely different approach that the objectivist can adopt, one in which we attempt neither to reduce temperature to another property nor to identify it with some property (that which defines temperature essentially). Instead we simply revise the concept of temperature. We replace the existing concept with a new one. The old concept, we find, is inadequate – perhaps there are no objects that instantiate the alleged property, or perhaps the concept, while performing some tasks adequately, is not up to the range of jobs required of it. It requires superannuating and replacing by a fresher concept, one better suited to the tasks.

The way I have defended the Locke-Descartes dispositionalist view, a revisionary approach is only to be expected. For the old concept of colour is defective. Objects are represented in experience as having that kind of colour, but no object in fact has it. If we want to talk about objects having colours, we need to invent a new sense of colour or modify the old. The dispositionalist sense is just such a modification. The bald statement that the old concept is defective needs qualifying. It is defective for some purposes, but not for all and certainly not for some of the most important ones. It is certainly not true that it is hopeless. On the contrary, it still allows one to make judgements that are very useful to make. It is often claimed, sometimes by the highest authorities, that humans need illusions and myths to live by. Whatever the case in morality and politics, it is true of colour perception.

Given that we have rejected the simple objectivist-realist view of colour but still wish to maintain that physical objects are coloured – bananas are yellow, roses are red, claret is purple – we seem to have two options: to maintain objectivism but to identify colour with some physical property, either of a microstructure or of light, or alternatively to endorse a dispositional (person-relative) analysis and thereby give up the objectivist quest.

It may not seem so at first glance, but whichever option we choose, we have to give up some portion of the original realist account. The dispositional view is an anti-realist one. It implies that what counts as the 'real' colour of an object is the colour it appears to have or would appear to have to observers of the right kind. In some sense, objects would have such properties in the absence of perceivers, but conceptually the property is related to perceivers. On such an account the 'real' colour is conventional, which of course is not to say that it is arbitrary.

On the other hand, those candidates usually offered as reductions also require modification of some part of the realist account. The causes of the colours objects appear to have are many and varied. The most plausible candidate for reduction will be the object's light-modifying powers, or the effect it has on the light. David Armstrong has sought to identify colour with some characteristic pattern of light at the object's surface (at least for surface colours); J. Westphal has argued that a more promising approach is to try to identify colour with a light-modifying disposition, e.g. with a disposition to reflect (or absorb) certain proportions of 'white' light, or, if one prefers, certain proportions of light of the wavelengths from the visible spectrum.[2] Objects with neutral or achromatic colours, such as whites, greys and blacks, are ones which reflect all wavelengths to (roughly) the same degree. Objects with chromatic colours are those objects which differentially reflect or absorb light at different wavelengths. Accordingly colour is to be identified with some feature of an object's reflectance curve.

Both accounts, however, give up some portion of the realist account as I have described it. On Westphal's account, colour, although objective, is a dispositional property, not an intrinsic property of the object. On both

2 Armstrong (1969); Westphal (1987). See my Chapter 3.

accounts, colour is a relational property, defined relative to the light that is incident or reflected/absorbed. On the realist account, colour is a property of the object, a property the object has whether or not there is light: a property similar to being square, being hard-edged (or curved), being pointed and so on.

It is tempting to respond to this point by saying, that 'so much the worse for the "natural view"': not for the first time and certainly not for the last time have 'natural' expectations been upset. Moreover, that there occurs this conflict between the natural view of colour and the reductionist view is not altogether surprising if we reflect on what typically happens in scientific 'reductions'. Usually the reduction of one property to another, or one set of laws to another, does not leave the original property or set of laws intact. More often than not, the new reducing property or set of laws leads us to revise our conceptions of the old property or old laws. Accordingly, if some aspect of reflectance is identical with some aspect of colour, we should not be surprised that we have to give up some part of our conception of colour.

But if we are prepared to consider a revisionary approach to colour, why should we adopt the dispositionalist view? Why not choose the objectivist view? Perhaps we could follow Smart and identify red with some disjunctive set of physical features

Red $= P_1 \vee P_2 \vee P_3 \vee \ldots$

where P_1 is spectral reflectance, P_2 spectral transmittance and so on. Alternatively we could say that red is to be identified with spectral reflectance in the case of surfaces, transmittance in the case of volumes and so on.

In principle there is no reason why not. Indeed, it is fully in the spirit of my approach to do so. Given that our experiences represent objects as having certain virtual colours, it follows that objects have a dispositional power to cause experiences that so represent colours. Coloured objects, that is, have distinctive dispositional properties: powers to appear in distinctive and characteristic ways. Those powers are properties of great interest to us, and they remain so whatever their causal basis. If a philosopher wishes to go on and add that there is a physical property in the object that we should call 'red' ('blue' . . . , as the case may be), then there is no reason why he should not. It is just that we would need to distinguish between two kinds of colour – physical colour and dispositional colour – just as we distinguish between absolute size and angular size.

152

However, if an objectivist wishes to say that colour is a physical property, say, a spectral reflectance property or a disjunctive property, she needs a justification for calling it 'colour'. A reductionist supplies such a justification by showing that there is a set of colour laws which is reduced to a set of deeper laws. An essentialist shows that there is a concept of colour implicit in our conceptual practices, of such a kind that we can identify colour as 'the property of objects which plays such-and-such a causal role'. What that causal role is will be defined by some of the colour laws which the reductionist appeals to. A revisionist, on the other hand, wishes to replace the old, inadequate concept with a new one. In principle this is fine. A dispositionalist such as Locke or Descartes can scarcely object. He is in the same line of trade. But in order for what is being done to count as revision and as replacement of the old concept of colour with a new concept of *colour,* there has to be something about the new concept that justifies calling it 'colour'.

Such a justification would need to refer to the set of practices and activities within which the old concept of colour is embedded. We can extract from those practices and activities a set of principles involving colour which comprise either our commonsense familiar knowledge about colour or those colour facts and laws which have been discovered in various fields of colour science.

Any adequate theory of colour has to provide some account of these principles. For the purest of reductionists, all of these colour laws and colour truths will be meant to be explained by, or reduced to, the proper set of 'reducing laws'. For the others, the original set of colour 'truths' may be refined, qualified or rejected – but reasons need to be given. If some of the old principles are to be rejected, some explanation is called for as to why these principles formed part of the previous store of 'knowledge'.

What is claimed here may run counter to some of the views expressed by Feyerabend.[3] I am prepared to live with that, but I should also say that I agree with him that when we have a replaced an old theory with a new one where the latter contains concepts that are revisions of some of the old, it is not a condition of the new theory's success that it contain the old laws or the old concepts. That would be absurd if it is a revision that we are describing. Nevertheless, if the old theory has been successful, there is an onus on advocates of the new to explain why the old was

3 P. K. Feyerabend (1989), 'How to Be a Good Empiricist', in B. A. Brody and R. E. Grandy (eds.), *Readings in the Philosophy of Science,* 2nd ed., Englewood Cliffs: Prentice-Hall, pp. 104–23.

successful or why it was so widely accepted. As far as I can see, there has been, historically, no shortage of attempts by such advocates to provide such explanations. But had it been true that scientists had not tried to give such explanations, then they ought to have done so – and Feyerabend should be the last person in the world to say that we should always accept without criticism what scientists do.

Both the dispositional analysis of colour and the realist-objectivist account embody revisions of the natural, standard account of colour. What each of them should be interpreted as providing, I would argue, is an account of different aspects of the natural account of colour. The natural account presupposes certain assumptions that are false. Despite this, there are different aspects to colour each of which serves a valuable function (or 'each of which has a point'). There is no reason in principle why there should not be two concepts of colour: an objectivist-realist one and a dispositional one. Just as we distinguish between absolute size and angular size, inertial mass and gravitational mass, rest mass and (non rest) mass, so we should distinguish between, say, absolute colour (intrinsic, proper, real . . . colour) and dispositional colour.

Nevertheless, the way the debate proceeds between proponents of these two accounts, they are often seen as mutually exclusive. The best argument for the dispositional account often seems to be that no successful reduction can be found, that there is no plausible candidate. The best refutation for the dispositional analysis seems to be that a successful candidate has been found. The dialectic, however, is misfounded. It could well be that neither provides an adequate full account of colour. Each provides, at best, an account of only one aspect.

Of course, other arguments might be provided to show that each analysis is defective as an account of any aspect of colour. For example, one objection to physical reductions is based on the premise that for each colour there is no single physical property either of the surface or of the surface-in-relation-to-light. As we saw, this leads J. J. C. Smart to treat colour as a disjunctive property: x is yellow $=$ x is P_1 or P_2 or P_3 or . . .[4] Most reductionists reject this device because they build in a restraint to the reduction: that the reducing property be a single property and not a disjunctive property. And the ground for this, it seems to me, is that this restraint is part of the unreduced concept. (It is one of 'our strongest intuitions' about colour.) However, if what we are trying to do

4 Smart (1971).

is seen as a revision, and inescapably so, then this restraint lapses. Smart's conception might be made to work as a conception of objective colour. The only thing is, to adopt this strategy requires one's admitting the viability of, and necessity for, another concept of colour: the dispositional concept. Just as important, once that is conceded we would need to ask why in addition we should have the disjunctive-objectivist account. That it is a revisionary account, as we have seen, is not sufficient grounds to reject it. However, it does place an onus on the revisionary to provide some justification for the revision.

Moreover, once we get down to justifying the objectivist (revisionary) account, we may well find that there are few if any serious purposes served by having the objectivist concept. In other words, the situation may well be as follows: the old concept needs revising: nothing can serve all the purposes for which it was intended. For the viable purposes, the dispositionalist concept is appropriate. For the other purposes, nothing will do.

2. COLOUR TRUTHS

Whether one's aim is to give an account of what colour is essentially or to give a reductionist account, or yet again a revisionary account, a defence of whatever story one gives must make reference to the 'natural view' of colour. This latter view is not just the view of the 'plain man' but is that conception of colour implicit in our colour-conceptual practices, both those involving the use of colour language and those involving colour perception.

That there is this need is shown by the fact that we are biological creatures with colour vision and that colour vision has played an important role in our lives. Any account of colour as an objective physical property needs to relate that physical property to the capacity of those with colour vision to perceive colour. This is just as true in the case of the physics of weight and of forces and of laws in relation to perceivers' perceptions of force and weight. Some such account can be given. The big difference between the physics of weights and the physics of colour is that in the former case, unlike the latter, once we have told the story about how the two are related we can largely forget about the perceivers. In the case of colour we cannot do that. If we forget about the perceivers, there is no story left to tell. Well, actually this is an exaggeration. The things to say are very minor.

Through the development of different aspects of colour science over the past two hundred years, we have discovered a modest wealth of information about colour. Summarising very briefly, that information can be grouped under different labels:

(a) Colorimetry
(b) Colour specification
(c) Mechanisms of colour vision
(d) Colour psychology

Colorimetry predominantly involves the mixing of lights and matching one colour sample with another, one produced by a mixture of lights. In this way one can provide a system of colour specifications. Both sources of information have been important in uncovering the mechanisms underlying colour vision, mechanisms which are, in the state of knowledge today, a combination of those described by Maxwell and Helmholtz for the photopigments in the retinas and those described by Hurvich, following Hering, for the neural cells.

In developing these fields of colour science, one is trying to build up a store of colour facts which contribute to our understanding of the perception of colour, as well as to provide an objective specification of colour. With both aims, the scientific account has to take account of a range of colour facts that hold of the practices and behaviour of colour-perceivers. That is, before we discovered any detailed scientific knowledge about colour, we had – and still have – a considerable body of knowledge about colour.

It is easy to see that the science of colour and of colour perception has both filled out the details of some of the colour principles described previously, e.g. in respect to the internal relations and to the conditions under which colour is perceived,[5] and in some case modified them. Furthermore, the discovery of colour-mixing laws and of the mechanisms underlying colour vision has added to our knowledge of colour. Accordingly we can put in summary form a list of the range of colour principles that we have both from detailed scientific work and from ordinary experience aided by science:

(A) Science
    (a) Colorimetry
    (b) Colour specification
    (c) Mechanisms of colour vision

5 See Chapter 5, Section 2 ('Conceptual Splitting').

(B) Ordinary Experience Supplemented by Science
   (a) Simple colour truths
   (b) Internal relationships
   (c) Causal truths: (i) objective; (ii) psychological
   (d) Principles of harmony, balance, contrast
   (e) Conditions of perception: varieties with illumination/distance,
       constancy, contrast etc.

Any adequate theory of colour will need to make sense of these principles. One possibility is that there is no single determinate concept of
colour that we can describe and that will satisfy all of the roles set down
above; that instead there is a family of interrelated concepts that in
our ordinary pre-theoretical practices are not clearly distinguished –
for the very practical reason that for many purposes there is little or no
point in distinguishing them. There may of course still arise new kinds
of situation in which it is necessary, or at least beneficial, to make the
distinctions: either for the scientific study of colour or for the detailed
pursuit of certain practical colour-related activities, e.g., in the fields
of art and design, in painting, in lighting, in the theatre and so
on; or, finally, for philosophical purposes, in providing a theory which
interrelates those different activities and studies, even in very schematic form.

Those in the Locke-Descartes-Helmholtz tradition who emphasise the
need for a distinction between colour-as-in-physical-objects and colour-
as-in-experience are best interpreted as thinking that there is no physical
feature in physical objects that satisfies all the requirements (that serves
all the required roles) of colour. Oversimplifying, there is no set of
features of physical objects which both make-true sentences such as 'ripe
bananas are yellow', 'Perth skies are blue', 'Granny Smith apples are
green', etc. and which, as a group, have the right kind of internal
relations to each other. In saying this I am being somewhat generous to
Locke, Descartes and Helmholtz. It might be more accurate to say that
what they believed was that there is no set of features of physical
bodies that both makes the sentences true and also has the richness and
sensuousness and variety and texture that we take colours to have. I
happen to think that they were right to think so, but, for a variety of
reasons, I have chosen to express the point in terms that will appeal to
the less poetic among us. The point will hold even for the nonromantics
who shy from appeals to these elements of subjectivity. Whatever the
historical facts about those in the Descartes-Locke-Helmholtz tradition,

157

we can reconstruct their position so as to provide a reasonable defence of the distinctions they wished to make.

3. COLOUR CONSTANCY

Included among the colour principles discussed in the last section is the phenomenon of colour constancy. It is an aspect of colour that we need to provide some account of. Indeed it, together with the phenomenon of colour contrast (successive and simultaneous), comprises some of the most important and intriguing aspects of colour.

There is no question that colour constancy takes place. What is not so clear, however, is the extent to which it occurs or how we are to understand exactly what colour constancy is. Very broadly, we may say that there is a tendency for an object that is one colour, white, say, to appear the same under a wide variety of conditions and illuminations. It is often pointed out that a white piece of paper in shade still looks white and not grey. The effect is more dramatic if we arrange conditions such that the portion of the white paper in illumination and the portion in shade can be separately seen and the eye 'deceived into thinking' that each is under the same illumination. The two portions look very different, and one does look grey.

However, although we can all agree that there is something very dramatic going on, it is not at all clear what it is and how it should be described. First of all, it is possible that the effect is not one of constancy at all. For example, perhaps that which is physical white (i.e. the physical property possessed by the physical object's surface) is not some property that is independent of the illumination: perhaps it is a disposition to reflect a certain proportion of the incident light or to reflect/absorb differentially certain proportions of the incident light. Or, more plausibly, it is a disposition to reflect a certain proportion of a certain level of light, where that level is determined by the pattern of the distribution of light over the total scene. It could be that insofar as judgements such as 'that paper is white' are true, what makes them true is a disposition that relates the piece of paper to the whole scene of which it is a part. That is, it involves a three-part relation among the paper, the scene and the overall illumination.

In the second place, the standard description of colour constancy, as with all other constancies, is framed in terms both of an object's having a certain objective property and of its appearing a certain way. It presupposes that an object is F and appears F under certain conditions, presumably standard ones, and that under a wide variety of other conditions it has a tendency to appear the same way, i.e. to appear *F*. Unfortunately, what is seldom done, either in the description of constancy effects or in actual experiments, is to resolve certain crucial ambiguities. First, the expression 'looks round' can be interpreted in at least two ways: as expressing either an epistemic sense or a phenomenal sense. Or, putting this a different way, the expression may be used to refer to two different aspects of perceptual states: their epistemic character or their phenomenal character.[6] This ambiguity has been recognised by a number of writers, although their characterisation of it is often mistaken.

There is a second ambiguity which, though just as important, is rarely noticed. The problem is that in constancy experiments there is not just one objective property in question, but at least two. Take size, for example. When we consider the size that a person or the moon appears to be, we need to distinguish between the absolute size and the angular size. When we consider shape we need to distinguish between intrinsic shape and perspectival shape. In the classic example of a round coin on a table which is looked at obliquely, there is something elliptical: it is the perspectival shape. This shape is analogous to the angular size. It is unlike the coin's intrinsic circularity in that it is defined relative to a point of view, the point from which I am looking and from which another could look. It could be characterised in terms of a shape drawn on a transparent screen placed at right angles to the line of sight. When I look obliquely at a coin on the table, there are both a circular shape and an elliptical shape: there are an intrinsic circular shape and an elliptical perspectival shape. The point is brought out by the use in many psychology books of a two-dimensional drawing of a hoop. We are told that it looks round even though the figure is elliptical. Exactly: the figure does look round (in one sense) but is elliptical.

The distinction between being objectively *F* and appearing *F* (between being really *F* and appearing *F*) can apply both to intrinsic shape and to perspectival shape. There is no reason why the one object should not look circular in the intrinsic sense and elliptical in the perspectival sense. What is seldom made clear in the many discussions of constancy experiments is whether the regression is supposed to be towards the real (or objective) intrinsic shape or the real (or objective) perspectival shape. A good illustration of the problems one can get into is provided by

6 For a discussion of the ambiguities, see J. B. Maund (1986), 'The Phenomenal and Other Uses of "Looks" ', *Australas. J. Phil.*, 64, pp. 170–80.

Gilinsky's discussion of his experiments on people's judgements of size.[7]

On the face of it, it would appear that the fact of colour constancy favours an objectivist account of colour. It would seem that it justifies the view that there is an objective property of objects and that it is towards the objective property that the regression occurs. Of course we would need to sort out which objective property it is – whether it is an intrinsic property or one relative to a point of view – but presumably that could be done. Indeed in D. R. Hilbert's defence of anthropocentric realism, an appeal to colour constancy plays an important part.

It is not at all obvious, however, that a nonobjective dispositional view cannot handle the facts of colour constancy. If colour is defined by the way it appears, and moreover by the way it appears in certain privileged illuminations, e.g. those of most importance for colour-perceivers, it is not at all unreasonable to expect that under other illuminations there might be a tendency for the appearance to be modi-fied in the direction of the standard appearance (understood as the appearance in the privileged illumination). In the second place, if we do admit the virtual-property concept of colour, there is no reason why the appearance should not regress towards the virtual colour. Virtual colours are of course 'objective' colours: they are objective properties that do not exist, just as phlogiston and caloric are objective natural kinds that do not exist. Given virtual colours, the regression could be to those. An analogy may help. We may not believe in Satan. Nevertheless we can believe that people such as Jack Nicholson can look satanic. We can also very reasonably hold that, as certain conditions change, a person that I do not like looks more and more satanic. For example, the more he disturbs me, the more satanic I find that he looks. Here we have a regression to the standard satanic look, epitomised in Jack Nicholson.

As far as making sense of the eye and the neural mechanisms is concerned, there is no difference between an objectivist and a disposi-tionalist account. In either colour perception or shape perception, the eye produces (eventually) states which represent certain states of affairs. These internal states have a certain character which makes them apt to represent objective affairs. As I argued previously, their having that character makes them apt also to represent a dispositional property: the power to appear a certain way. Reflection on the characteristic appear-ances of squares, circles, ovals, triangles etc. should convince us of this.

7 See A. S. Gilinsky (1955), 'The Effect of Attitude upon the Perception of Size' *Am. J. Psych.*, 68, pp. 173–92. This is discussed in Eleanor Gibson (1969), *Principles of Perceptual Learning and Development*, Englewood Cliffs: Prentice-Hall, pp. 363–8.

I have written of the *aptness* of the states to represent certain states of affairs. What makes it the case that they do in fact represent one state of affairs and not another, it needs to be stressed, depends on other things, e.g. on the range of beliefs, practices, conventions etc. of the people whose states they are.

4. OBJECTIVIST VIEWS AND APPEARANCES

The set of colour principles described above comprises five classes of colour 'truths' drawn from our ordinary knowledge of colour, supplemented by the findings of several scientific fields: (a) simple colour truths; (b) internal relationships; (c) causal truths, both physical and psychological; (d) principles of harmony, balance, contrast etc.; and (e) conditions of perception.

In previous chapters I placed great emphasis on the set of internal relationships among colours – the relationships expressed in the (various) three-dimensional colour array. As it happens, there are no physical features that stand in those relationships. What we are forced to say is that the set of ordered samples appears to be colour-related, as expressed in the three-dimensional colour array. The full force of the position on virtual colours is that the virtual colours stand in a set of relations, and those relations are virtual. Of the samples that appear to be coloured, they also *appear* to stand in a set of ordered relationships – but apart from their power to appear, they do not actually stand in any such set of relations. This fact about colours and the way they appear brings out a problem for the objectivist who wishes to say that the appearance picks out the physical feature only accidentally and not essentially. The problem is that the coloured samples do not just appear coloured: they also appear to stand in the ordered relationships. We would have to say that this feature of colour appearance also picks out, albeit accidentally, a set of relationships among physical features. But there is no such set of relationships among physical features. Accordingly anyone who wants to maintain an objectivist position with respect to the property colour would need to hold a dispositionalist position with respect to *relations* between colours – a paradoxical position, to say the least.

The pluralist framework for thinking about colours allows a possible but not a mandatory place for an objectivist concept. It has been argued by some objectivists, however, that there are certain features of colours that demand an objectivist concept; that at least for handling these features, a dispositional concept is inadequate. For example, some of the colour truths above attribute a causal role to colour, e.g. in colour perception. Accordingly an objectivist concept is a perfect candidate for satisfying such a role. For it can specify a physical feature that can exert the right kind of causal power. It is not true, however, that a dispositional concept is to be excluded on this ground. As we saw earlier, a dispositionalist might adopt a mixed rather than a pure dispositionalist account. There are two kinds of dispositional account to choose from:

(1) To be red is to have the power to appear red in standard conditions;
(2) To be red is to have some feature whereby one has the power to appear red in standard conditions.

The second, mixed form retains the emphasis on something's being red, on its having the right kind of power, but it allows that the object, in having that power, has some feature (which may be different in different objects) which is the basis for that power. Clearly on this analysis the underlying physical feature has all the causal powers one could wish. The mixed dispositional analysis combines this with the advantage of keeping colours tied to the way they appear. Even the dispositionalist who adopted version (1) might insist also that on this account being red is causally relevant to the way things appear. For according to that, being red is having a certain power, and that power is a causal power, and for the problem under consideration it is the best kind of power: it is the power to appear red. Causal powers are just that: causal powers. It therefore seems that the objectivist account has no decided advantage over the dispositional account.

Another consideration thought to benefit the objectivist account is that it captures our intuition that colour, at least in the case of opaque surfaces, is an intrinsic property of the surface, like its shape. It may not be the sort of physical feature which we had thought it was, but at least it is a property of the surface and it is intrinsic, unlike what it would be on the dispositional account.

This argument won't do, for several reasons. First, if the objective physical property is an aspect of the object's spectral reflectance curve, then it is not an intrinsic feature of the surface. It is a light-relative property. The spectral reflectance curve sets out the relative proportions of light at each wavelength of the visible spectrum that is reflected or absorbed at the body's surface. The property has no meaning apart from the reference to the visible spectrum. Of course there are physical features of the body's surface that are causally responsible for the object's power to absorb/reflect differentially light from the visible spectrum, but, on the account that we are considering, they do not constitute the colour. On the other hand, if we were to choose a different physicalist option and identify each colour with the intrinsic feature of an object's surface, then we would preserve the intuition that colour is an intrinsic feature of the object's surface but would fall foul of another intuition. It is also one of our intuitions that red, say, is a single property, that it is a single property shared by all bodies that are red, and not a disjunctive property. On this objectivist option, however, it would have to be a disjunctive property. Not only would red have to be a different property for surfaces from the property it is for volumes or light sources, but it is not a single property for surfaces. There is no one physical-chemical feature that all red bodies share, nor any single feature shared by blue (yellow, green, orange . . .) bodies (see Nassau).[8]

On the other hand, once we turn to the dispositional account, we see that both intuitions are preserved, or at least − and this is just as good as far as the intuitions are concerned − an explanation is provided for why we have these intuitions. Our visual experiences of red represent to us objects as red. What sort of red? Virtual redness. That is, our experiences represent to us objects as having intrinsic single colours. As it happens, the objects do not have those colours, but it is perfectly intelligible why we have the intuitions that we do about colours. Those intuitions reflect the kind of colour that we experience objects as having, i.e. the kind of colour experiences represent to us objects as having.

It follows therefore that the objectivist notion of colour has no advantage over a sensible dispositionalist view − this is, with respect to that class of 'colour truths' which were most favourable to the objectivist analysis. However, even if we were successful in finding a set of colour truths in this class that favoured the objectivist analysis, it would not mean that there was no need for a dispositional account of colour, any more than the fact that there is such a property as intrinsic size means that there is no need for a concept of angular size. Both concepts have roles to play.

It would not matter in the least if Westphal or Armstrong or Hilbert were successful in providing a justification for having an objectivist account of colour, for we would still need to identify and recognise a different kind of colour, dispositional colour. All that they would have done was show that the dispositional account was not alone in the field. And the reason for insisting on this is that, if we reflect on the set of

8 K. Nassau (1983), *The Physics and Chemistry of Color*, New York: Wiley.

colour principles or 'colour-truths', we find that there is a wide body of them for which we need the dispositional account.

The important point is that coloured objects have characteristic appearances and that those appearances are of great interest to us. It is because we have that interest that we need a concept of dispositional colour – the power to appear in characteristic ways. It is because of the way colours appear that they are important to us both biologically and socially. It is because colours have a characteristic appearance that:

The colours can be ordered systematically in colour arrays;
They have emotional effects;
Principles of harmony and contrast apply;
There are principles governing phenomena of colour contrast.

It is true that physical features both of physical objects and of retinal cells contribute causally to these phenomena, but central to all of these colour principles is the way colour appears.

There is an additional reason for requiring dispositional colour. Physical surfaces have distinctive ways of appearing, ways differing from those for volumes and films and light sources. Nevertheless they are all modes of appearing for colour. What makes them all examples of colour can only be understood in terms of them as *appearances*. The account that makes most sense of these modes of appearance is the dispositional account, one that unites these ways of appearing into dispositions to appear.

5. MODES OF COLOUR APPEARANCE

As Jacob Beck points out in his book *Surface Color Perception*, D. Katz was the first to attempt to describe and treat systematically the different modes of colour appearance. This he did in his influential book *The World of Colour*. In this he claimed to identify eleven modes of appearance, including film colours, surface colours, volume colours and luminous colours. Katz went on to describe various aspects of each mode of appearance, some being common to several or all and others being peculiar to one or to some.[9]

There is some controversy about the precise number of such modes of appearance and about the number and nature of the aspects of the modes,

9 J. Beck (1972), *Surface Color Perception*, Ithaca: Cornell U.P., pp. 16–32; D. Katz (1930), *The World of Colour*, trans. R. B. Macleod and C. W. Fox, London: Kegan Paul, pp. 7–94, esp. 7–23.

but it is clear that there are at least five important modes of appearance: film, surface, volume, illuminant and illumination. Secondly, it is clear that some attributes or aspects are shared by some modes and others are not. The attribute of hue – red, blue, green, yellow – applies to each. Brightness applies to film and luminant and illumination colours but not to surface and volume colours. To the latter but not to the former, lightness applies. Beck followed the Committee on Colorimetry of the Optical Society of America in saying that saturation applies to all modes of appearance.[10]

However, in the Munsell Colour System and the Natural Colour system the dimensions of saturation and lightness are replaced by other dimensions. In the Munsell system the dimensions are chroma and value (which roughly correspond to saturation and lightness respectively). In the Swedish Natural Colour System the dimensions are chromaticness and whiteness/blackness. One way of thinking about these different systems is to see them employing different systems for mapping colours. Each colour gets a location in each colour space, but there are different ways of ordering the colours. (The fact that there are these different systems does not in itself count against the reality of any of the attributes, although it does count against Bernard Harrison's claim that all it can be to be a given colour is to occupy a certain locus in 'the' 3-dimensional colour space.)[11]

I raised the possibility previously that perceived colour could be reduced to some objective physical feature, albeit a different feature for each attribute of each mode of appearance. That is, red for surface colour would be a different physical property from red for film colour, volume colour, illumination colour and luminous-source colour and so on. I argued that given certain restraints on colour-as-it-appears, no such reduction would work, and certainly not for surface colour. That mode of appearance provides, however, the best chance for success. Objectivists tend to concentrate on surface colour, and that is understandable. Less so is the tendency to downplay film colour – the colour seen through a small aperture held close to the eye so that it is not a precisely localised colour. Film colour, with qualification, comes close to corresponding to a retinal pattern, suitably defined.

Let us consider opaque physical surfaces whose characteristic appearance is different from that for light sources. Now, if we look at physical

10 Beck (1972), pp. 18, 24.
11 Harrison (1973), p. 86. See also my Chapter 2, Section 5.

surfaces through a small aperture we will see what is called a 'film colour' or 'aperture colour'. This colour will have a mode of appearance different from that of the surface. Actually there are two kinds of aperture colour one can see, depending on how close the eye is to the aperture. The film colour is a colour that is hard to localise: it is some distance behind the screen with the aperture. It is a hard-to-localise film that is seen to have the colour. On the other hand, if the screen is held a little further away, one sees the aperture colour as a spot of colour localised on the screen, as part of the screen. Its character will be different from, though related to, the colour of the surface seen through the hole, although it will be related as well to the colour of the surrounding screen.

Now it may be true that a brownish surface colour will appear yellowish through the aperture. The yellow colour is not a surface colour, yet it too is a property of the surface. That physical surface has the power to appear yellow when viewed under those circumstances. It has that dispositional property, the power to have that aperture colour, i.e. the power to appear *that* way under those circumstances.

It is just as objective a feature of a brownish surface that it has a yellowish aperture colour and not a green one or red one as that it is brownish when seen in normal circumstances without an aperture. It won't do to say that the yellowish way it appears through an aperture can be explained as being the same as yellowish surfaces appear when seen normally. For they don't appear the same at all. Aperture colours have a distinctive appearance, one quite different from that for surface colours. It is true that there is some aspect of the aperture colour that is similar to an aspect of the surface colour that justifies calling them both yellow. It is not true, however, that surface colour provides the primary sense of colour and that aperture/film colours are secondary. Both are colours in their own right, colours between which there are certain similarities. It is plausible that there is a close correspondence between aperture colour and retinal effect – at least for certain surrounds – but there is no question that physical surfaces have the disposition to appear to have characteristic colours when viewed through apertures.

It is obvious that surface colours are of crucial importance to biological organisms such as ourselves. Film colours are much less so. They are normally seen as artefacts of laboratory situations or perhaps as artificially produced by artists and designers whose job it is to produce the right, or at least appropriate, colour effects. Notwithstanding how they are usually produced, film colours are objective too. At least they appear as much part of the objective world as do surface colours and volume colours. Moreover they have affinities with the colours of light sources and with illumination colour, and these are important as naturally, if infrequently, occurring features of the physical world. So film colours require theoretical treatment too. Now, whereas there is some plausibility to the notion that surface colour does correspond to some light-relative physical feature of the surface, there is no plausibility whatsoever to the idea that for film colour or illumination colour there is a single light-relative physical feature. For film and illumination colour, samples that are all red (or blue, yellow, orange etc.) are samples constituted by different proportions of light. What unites the red samples (and what unites each of the other colours) is, at best, the capacity to excite, in similar proportions, photopigments similar to those possessed by humans.

So it would follow that even if the reduction for each mode of appearance satisfied the first set of restraints upon colour appearance, the candidate for reduction would, in the case of surface colour, be a property of the surface, but in the case of film colour a psychophysical property, even though both kinds of colour *appear* as objective features of objects in the physical world.

Secondly, there would be raised the question of why the same terms for hues – red, yellow, blue, green – should apply to surface colour, film colour, volume colour, illumination colour and so on. What justifies our using the same term 'red' for each? The dispositionalist has a ready answer. In the case of hues, it is the fact that each kind of physical feature has the power to appear a similar way that justifies the use of the hue term. It needs to be acknowledged that other dimensions, such as saturation and brightness, do not apply equally to all kinds of appearance. Even this concession can, however, be turned to the dispositionalist's advantage. For even if the dimensions are different there is still an analogical relationship that holds between them, and for that the dispositionalist account is also appropriate.

One might reply that it is only accidental fact, explained historically, that we use the same term 'red' for each of surface colour, illumination colour, film colour and so on. There is a similarity in the way each objective feature appears that makes us use the same term 'red', but what redness is essentially is what objective feature is the causal basis for its appearing a certain way. Being red, it will be argued, is not constituted essentially by that appearance.

Well of course one can say this. Indeed, one is forced to say this if one wishes to retain an objectivist account of colour. However, to think that one has thereby routed a dispositional account of colour is to delude oneself. One can assert that what one is trying to give an account of, in giving an account of colour is an objective property that is not defined essentially by the way it appears. But this leaves it open for the dispositionalist to reply that you are welcome to that but that what he or she is doing is giving an account of colour for which the way it appears is essential – and only the dispositional account is appropriate. The point being made by the dispositionalist here is not simply that it is the natural concept of colour for which appearance is essential, but that there is a need for a concept of colour for which appearance is essential. It is quite open for the objectivists to continue with a very different task, but they need to be aware that this is what it is.

Of course if what one is trying to do is to give an account of the sort of colour that is contained within our conceptual and linguistic practices as colour-perceivers, then the fact that we take ourselves to be justified in using 'red' with respect to all modes of colour appearance would seem to support the dispositionalist, in this task.[12]

6. CONCLUSION

Within the pluralist account of colour there is room for an objectivist concept of colour, but that does not mean that the (person-relative) dispositionalist concept can be dispensed with. On the contrary, we have seen that there are powerful reasons for thinking that a dispositional concept is necessary.[13]

There is strong reason, moreover, to prefer what I have called a 'mixed' dispositional concept. Blue$_D$ objects are objects which possess some feature by virtue of which they look blue$_I$, that is, they look blue in the intrinsic sense, i.e. in the virtual-colour sense. This analysis has the virtue of helping to explain why colours (dispositional colours) play a causal role in perception, why the causal feature does not have to be the same, either for surface colours or for all kinds of colour (light sources, volumes, surfaces and so on). And it ties colours to the way they appear.

12 For the recognition both of the importance of appearances and of their diversity, I am grateful to Paul Green-Armytage, and specifically to his 'Brightness, Whiteness and Lightness', Colour Report F26, Scandinavian Colour Institute (1983), and 'The Specification of Colours', invited paper at the Illuminating Engineering Society of Australia, 30th National Convention, Perth (1984).

13 An even stronger claim for the necessity of dispositional concepts is made by John Harvey (1992), 'Challenging the Obvious: The Logic of Colour Concepts', *Philosophia*, 21, pp. 277–94.

It does also fit what Descartes and Locke sometimes said, e.g. Descartes's saying that, speaking carefully, to say that a physical object is red is to say that it has some unknown nature which gives it the power to produce sensations of red.

Since the dispositional concept needs to be specified in terms of the way colours appear, an account of this disposition must make reference to virtual colours, and then in turn to phenomenal colours. These colour concepts, therefore, have an important role to play in forming how we should think of colour. Although this claim has already been supported in this text, there are certain serious objections that have to be considered. They are the subject of Part III of this book.

Part III

Colours and consciousness

Given that colours, as we normally think of them, are virtual properties, how, if at all, should we adjust our ideas in thinking of colours? If normally our perception of colour involves 'false consciousness', what is the right way to think of colours? The answer to that is that for many purposes we should think of them in the same way as we always did. In the case of colour, unlike other cases, false consciousness should be a cause for celebration.

For some purposes, however, we need to develop a more comprehensive account, a pluralist account of colour. The different elements of the virtual concept of colour reflect different functions that this concept is meant to play. Given these different functions and the fact that there is no property that satisfies all of them, it is open to us to develop a pluralist account of colour in which different concepts of colour take over different functions.

This pluralist framework may be thought of as fulfilling two tasks. First, it provides a descriptive account of how our concepts of colour have been, and are in the process of, evolving. Second, it provides a framework within which colour can properly be thought of. It did not have to be this way, but the two tasks, at least for colour, are related.

This framework has the advantage of allowing a place for an objective concept of colour, although it also leaves it open whether there is a genuine candidate. Whether or not there is any point in having an objective concept, there is, as we have seen, a need for a dispositional concept, one tied to the appearance of colour. The dispositional concept is a crucial part of the pluralist framework. But once we become enlightened by accepting the theory of virtual colours, how should we then think of the dispositional concept? What exactly does the exercise of the disposition consist in? What exactly is the content of the dispositional concept?

The right answer is that there are two parts to the dispositionalist

171

concept. One part refers to the way objects appear, and the other to the feature, whatever it is, which is the causal basis for the appearance. That is, the disposition is not pure but 'mixed'. Blue$_D$ objects are objects that have some feature by virtue of which they look as if they are blue, i.e. blue in the intrinsic sense, i.e. blue in the virtual-colour sense. The content of the dispositional concept thus presupposes the virtual-colour concept. This means that there is point in retaining this concept, even though I know that no objects have the property. The fact that I do not believe that this property of intrinsic blueness is ever instantiated does not mean that I should give up the concept, any more than disbelievers in Satan should give up the concept of *satanic*.

This answer is perfectly reasonable, as far as it goes. The use of the virtual-colour concept to describe things requires me to adopt the naive attitude to colour or, as I prefer to say, the engaged attitude typical of the playgoer who, at the theatre, suspends his belief that 'it is all a pack of lies'. Of course as a philosopher I need to understand why I have this virtual-colour concept and what role it plays, and for that I need to understand an account that makes reference to phenomenal colours. But none of that stops me from continuing to employ the virtual-colour concept, whether as scientist, artist, consumer, town-planner, interior decorator or philosopher. As for serving their functions as signs or as being aesthetically or emotionally significant, virtual colours are as good as real colours.

Any adequate theory of colour, however, requires understanding how it is that the content of our experiences can be colours that do not in fact exist. How can this be so, and why is it beneficial? The answer to those questions depends on making reference to phenomenal qualities, that is, to qualia. The explanation for why our experiences represent objects as having virtual colours is that our visual experiences contain sensory representations. These typically represent objects in the physical world as having (virtual) colours, and they do so because the representations have the character implicit in three-dimensional colour arrays. The representations do not have the virtual colour – they have the right kind of structure, but they are not physical. What they have are phenomenal colours, that is, qualia.

It needs to be stressed that this account does not require colours, either phenomenal or virtual, to be projected into space. Just as they represent objects as having virtual colours, so they represent objects as having spatial properties (and relations) through themselves having phenomenal spatial properties.

Thus the pluralist account, which allows for a dispositional concept of colour, requires in order to make sense of that concept both virtual colours and phenomenal colours. For its reliance on the sensory, phenomenal component, however, the pluralist account is open to attack on two sides. Some wish to reject it in favour of neural states and their character. Others attack it from a different viewpoint, arguing that, because of the central role in the language of community and culture, the explanatory role of such notions is suspect. Such arguments tend to come from cultural anthropologists or from philosophers deeply influenced by Wittgenstein. In the final part of this book, these two forms of criticism will be confronted and, it is hoped, set aside.

8

Colour qualia

When we have colour experiences, typically we form sensory representations of the world. These representations represent objects in the physical world as having (virtual) colours, and they do so because the representations have the character implicit in three-dimensional colour arrays. The representations do not have virtual colours (they have the right kind of structure, but they do not have the right causal powers),[1] but they represent physical objects as having those colours. What the representations have are phenomenal colours, that is qualia, in the full-bodied sense. Sensory representations, in other words, have the phenomenological character that physical objects might have had but do not.

Physicalists would deny that we have to admit the existence of states with any such phenomenological character. The strength of this position would depend on the possibility that for each colour-perceiver there exists a system of neural states which stand together in the right kind of relationships, such that they would justify the claim that they form a system of open-qualia. It could well be that, with respect to the neural processes underlying colour perception, we could construct a vector phase space and populate it with colour correlates such that they comprise a system in that vector space with the right kind of character.[2] If so, then there would be neural states that have the same form as virtual colour and as phenomenal qualia. Given this, we may wonder whether it is necessary to suppose that there are phenomenal qualia. Perhaps the neural-'qualia' could perform the task of explaining why we have the virtual-colour concept that we do.

The proper response to the physicalist is that whatever the character of the system of neural states, it is not the right character. What it lacks is the phenomenological character that the sensory representations have

---

1 That is, they do not have the properties which the virtual-colour concept specifies: they do not have what it takes to make the virtual colours actual.
2 See Patricia Churchland (1986), *Neurophilosophy*, Cambridge: MIT Press.

and that physical objects might have had but do not. The point about the character of virtual colour is that it enables us to think of virtual colours as features which physical objects, such as lakes and rivers and eyes and lips, might have had but do not. Whatever the character of the neural states, i.e. the system of vectors in neural phase space, it will not do the job.

The task that needs to be done was clarified by introducing the notion of open-qualia. These are the qualitative features that we experience trees and lips as having. They are not defined as phenomenal qualities, as features of our experience; indeed, the point of the notion is to leave open whether they are phenomenal or physical. There might well be a structural similarity between the system of neural states and the system of virtual colours, but that leaves the neural states far short of being open-qualia.

The best explanation for why virtual colours play the role that they do is that we have sensory representations with intrinsic features that are qualia. This means, I suggest, that we have an argument to add to those provided by other philosophers for the existence of qualia. It is the aim of this chapter to defend this argument, especially against the physicalistic challenge described above.

1. QUALIA

Qualia are usually introduced by contrasting them to physical states. The claim is made that there is a range of mental states, e.g. visual experiences, experiences of taste and of smell and so on, which have a phenomeno-logical character which cannot be captured by a functionalist account of mental states or by any physicalistic account. In the words of Frank Jackson, a self-confessed 'qualia-freak':

Tell me everything physical there is to tell about what is going on in a living brain, the kind of states, their functional role, their relation to what goes on at other times and in other brains, and so on and so forth . . . you won't have told me about the hurtfulness of pains, the itchiness of itches, the pangs of jealousy, or the characteristic experience of tasting a lemon, smelling a rose, hearing a loud noise or seeing the sky.[3]

The qualities of states that give them their phenomenological character are called 'qualia'. For many, the existence of qualia is simply self-evident. Only a madman would deny them. Or, to put it more accu-

3 Frank Jackson (1990), 'Epiphenomenal Qualia', in William Lycan, *Mind and Cognition: A Reader*, Cambridge, Mass.: Blackwell Publisher, pp. 469–78.

rately, for me to deny that I have them I would have to be mad. That is the rub. For those who believe in qualia, it seems that the best evidence for them is one's own experience. Unfortunately, there are others who deny qualia. Presumably for them their own experience is not enough.

However, a range of arguments have been offered. Perhaps the most well known is the celebrated Inverted Spectrum Argument; a second is the Knowledge of Physical Information Argument: someone could know all that it was possible to know about the physical world, including the physical truth about neural processes, but still lack a certain piece of knowledge, e.g. what a rose smells like. A third is the Phenomenological Argument.

The last argument is based on making sense of perceptual experience from the first-person point of view. It reflects an attempt to make sense of the phenomenology of experience. It is, I hold, not only the most powerful of the arguments for qualia, but it lies at the heart of the other arguments, including variations of the classical 'argument from illusion'. It is important to recognise this, for without it the responses of the physicalists and the functionalists, that the arguments are question-begging, will seem hard to meet.

One person who has realised the centrality of the phenomenological argument is Gilbert Harman. It is in a recent paper, 'The Intrinsic Quality of Experience', that he makes this point and claims to produce a refutation of the argument.[4] Harman's objection is certainly a very powerful one. Indeed, his paper has been widely taken as presenting a decisive rebuttal to the qualia-defender. The objection is in fact very similar to that mounted by Michael Tye.[5] Their challenge is important not least because it meets the qualia-defender on her own grounds. These philosophers appeal to introspection and to the phenomenology of experience to challenge the claim that in perceptual experience one is aware of intrinsic qualities of one's own experience.

The fact that this objection appeals to the phenomenology of experience is important. I take it that appeals to one's own experience are crucial and, far from being questionable, are indispensable. This is not to say that they are incorrigible or license indubitable statements. Far from it. Nevertheless they provide evidence, and sometimes the very best evidence.

4 Gilbert Harman (1990), 'The Intrinsic Quality of Experience', in James Tomberlin (ed.), *Philosophical Perspectives*, 4, Alascadero: Ridgeview, pp. 31–52.
5 Michael Tye (1992), 'Visual Qualia and Visual Content', in Tim Crane (ed.), *The Contents of Experience*, Cambridge: CUP, pp. 158–77.

In the light of these considerations it is crucial whether the Harman-Tye challenge can be met. Before examining their objection, however, it will be necessary to be clear about whether the issue is between qualia theories and functionalism or between the former and physicalism.

2. QUALIA AND FUNCTIONALISM

It is unfortunate, even if understandable, that arguments about qualia have tended to become set in the context of functionalist accounts of mental states. Influential in this have been papers by Block and by Fodor and Block, in which they argued that there are states or experiences whose existence is incompatible with functionalism.[6] One of the major arguments used was the Inverted Spectrum Argument. This was intended to show that there are experiences with qualitative character and functional roles, such that it is possible for functional roles to be interchanged while the qualitative character remains the same.

This problem has spawned a considerable literature, much of it confusing and inconclusive. It is necessary to separate two questions. One is whether the argument shows that there exist states with qualitative character (qualia realism is true); the other, whether their existence is consistent with functionalism. These two issues need to be kept separate, for it may well be the case, as Sydney Shoemaker has argued, that the existence of qualia can be accommodated within the framework of functionalism.[7] For our purposes it is the existence of qualia that is of greatest relevance.

Not only is it crucial that these issues be separated, but it is lucky that they can be. For I take functionalism to be a morass that is best avoided. Not that functionalism is necessarily wrong. I agree with Elliott Sober that if we take it as the view that all mental states are essentially defined as functional states, then either it is trivially true or it is bizarre.[8] Unless we are prepared to specify what kinds of functions are involved, i.e. unless we say more than that the states are related to 'inputs, outputs and other internal states', then the thesis has little content. Once we do specify the functions, then it seems bizarre. In biology, for example,

6 N. Block and J. Fodor (1972), 'What Psychological States Are Not', *Phil. Rev.* 81, pp. 159–81, esp. 172–4. See also N. Block (1980), 'Troubles with Functionalism' in Block (ed.), *Readings in the Philosophy of Psychology*, Cambridge: Harvard U.P., pp. 268–305.
7 S. Shoemaker (1982), 'The Inverted Spectrum', *J. Phil.*, 79, no. 7, pp. 357–81, and (1975), 'Functionalism and Qualia', *Phil. Stud.*, 27, pp. 291–315.
8 Elliott Sober (1990), 'Putting the Function Back into Functionalism', in William Lycan (ed.), *Cognition: A Reader*, Cambridge Mass.: Blackwell Publisher, pp. 97–106.

there is a useful notion of function, but it would be absurd to expect all biological states to be functional ones. Why should we expect all psychological states to be functional? (The difficulties faced by functionalism in this context have recently been described by Edmond Wright.)[9]

One of the major difficulties with discussions of the Inverted Spectrum Argument is that we rarely find spelled out exactly what the thesis of functionalism at issue is, or in particular what the functionalist analysis of 'visual experience' is. As in many another philosophical debate, we find the dialectic turning on onus of proof. The anti-functionalist is often left with the onus of showing that no possible functionalist account would work, without the functionalist's actually specifying a precise functional analysis.

One way the dispute can become trivial is if the functionalist is allowed to appeal to the possibility that the ultimate features of the world are not intrinsic states and features but powers. Such a possibility has been suggested by Harre and Madden and more recently by B. Ellis.[10] Someone who held such a view could present a functionalist's view of everything.

Perhaps the greatest problem, however, is this. When specifying functionalist accounts of mental states, we need to distinguish between broad and narrow specifications.[11] A broad description of a mental state makes reference to some feature of the person's environment, either a general kind, e.g. H_2O, or some particular, say, Mr Clinton or the Melbourne Cup (of 1994). Accordingly we can distinguish between broad and narrow varieties of functionalism, reserving each for the appropriate kind of mental state.

This leads to a problem when we turn to qualia. Let us suppose that there are qualia. A specification of the functional role of visual experiences could then make reference to the qualia themselves. Broad mental states are taken to refer to the person's environment, which is normally taken to be the external environment. However, if we can make sense of an internal 'environment', or an internal set of events which the person has access to, then there is no reason why broad mental states

9 Edmond Wright (1993), 'More Qualia Trouble for Functionalism: The Smythies TV-Hood Analogy', *Synthese*, 97, pp. 365–82.
10 R. Harre and E. H. Madden (1975), *Causal Powers: A Theory of Natural Necessity*, Oxford: Blackwell; B. Ellis (1992), 'Scientific Essentialism', Victorian Centre for History and Philosophy of Science, La Trobe University, preprint 1/92, August.
11 See F. Jackson and P. Pettit (1988), 'Functionalism and Broad Content', *Mind*, 97, pp. 381–400.

should not refer to these as well. According to the qualia-defender, the qualia are just such internal events.

The point is this. Normally with respect to a mental state we distinguish between the content of the state (the intensional content) and the intrinsic features of the state whereby it carries the content. The content, for a broad state, will usually make reference either to some particular or to some general kind in the external environment. But of course sometimes the state can be self-referential or alternatively can refer to some internal state(s). The 'broad' characterisation should be extended to such cases as well. Instead of the broad/narrow classification, it would be better to use a focused/unfocused or a targeted/nontargeted classification. The crucial point is whether or not the mental state has a target or focus, be it external or internal.

The extension of the broad/narrow classification is highly significant for the spectrum-inversion case. The point of the inversion depends on a distinction between a qualitative state and its functional role. We are asked to imagine that the two should come apart: that *that* qualitative state should interchange its functional role with another. But even if there are inner intrinsic qualia in the strongest possible sense, it will be impossible for the two to come apart. For the specification of the functional role is a broad one or a targeted one. Hence the functional role makes reference to the qualitative state. It is no more possible for a different qualitative state to play that role than it would be for a doppelganger jockey on twin-earth to dream of winning our-earth's Melbourne Cup or, if you prefer, express remorse for losing our-earth's Melbourne Cup.

The upshot is that if the functionalist is allowed to help herself to any version of functionalism, no thought-experiment can possibly lead to its rejection. The thought-experiment is only relevant if we specify a particular version of functionalism. How effective this point is can be illustrated by reference to Shoemaker's 1975 paper 'Functionalism and Qualia'. Shoemaker says that any state functionally identical with a pain state will share with the pain state not only

(1) Its tendency to influence overt behaviour in certain ways

and

(2) Its tendency to produce in the person the belief that there is something organically wrong with him

but also

179

(3) Its tendency to produce qualitative beliefs in the person, i.e. to make him think that he has a pain with a certain qualitative character.

But of course the third functional role is one of which we have to ask: is it a pure functional role, or is it a targeted one – does it target a specific qualitative state? It seems to me that a defender of qualia in the strong sense would say that what makes the belief in (3) the belief that it is, namely a belief held by the person that he has a pain with a certain qualitative character, is that it focuses on that qualitative character. Hence, for the defender of qualia in the strong sense, the functional role specified in (3) is related to a particular quale. No other quale can occupy that functional role. (This point is also made in Howard Robinson's reply to Dennett's claim to relieve us of our qualia.) [12]

There is another way in which functionalism could be compatible with the existence of qualia. Even if one of the functions of sense-experience is, say, to enable one to latch on to certain objective properties of the physical world (to put it figuratively), there is a related function: to enable one to latch on to the objective features *in a certain way*. Why shouldn't the functionalist say that what happens in hypothetical cases of spectrum inversion is that those different functions come apart? My experience of blue no longer latches onto the same objective property that it used to. Now it latches on to a different property but the *way* it latches on to that is the same as the way it used to latch on to the other. In other words, after spectrum inversion there is a function that the experience of blue retains. The function has to do not so much with *what* it latches on to, but *how* it does the latching. Hence once again it is possible to be a qualia-realist and to hold on to functionalism. Thus spectrum inversion will count against functionalism only if the functionalist specifies the functional roles either as pure or narrow functions or as broad ones targeted on nonqualitative states. It is not clear that this can be done except in a broad, handshaking way. That is, it is not plausible that every function of every experience can be specified in such a way.

Visual experiences, like most other mental states, have a range of functions. It is not easy to pick out which functions are essential to making a specific mental state the state that it is. For some functionalists, e.g. David Lewis, it seems that all the functions are necessary. But this surely cannot be right. An experience of light blue things can give some

12 Howard Robinson (1993), 'Dennett on the Knowledge Argument', *Analysis,* 53, no. 3, pp. 174–7; Daniel Dennett (1992), *Consciousness Explained,* London: Penguin, esp. Ch. 12, 'Qualia Disqualified'.

people a coolish feeling. This is interesting, but it surely cannot be essential to the experience of light blue, even for those people. Visual experiences have in general two important kinds of function:

(1) They carry nonconceptual content, information about physical objects and their qualities. This is related to their causal interaction with the physical features, but it is not simply a matter of being caused by those features. As Dretske has pointed out, for information about P to be carried by state S, it is possible for something causally related to P, call it Q, to cause S.[13]

(2) They carry conceptual content. That is, the experiences fit in with the perceiver's cognitive and conceptual resources so as to provide the basis for judgements, especially judgements about the physical objects and qualities that are perceived.

But there are other functions as well:

(3) They provide a basis that enables one to act in relation to objects in space.
(4) They remind us of previous sense-experiences, e.g., your gleaming cup reminds me of how mine looked when it was new.
(5) They serve social functions, e.g., they provide a basis that enables one to communicate freely with others and to orient oneself towards, with and against other people.

Are all of these essential? Are any of them? The right answer, it seems to me, is that our visual experiences can be described in different ways and that different descriptions are connected with different functions. For example the sentence 'X looks blue to me' can be interpreted in at least three different ways: epistemic, phenomenal and comparative.[14] It is at least plausible that these three types of description go with three different functions: that for some description of the experience, some function is essential.

Whether all these functions are essential, or, more plausibly, under different descriptions different functions are essential, the crucial question becomes whether all of the functions can be described in a qualia-free way. To answer this question we may be able to appeal to the Spectrum Inversion Argument, or other arguments, but now the debate is not between qualia realism and functionalism, but between the former and physicalism. And so it should be.

The difficulty in using spectrum inversion to prove, against the physicalist, the existence of qualia is that the description of spectrum inversion is the description of a possibility of an inversion. We need to determine what kind of modality is involved. Two obvious candidates are logical

---

13 Dretske (1981), pp. 38–9.   14 See Maund (1986).

and epistemic possibility. The problem with epistemic possibility is that it does not seem strong enough to discount putative identities between properties. It is epistemically possible that water is not H_2O but has a different composition (the atomic theory, that is to say, is seriously flawed). Epistemically water might have turned out not to be H_2O, but it is still true that water is H_2O and, given that it is, that it is essentially H_2O. The problem with relying on logical possibility is that the resulting argument will either beg the question or will not convince those who require to be convinced. The physicalist opponent may refuse to admit the logical possibility, saying that the qualia-theorist's belief that it could obtain is based on his intuition that there are qualia. For someone with a counterintuition the possibility will not be obvious.

It would appear that the Spectrum Inversion Argument is really an expression of a point of view, one which, if defensible, is so for independent reasons. The strongest source of such reasons is what Gilbert Harman calls the Phenomenological Argument. As Harman rightly points out, it is this argument that lies at the heart of most (and probably all) arguments for qualia.

3. HARMAN AND THE INTRINSIC QUALITY OF EXPERIENCE

One of the most significant features of Harman's opposition to qualia-theorists is that, like Michael Tye, he grounds his argument on an appeal to the phenomenology of experience, thus meeting the defender of qualia on her own ground.

Although Harman's objection is framed in terms of functionalism, the point of his argument is to undermine any argument for qualia. This is far more radical than, for example, Shoemaker's position, which is that there exist qualia but that their existence is compatible with functionalism. Harman claims to show that the most popular arguments purporting to demonstrate that functionalism cannot account for the subjective feel of experience are fallacious, and for the same reason: they confound an intrinsic quality of the intentional object of an experience and an intrinsic quality of the experience itself.

The first of the arguments for qualia is that we are directly aware of intrinsic features of our experience, where this awareness cannot be accounted for on the functionalist view. The second is that a person blind from birth could know all about the functional role of visual experience without knowing what it is like to see something red. The third is that functionalism cannot account for the possibility of an inverted spectrum.

I shall argue that Harman's objection is itself flawed, and that it rests on a faulty interpretation of his opponent's position. I shall concentrate on his treatment of the first of those arguments for qualia, since the element crucial to it and Harman's resolution of the difficulty are equally vital to the other arguments. The first argument, set out in greater detail, runs as follows:

When you attend to a pain in your leg or to your experience of the redness of an apple, you are aware of an intrinsic quality of your experience, where an intrinsic quality is a quality something has in itself, apart from its relations to other things. This quality of experience cannot be captured in a functional definition, since such a definition is concerned entirely with relations, relations among mental states, and behavioural output.[15]

The argument fails, Harman holds, through confounding a quality of the intensional object of an experience with a quality of the experience itself. We cannot, he maintains, be aware of any intrinsic features of our experience. We can only be aware of the content of the experience, i.e. of the intensional objects of our experience and of their intrinsic features.

Not only does Harman not deny, he insists, that visual experiences have intensional (i.e. representational) content, that they also have intrinsic features, and that it is by virtue of having intrinsic features that they have the intensional content. His claim is that the perceiver is never aware of the intrinsic features, only of the content. Does Harman provide what can count as a proof for this claim? To begin with, he points out the fact of the intensionality of experience:

Our experience of the world has content – that is, it represents things as being in a certain way. In particular perceptual experience represents a perceiver as in a particular environment.[16]

The representational content of the experience is its intensional object. An important feature of the way things are presented in perception is that this is not always the way things actually are. Eloise, for example, can see a tree as green and brown when it is neither, or when there is no tree there. Eloise, we may suppose, is aware of the tree as a tree that she is now seeing,

15 Harman (1990), pp. 40–1.   16 Ibid., p. 34.

183

So we can suppose that she is aware of some feature of her current visual experience . . . she is aware that her experience has a certain content . . . she is not aware of those intrinsic features of her experience by virtue of which it has that content.[17]

Indeed, Harman does not believe that she has access at all to those intrinsic features of the mental representation that makes it a representation of seeing a tree. Things are said to be different with paintings. In such cases Eloise can be aware of those features of the painting that make it a painting, say, of a unicorn, as well as the content of the painting. In the case of visual experience, however, she is aware only of the intensional or relational features of her experience, not of the intrinsic, nonintensional features.

The crucial part of Harman's argument comes when he rejects the contention of the sense-datum theorist that perception of external objects in the environment is always indirect and mediated by a more direct awareness of a mental sense-datum. This claim, Harman insists, runs counter to ordinary visual experience! When Eloise sees a tree before her, the colours she experiences are all experienced as features of the tree and its surroundings. 'None of these are experienced as intrinsic features of her experience. Nor does she experience any features of anything as intrinsic features of her experience.' To confirm this, Harman asks us to perform a simple thought-experiment:

Look at a tree and try to turn your attention to intrinsic features of your visual experience. I predict you will find that the only features there to turn your attention to will be features of the presented tree, including relational features of the tree 'from here'.[18]

The alternative view, set forth by the sense-datum exponents, is not the result of phenomenological study but rather is the conclusion of an argument, e.g. the argument from illusion. But this argument, it is claimed, is either invalid or question-begging.

4. THE INTENSIONALIST ACCOUNT

To assess these claims by Harman, we need to be clear about what exactly the qualia-theorist is committed to. According to the account set out in this book, the sensory qualities, or qualia, that are components of the visual experiences are qualities which one takes naturally and nor-

17 Ibid., p. 38.
18 Ibid., p. 39.

mally to be qualities of physical objects such as trees. One is not, in the normal course of events, aware of them as sensory qualities, nor as features of one's experiences. Yet for all that, they are sensory qualities.

The account of sensory experience required is one that has been ably defended by Moreland Perkins.[19] For him, the visual experience is an act of sensory awareness which is an awareness of a sensuous quality, e.g. of sensory red. This sensuous (i.e. sensory) quality is a constituent of the act of sensing and has no existence independent of the act. Moreover visual experiences are not, typically, awareness of isolated qualities. More typically a sensory experience, e.g. the visual experience of a deeply foliated tree, consists of a complex arrangement of sensuous qualities, e.g. of an organised pattern of green and brown colour expanses in a three-dimensional visual field.

The important point is that when one is aware of intrinsic features of one's experience, then what one is aware of are the sensuous qualities, qualities which one typically and straightforwardly takes to be qualities of physical objects. Harman and Tye both give great weight to what they term (following G. E. Moore) the 'diaphanous' character of visual experience, viz. that one is only ever aware of the object of the experience, never the experience. If I try to describe the visual experiences I have when I look through my window, then the only features I can describe are features of the objects. All that I am aware of are the trees in the garden, the black birds in the foliage, the dog on the ground, the wooden window frame, etc.

But the 'diaphanous' character of the experience is not denied by the qualia-theorist. She holds that the sensuous qualities add up to the object component of the act of awareness. All that one is sensorily aware of are those sensuous qualities – colours, shapes, textures – which one naively takes to be qualities of objects. The qualia-defender agrees that in attempting to describe one's visual experiences, all that one has to describe are features which one straightforwardly takes to be features of objects. She argues that these features, which might well have been features of physical objects, are in fact not – witness the argument about virtual colours. What they are are sensuous qualities, qualities that are components of acts of sensory awareness.

A common objection to this treatment of sensory qualities rests on the belief that it is self-contradictory to apply an act-object analysis to visual experience and yet hold that the object is a sensuous quality that is

19 Perkins (1983).

185

internal to the experience, i.e. does not exist independent of the experience. This objection is sometimes directed at sense-data theories of experience by those who argue that if the sensory quality is internal to the experience, it cannot be handled by an act-object analysis. Hence, so it is argued, the experience should be analysed as an adverbial sensing. This objection is misfounded. One can have an activity or process which consists in *sustaining* a state of affairs, so that we can think of the process as having a product where the product is a constituent of the process.[20] Its intrinsic features can be described, even though the product depends for its existence on the process that sustains it. Examples are:

(a) The activity that consists of my casting a shadow has an object 'my shadow' which is internal to the process. The shadow has describable features such as colour, speed and shape that it shares with other objects.
(b) The process of the waves approaching and breaking on the beach has such objects as particular waves with height, speed and so on.
(c) The activity of projecting silhouettes on a screen produces objects: the silhouette has a discernible shape and colour, even though it is sustained by a process of which the observer may be entirely unaware and which ceases once that process is interrupted.

In all of these cases the object is internal to the process or activity, but it still makes sense to identify the object as a distinct component of the process or activity. In a like manner, the sensuous quality, e.g. the sensuous red, is both the 'object' of the act of awareness and is internal to the act.

Given the considerations above, it may be difficult to see how Harman's predictions about the phenomenology of experience differ from those of the qualia-realist. Presumably they agree that included among the features attended to are green and brown colours – shaped, coloured expanses. Even if it is true that what one is attending to is a physical surface and not a sensory item, it is still true that what one is attending to, i.e. the physical surface, is a coloured expanse. Criticism of sense-datum theorists that they subscribe to absurd claims that in perception one is aware of shaped patches, say, of blue, and not physical objects, are wide of the mark. Physical surfaces are, or can be, patches of blue: they are coloured expanses. They are more than that, but that is beside the point.

Harman characterises the difference between himself and the qualia-realist in this way: for his account the coloured expanse is an intensional

20 See also ibid., pp. 286–95, for a similar argument.

object; for the qualia-realist, it is not. The important element in this distinction is that, construed as an intensional object, the coloured expanse need not exist even if it is true that the perceiver is having visual experiences of coloured expanses (i.e. experiences of green leaves, brown branches, etc.). For the qualia-realist, on the other hand, the coloured expanse must exist if one is having visual experiences of coloured expanses.

The weakness in Harman's account is brought out by the argument set out in this book. He cannot just say that the coloured expanse is an intensional object without saying what the intensional object is. That is, he must characterise the content that makes up the intensional object. There is an important point to be made here, one that Frank Jackson drew attention to in a related context.[21] It is never a solution to a problem to say that some state or activity has an intensional object. It is at best the beginning of a solution. One needs to be able to go on and say how the activity in question has *that* intensional object. It won't do, therefore, for Harman to say that content is given by such descriptions as 'green leaves', 'brown branches' and so on and leave it at that. He needs to provide an account of what 'brown' is, what 'green' is. If the argument of this book is right, then try as he might he cannot do that without reference to virtual colour.

The important difference between the intensionalist account and that of the qualia-realist comes when one tries to specify the content. In this respect, the contrast between Harman's account and mine could not be sharper. I agree that visual experiences have intensional objects, i.e. they have representational content, but I supply an account of what that content is. I spell it out in terms of virtual colour. Having done that, I provide an explanation for how visual experiences have a content which includes virtual colours. Part of the explanation is that there are colour qualia. Harman's version gives no account.

A further problem for the intensionalist is that we have different kinds of experience with the same intensional content. The facing surface of a coffee spoon can be both seen and felt as concave. An explosion can be both heard and felt. Watching a sporting event on television, one can sometimes see and hear what the player's curse is. The intensionalist has a choice here; either the content is the same for each experience, i.e. it can be specified 'purely' conceptually without reference to sensory experience, or the contents, despite first appearances, are different. Nei-

21 Jackson (1977), pp. 111–12.

ther option should be very welcome. If he chooses the first option, then presumably the content can be specified in terms of causal powers. If so, then it would follow that one is aware of the power through the exercise of this power, that is, through the having of the experience. Hence the perceiver would be aware of the experience, e.g. whether one is feeling or hearing the explosion. In other words, the experience is no longer 'diaphanous' in the sense employed by Moore, Harman and Tye. For now the perceiver can be said to be in the position of being aware of the mode of experience which carries a certain content.

The other option for the intensionalist is to say that the content is different for each experience. But now the problem is being able to specify what this difference is without making reference to sensory qualities, that is, to aspects of the sensory experience. Unlike the case of Eloise and her tree, it is hard for me, when I am attending to an explosion, to dissociate the explosion from the effect it has on me. Of course there will be physiological differences occurring in me when I feel the explosion, as opposed to hearing it, but it must be remembered that Harman's account is that the difference in experiences is to be accounted for by difference of intensional content.

It would seem that the intensionalist has serious problems specifying the intensional content in a purely conceptual way, i.e. without reference to any sensory component. Even if it is possible in principle to have perceptual experiences with pure conceptual content, they are not the sort of experience that we humans have (at least, not usually).[22] Given that we can distinguish, as we can, the different modes of perceptual experience by virtue of which the same pure conceptual content can be carried, then some explanation of how we can do so is required. The qualia-realist employs qualia to explain this. As far as I can see, the intensionalist has no explanation.

It may be possible to mount an even stronger argument, one that shows that it is not possible for all of one's experiences to have pure conceptual content. Perkins, in his book *Sensing the World*, provides a Kantian transcendental argument: a 'deduction' of the necessity for direct awareness of purely sensuous qualities if one is to have experience of the presence of a physical world.[23] This argument is highly plausible; however, for our purposes all that is needed is the weaker argument: that, as things stand, our perceptual experiences do not merely carry content that

---

22 Perhaps kinaesthetic perception is an example of perception without sensory components, but then it is not clear either that there is experience involved here.
23 Perkins (1983), pp. 320–40.

188

is purely conceptual. This is sufficient to provide justification for qualia-realism.

Finally, problems with the intensionalist account are shown up by the difficulties Harman has in dealing with the experience of pain. It is curious in fact that he takes pain to illustrate the importance of keeping clear the distinction between what we experience as intrinsic features of the intensional object of experience and those intrinsic features of the experience itself. Take the experience of having a pain in your right leg. It is very tempting, he holds, to confuse the features of what you experience as happening in your leg with the intrinsic features of the experience. The happening in your leg, Harman claims, is the intensional object of your experience: it is not the experience itself.

But what exactly is the intensional object of the pain experience, i.e. the content of the experience? Harman states that the content is that there is a disturbance of a certain specific sort in your right leg, and that this ought not be confused with the experience, which, if it is anywhere specific, is in the brain. But what exactly is the disturbance of a certain specific sort? What kind of disturbance, and of what specific sort? The right answer, it seems to me, is that it is a painful disturbance, and the specific sort is that it is a dull ache, a sharp pain, a pulsating pain or a pain that is piercing, throbbing, shooting, searing, splitting, bleeding, stabbing, stinging or smarting. That is, the intensional content of an experience of pain is given by something like 'I feel a sharp shooting pain in my stomach.' The content contains reference to a pain, to the location of the pain and to some quality of the pain, i.e. at least in part it makes reference to its intrinsic features.

If the vital issue is one about the phenomenology of the pain, that is, about our ordinary experience of pain, then what we feel located in the knee or head or stomach etc. is not a disturbance, but a pain. If I feel pressure in the tips of my fingers when I press on a table, then just as surely when I press on a hot stove I feel pressure, warmth *and pain* in the tips of my fingers.

Of course, given my understanding of the workings of the body and the role of the brain, I have a right to be puzzled about the nature of the pain. I believe that unless my brain is activated in the right way I will not experience pain in my elbow or head or left knee, but why should that show that what I experience in those parts of the body is not pain? After all, I will not experience the colour or shape of a tree before me unless my brain is suitably stimulated, but Harman denies that that shows that it is not colour or shape that I experience.

189

It may well be that Harman's account of pain is intended not as a description of the intensional content of pain experiences but as a proposal that this reflects the proper way to think about pain. Possibly the ordinary intensional content of pain experience should be treated as confused. That, however, is not the way Harman describes what he is doing, and it would be irrelevant to his project, which is to appeal to the phenomenology of experience.

Given the range of difficulties the intensionalist account has, it would appear that Harman and Tye have much more to do to show that the arguments for qualia are based on confusions. In particular, it has not been shown that the Phenomenological Argument is flawed.

5. MISCONCEPTIONS ABOUT QUALIA

The Harman-Tye objection suffered from misconceptions about what the qualia-realist is committed to. Such misconceptions are common. Another example, this time in relation to the specific case of colour, is the article by Evan Thompson on novel colours.[24] The article is instructive not only for the interesting material on the possibility of extending our colour experience, but also for the misunderstandings displayed about qualia.

Thompson traces the difficulties raised by the suggestion by Frank Jackson about the possibility of there being novel hues – different, that is, from red, green, blue and yellow. Jackson had used that possibility as part of his Knowledge from Physical Information Argument for qualia.[25] Thompson convincingly shows that such a novel hue could not fit into our current colour space, for the geometry of that space is closed. What would be required – and this seems a coherent possibility – is that we imagine a more complex colour geometry which includes our current colour space as a part. In addition, we would in the hypothetical situation need to establish a resemblance route between the hue and at least one of the already existing unitary hues.

It is crucial to Thompson's account that our current colour space with its geometry should form a part of the more complex space. For he accepts Wittgenstein's proposition that it is the geometry of the space that indicates in the first place that the qualities with which we are concerned are *colours*.[26] A space of qualities that had a radically different

24 Evan Thompson (1992), 'Novel Colours', *Phil. Stud.*, 68, pp. 321–50.
25 Jackson (1990), p. 469.   26 E. Thompson (1992), p. 334.

geometry would not be a *colour* space. In other words, it is essential to properties' being colours that they stand in internal relations to each other.

Against Jackson, Thompson claims that his exploration of novel colours shows how Jackson's intuition that there are (qualia) properties is misinformed and misguided in its treatment of colour.[27] This claim was made after pointing out that at the heart of Jackson's argument was an appeal to the individual's first-person perspective, one put more explicitly by another friend of qualia, Terrence Horgan: 'I take the intrinsic non-relational nature of qualia to be a self-evident fact, a fact which impresses itself upon most of us who actually experience these states.'[28] Why does Thompson think that this intuition by Horgan and Jackson is 'misinformed and misguided'? Because he takes the intuition about qualia to be:

that the intrinsic qualitative features the colours have qua colours . . . are purely phenomenal, non-relational and simple properties, accessible from the first-person perspective,

where, crucially, this is taken to rule out the claim that colours, as a system of colours, stand in internal relations to each other. This view the author labels the 'empiricist view'.[29] One does not, however, need to be an empiricist to be a qualia-theorist. Certainly one does not need to be that form of empiricist. More strongly than that, it is a curious view that Thompson holds the qualia-realist to be committed to. The claim that colours are intrinsic qualities is not inconsistent with the statement that there are internal relations holding between the colours. Qualia are universals, and there is no reason why there should not be internal relations between them. Certainly it does not stop a certain tone of blue from being an intrinsic quality of some particular. That there are internal relations between properties does not make the properties relational.[30] It does mean that the qualities are not simple, but one does not need to hold that qualia are simple. Qualia are intrinsic qualities between which there are relations. It would indeed be surprising for any qualia-realist to

27 Ibid., p. 343.
28 Terrence Horgan (1984), 'Functionalism, Qualia, and the Inverted Spectra', *Phil. & Phenom. Res.*, 44, pp. 453–69; see p. 459.
29 E. Thompson (1992), p. 342.
30 It is worth pointing out that, as Kevin Mulligan ([1991], 'Colours, Corners and Complexity: Meinong and Wittgenstein on Some Internal Relations', in Wolfgang Spohn [ed.], *Existence and Explanation*, Dordrecht: Kluwer, p. 81) has observed, if Kripke is right about identity, then a numerical difference between things would be such a relation.

hold that the different (universal) qualia did not form a structured system – that they did not bear relations to each other, e.g. of similarity and difference.

Nor is it at all clear that empiricists are guilty of holding the simple-minded 'empiricist view'. One of the most influential figures in providing a descriptive phenomenology of colours was Meinong. In describing the colour solid and its geometry, Meinong argued that the colours stand in internal relations to each other. Given that, it is significant that, as Kevin Mulligan points out,

Meinong, unlike Wittgenstein, took his account of the internal relations amongst colours to provide a scientific foundation for the empirical theories of colour developed by empirical psychologists.[31]

And indeed it is hard to see why an empiricist could not be happy with Meinong's descriptive phenomenology (or with Wittgenstein's). Why should we treat all empiricists not only as the same, but as if they are the most extreme?

Thompson also and quite rightly ascribes to the qualia-realist the view that the colours have features that are purely phenomenal, but he takes this to imply that we perceive colours 'floating freely'. We never perceive colours this way, he claims; we always perceive colours as properties of things in some visual context. He goes on to say:

When empiricists claim that the fundamental element of the perceptual experience is a sensation of colour they are simply mistaken ... The fundamental element of the perceptual experience is the seeing of a coloured thing.[32]

But it is Thompson who is mistaken. First of all, one does not have to be an empiricist to believe in qualia. But secondly, and more important, it is possible to believe that sensory qualities are fundamental elements of perceptual experience without believing that we perceive colours 'floating freely'. The accounts of Perkins for perception in general and the position developed in this book for the special case of colour demonstrate this.[33] Finally, was there ever anyone who did believe that we perceive colours 'floating freely', or at least that colour perception was commonly like this? I doubt it. Berkeley and Mach certainly did not. Almost everyone believes that 'we perceive coloured things': the question over which they divide is the question of what this consists in.

---

31 Mulligan (1991), p. 78. See also p. 81, where Mulligan discusses Meinong's view that 'numerical difference between colours is an internal relation'.
32 E. Thompson (1992), pp. 343–4.   33 See Chapters 1 and 2.

6. AN ARGUMENT FOR QUALIA

It is true that the emphasis on the first-person perspective is crucial for the qualia-realist. This is not to say, however, that one is relying simply on an intuition, one that says that there are qualia. For clearly that may be opposed by a counterintuition, one that says that there are no qualia.

The qualia-theorist relies on qualia to give an account of perceptual experience from the first-person perspective, and to relate that perspective to the third-person point of view. It is usually the qualia opponents who rely on their intuition that they have no qualia. But they must do better than that. They must give some account of experience from the first-person point of view. At least Harman and Tye acknowledge this and attempt to provide such an account.

The Phenomenological Argument, which, as we have seen, is immune from the Harman-Tye attack, is one form of argument for qualia. A closely related one is the traditional argument from illusion (in its many variations). Standard criticisms presuppose, not unreasonably, that the argument from illusion is presented as a demonstrative proof, set out with certain premises leading to a conclusion that in ordinary perception we take to be veridical, that the perceiver is not immediately aware of a physical object or state of affairs. (Harman, in the paper discussed above, certainly makes this assumption when he criticises the argument.)

There are two crucial steps in the argument from illusion. One involves showing that, for some nonstandard case of perception, e.g. involving illusion, hallucination, time gaps or whatever, the thing of which one is immediately aware is either a non-physical item or alternatively is a quality which no physical object in the context has. The other crucial step is involved in extending the point from the nonstandard case to veridical ones. In the latter case too, what one is immediately aware of is either some nonphysical item or some quality which the physical object lacks. Cast as a demonstrative proof, the argument seems easy to refute. Even if the first step goes through, it is logically possible that veridical cases are different, even if phenomenologically they are the same. There is no contradiction involved in denying the second step. And as far as the first step is concerned, it seems to require a principle that is implausible, to say the least:

If X looks blue to A, then there must be something which is blue.

Such a principle is hard to sustain. Does anyone think that because something looks rusty, then there must be something there that is rusty, or because something looks metallic, that one must be aware of something that is metallic? Surely not.

It is a mistake, however, to construe the argument in such terms. In the hands of its most careful exponents, it is not intended as a demonstrative proof. Its strength depends on its phenomenological appeal.[34] Moreover there are three crucial steps, not two. The first involves the analysis of one's experience: in seeing a tree before me I am aware of certain features: brown, shaped expanses in a complex arrangement. (As we saw earlier, in Section 4, the use of 'expanse' does not rule out the possibility that the expanse is physical.) Given that analysis of veridical perception, a similar analysis is called for with the nonstandard case: I am likewise aware of brown, shaped expanses. In this case, however, the expanses are not physical. Therefore in the veridical cases too they are not physical. The phenomenological similarity is employed in each of the last two steps. We should also note that the argument may be construed as beginning with the claim that

I am aware of physical objects and aware of them as green and brown expanses.

With that beginning, one tries to make sense of the similarity of veridical and nonveridical experiences. Here it is a mistake to set out the reasoning from acceptable premises to warranted conclusion. The reasoning is more like beginning with an assumption, moving to a conclusion and then going back to revise the initial assumption so as to make the best sense of things. Although there is some parallel between this kind of reasoning and arguments that involve inferences to the best explanation, there are important differences. I claim that this kind of reasoning is quite widespread and deserves greater recognition. It takes place in science and is common (enough) in philosophy.

It should be noted that Harman, a critic of the argument, must himself depend on some such argument as this one. Why say, for example, that our experiences have intensional objects? Presumably because on occasion an object which is not blue appears blue; an object whose border is not fuzzy appears fuzzy. When I press on one eyeball, two images of the things on my table appear. These are not real objects. There is no fuzzy-bounded actual object, no actual duplication of cups, pens, punches and so on. In both veridical and nonveridical cases, one is aware of an intensional object.

34 For a similar point see Paul Snowdon (1992), 'How to Interpret "Direct Perception" ', in Tim Crane (ed.) (1992a), *The Contents of Experience*, Cambridge: CUP, pp. 48–78.

7. A NEW ARGUMENT FROM ILLUSION

Once we understand the point of the argument from illusion, we can see that it is far more formidable than is customarily believed. As traditionally conceived, the argument can be put into something like the following form:

(1) There are nonveridical situations in which something x appears to be, say, purple when it is not.
(2) There are veridical situations in which things that appear purple are purple.
(3) The purple that x appears to be is the same purple that those objects in veridical situations appear to be.
(4) Object x could not appear purple unless there is something which is actually purple.
(5) Object x is not purple.

Therefore

(6) The perceiver is aware of some sensory item that is purple under nonveridical conditions, as in (1).

Therefore

(7) The perceiver is aware of some sensory item that is purple even under veridical perceptual conditions, as in (2).

This argument is often derided. It is easy to point out that there is no problem in imagining (4) to be false. It is often true that something that is not metallic looks metallic. Do we have to suppose that therefore there has to be, in such cases, something that is metallic? Obviously not. The argument so framed is unsound. But we cannot stop there. We need an account of appearances, of what it is to appear F, of what it is to look red or look round or look metallic. We need to take into account the fact that we can and need to make a distinction between different kinds of 'looks': phenomenal, comparative and epistemic.[35] And we need to give an account of the relationship between them and of the differences between them. The point of a significant argument from illusion is not that it provides a demonstrative proof for the existence of qualia, but rather that it provides (something like) an argument to the best explanation, and in particular that it makes the most sense of such distinctions as these.

When something that is not metallic looks metallic, it is not necessary to believe that there is something else that is metallic and that explains why the object in question looks metallic. To be sure, that would be

35 See Maund (1986).

crazy. But it is the beginning of a good explanation of the situation that there does exist something that has a feature which is the same feature of which one is aware when metallic things look metallic. Of course there may be other explanations, and if all we are concerned with is the look of metallic things, there may not be much to choose between the explanations. The situation changes, however, when we turn to colour appearances.

As we have seen, there is good reason for thinking that the colours we perceive objects as having are not identical with any physical characteristics of the object: we can order different samples of colour-as-it-appears so that colours constitute an ordered three-dimensional colour system, a system with a distinctive structure and character. That structure and character, it turns out, is intensional, or, as I prefer to call it, virtual (it could be intensional without being virtual). There is no system of objective features possessed by the ordered samples that has this structure and character. In particular, there is no system of features associated with spectral reflectance curves that make up such an ordered system.

Once we recognise the virtual character of systematic colour arrays with respect to colour-as-it-appears, we can see how an updated argument from illusion can be successfully mounted. Crucial premises in the traditional arguments were statements about nonstandard cases, e.g. illusions, hallucinations, after-images. It was always possible, however, for critics of the argument to reject the move from what applies to the nonstandard case to the standard cases. Many of these critics would insist that the nonstandard case is described by contrast to the standard case, and hence cannot be used to undermine the standard cases of perception. Whatever weight such criticism had is removed, however, once we replace the usual premises about illusions or hallucinations or after-images with premises about the colours *all* physical things appear to have. Now, the premises are that the mountains, the sky, the oceans, the bananas and apples and oranges, the ceiling of the Sistine Chapel and so on all appear to have colours that they do not have – some are rich, vivid purples and reds and golds. They certainly appear to have these colours. They do not have them. These facts vastly strengthen the claim that in perception what we are aware of, directly, are sensory items and that it is these that possess the rich purples and reds and the pastel greens and blues and so on. (The sensory items are either sensory particulars or sensory qualities.) This claim makes the most sense of these facts.

True, it may need to be admitted that it is part of the concept of something's being a rich purple that the object have certain causal features and that the sensory items do not possess such causal features. But the right response to this is to admit that the sensory items do not have the rich purples and reds (in this sense): what they have is that vivid feature that we are understandably inclined to take as rich purple but is not. It is that vivid, rich feature that represents physical objects as being purple and gold or red and so on. This hypothesis is part of the story that makes the most sense of the perceptual and phenomenological facts.

The crucial point in this argument is that the emphasis is on making sense of perception in one's own case. From my own point of view, it appears to me that I see physical objects having one or more of a rich variety of colours: reds, purples, blues, yellows, golds, and so on. It certainly appears that apples, plums, wines, tapestries, sunsets, etc. have some of these rich colours. It turns out that they do not. The best explanation for why I should have experience of this kind, and that the physical world should be the way it is in lacking these qualities, is provided by the hypothesis that those physical objects induce in me sensory states which represent objects as having those colours. They do this because those sensory representations have the qualitative features that I take physical objects to have.

8. THE SIGNIFICANCE OF THE FIRST-PERSON POINT OF VIEW

It is in trying to give an account of one's own experience that colour qualia are important. It is important in this context to be clear about the methodological significance of this appeal to the first-person point of view. The appeal is not a priori, nor does it rely on incorrigibility. On the contrary, it appeals to experience, and to experience that can be mistakenly described. Secondly, in stating claims about what it is like for me to perceive things and to perceive colours, I am not making a statement that might be thought of as part of a folk theory of perception. What I am doing is appealing to the experience of someone who is an expert in perceiving, and each of us, however humble, is an expert in that. This expertise is by no means incorrigible, but neither does it count for nothing.

There is no question that I know what it is like for me to see objects, to see churches, to see rabbits and green meadows and so on. I experience seeing, and I can experience not seeing, e.g. by closing my eyes. I know from my own point of view what it is to see a church spire. I see a church spire related to other objects and at a certain distance from the

197

point of view from which I look. There is little doubt that in order to undergo this experience certain neurophysiological processes must take place. Nevertheless, whatever the experience is, it is distinct from a neurophysiological process.

It could be that a creature could be designed to so behave that it acts as if it had such experiences when in fact it has no such experiences. But it is surely impossible for me to say of myself that it is with me merely 'as if I had such experiences'. The point about qualia is that I am able to explain in my own case what is going on, and in particular can resolve certain problems. For example, (1) why is it that I am inclined to think that there are flowers, trees, etc., with colours which I see them as having, when in fact they do not have them? (2) Why am I inclined to think the same things have colours and shapes, and that I see objects as having both shape and colour?

The explanation is that as the result of the brain's being affected there form for me representations, ones of which I am aware. These representations have both representational properties and intrinsic non-representational properties.[36] The representational properties refer to states which are represented: typically objective states of affairs, e.g. the presence of shapes and colours. There are two ways that these states come to perform representational tasks:

(1) Linguistically: I get trained by initiation into the linguistic community to take these states as representing objective states of affairs and properties. This is a causal process whose efficacy does not rely on the members of the linguistic community having more than rudimentary knowledge of how the effect is achieved.

(2) Intuitively: these states come to match objective states which typically they are caused by, and which guide a perceiver in the way he or she negotiates a way in the world. That they match explains why a perceiver's negotiation is successful. It is not necessary that the perceiver be aware that there is a match. (See Maund [1993] for a defence of this.)

Thus it is that the representational states come to have their representational status. It also helps us understand why our colour concepts have the character that they do. In the account given earlier (Chapter 4) of the natural concept of colour, a crucial part was played by the first-person point of view: my knowledge of what it is like to see something, and in particular what it is like to see colours. In the account of the

36 This view is defended against standard objections by Barry Maund (1993), 'Representation, Pictures and Resemblance', in Edmond Wright (ed.), *New Representationalisms*, Aldershot: Avebury, pp. 45–69.

natural concept of colour I argued that implicit in it was a certain view of perception. The way to understand this is to say that language-users engage in a set of conceptual practices that constitute their concept of colour. Embedded in those practices is a certain view of perception. As part of that view, colour is taken to be the kind of property which ordinary perceivers recognise objects as having. As a member of this community of perceivers, I have the ability to recognise the colour of objects.

It is part of the concept of colour qualities such as yellow, blue, etc., that they can be recognised by myself as a typical competent perceiver. My ability to recognise an instance of redness is related to the fact that redness is the sort of property that is presented to me in perception. I know what it is like for something to be blue: I recognise objects as blue. It is this first-person knowledge which is implicit in the ordinary concept of colour and which can also be exploited in the argument from spectrum inversion. In particular, it enables us to do more with this thought-experiment than our earlier examinations promised. The possibility of spectrum inversion was meant to apply in the case where the neural processes have the same structure as the virtual colours and hence as one's visual states. Now, even if others point out to me that the neural processes have the same structure as my visual states, that need not disturb me. I distinguish the form from the content. There will be neural stuff and phenomenal stuff, each having the same form. This distinction should not be problematical. For those who wish to say that colours are represented by vectors in neural phase space, they should accept the possibility of such vectors being transformed into vectors in a different phase space. Indeed, Patricia Churchland insists that such transformations take place. Given such transformations, there can exist a range of different phase spaces which have the same formal structure. It is clear that they will be distinguished by having different content.

If we try to identify some physical characteristic that provides the objective basis for colour judgements, that is, that provides an objective basis for the objectivity of colour judgements, then there is a range of possible candidates:

(1) An electronic microstructure
(2) A quality of a reflectance curve: a disposition to affect/modify differentially incident light
(3) A disposition to induce a characteristic triplet of cone responses
(4) A disposition to induce a characteristic triplet of 'lightness'-efficiency values
(5) A disposition to induce a characteristic triplet of neural responses

An important restraint on one of the candidates being the right one is that it forms a system with fellow states (properties) such that the states collectively have the right kind of structure or form. That is, each objective state must occupy a distinctive place in the system which corresponds to that system of the colour solid reflected in the subjects' colour judgements, that is, to the system of virtual colours.

It is true of none of the first three objective characteristics that they comprise a system collectively with like properties that has the right kind of structure. Arguably it is true of none of them. Nevertheless it *could* have been the case that physical bodies did have the right kind of physical property that has the form of virtual colour. Indeed, it could have turned out to be true for all of the candidates above that they had the right form. Even if they did, we would want to distinguish between these five systems of interrelated properties, saying that though they share the same form, they are materially different.

It could also be that with respect to the neural processes underlying colour perceptions one can construct a vector space and populate it with colour correlates such that they constitute a system in thatzl vector space with the right kind of character. This too would provide us with a system that has the same form but different matter (stuff) from both virtual colour and phenomenal colour; call it 'neural colour'. It seems obvious to me that, in trying to understand our own colour experiences we would be justified in distinguishing neural colour from phenomenal colour, just as it seems unproblematical to distinguish between the different kinds of physical stuff.

The centrality of the first-person point of view is highly significant. Putnam, in his discussion of the possible identification of phenomenal states and neural states, wrote that prior to the 1960s (when Quine's influence began to be felt) philosophers 'knew' the identity theory to be false 'a priori': a sensation could not be a brain state. Putnam writes that once we have recognised, following Quine's guidance, that most of what we regard as a priori truth is of a contextual and relative character, 'we have given up the only good "argument" there was against mind-body identity'.[37]

It should be noted that my argument does not appeal to a priori truths. It appeals to experience. I know in my own case that there is a difference between neural processes and experiences. To deny that there is would

---

37 H. Putnam (1981), *Reason, Truth and History*, Cambridge: CUP, pp. 82–4.

require me to think that I was crazy. Possibly I am crazy, though methodologically I could hardly accept that I am, but no good argument is available to show me that my qualia do not exist. In the case of other people, it may be that they do not have qualia. Nevertheless I find that many claim to have them just as I do, and it would be only respectful of persons to believe that what they say is true, failing reason to think that what they say is false. And that, as we have just seen, is lacking.

9. PHYSICALIST OBJECTIONS

I said that I know in my own case that my experience of seeing a church spire in a meadow is distinct from my undergoing or having a neurophysiological process, even if features of the experience can be represented in features of the neural process (i.e. for the latter we can construct an n-dimensional phase space in which each experience feature is located). Even if the experience were the neurophysiological process, it is the process experienced in a certain way, one that only the subject has, and it is still true that the process has two types of distinct properties: (i) neurophysiological features and (ii) experiential features.

This kind of thought is often challenged on either of the following grounds: first, what we know as distinct are in fact (a) the object seen, e.g. the church spire, and (b) the neural process; but this is not inconsistent with saying that the neural process is identical with the experience. For it is not the church spire but the experience of seeing a church spire (or seeming to see one) which is supposed to be identical with the neural process. That the neural process associated with seeing a green triangle is neither green nor triangular is only to be expected.

Secondly, in the case of other identities such as light and electromagnetic radiation, lightning and electrical discharge, gas temperature and average kinetic energy, we need to distinguish intensional contexts from extensional contexts. In an extensional context what holds true of one side of the identity need not hold true of the other. The context 'x appears F' is an intensional context. Accordingly the fact that a neural process does not appear the same as a visual experience does not show that they are not the same.

The second objection is really a replay of Harman's objection and invites the same response. Labelling a context 'intensional' has the appearance of resolving a problem when often it simply postpones it. For reasons given earlier, the attempts by such philosophers as Harman and

Tye to spell out the intensional content without making reference, hidden or not, to sensory qualities does not work.

The problem with the first objection is that if the experience of, say, seeing a green triangle does not entail the existence of something green and something triangular (and I agree that it does not), what does it entail? Or, putting it another way, what characteristics does it have? There must be some features of the experience by virtue of which I identify it as 'seeing something green and triangular' rather than 'seeing something red and devil-shaped'. The physicalist, in order to overcome this problem, must eliminate all features of the experience apart from features of the neural processes. Presumably, as Harman suggests, the experience can have intensional content. Either the perceiver is aware only of the content and not the intrinsic features; or she is aware of the neural processes but not as neural processes: she is aware of them as features of physical objects.

The first option is Harman's, and it cannot be sustained. The second option is nonsense, if interpreted literally. There is a way of stopping the latter from being nonsense, but that way does not eliminate the phenomenal qualitative states. What might be said, to avoid the nonsense, is that one is aware of neural states as phenomenal states, and of the phenomenal states in turn as features of physical bodies. The best way to understand this possibility is as follows. The perceiver is not aware of individual neural processes. What he is aware of is the body of neural states as a visual field of sensory qualities. The sensory qualities are attributed to physical objects.[38] If this does not make sense, it does not greatly matter. What I insist upon is that if this is coherent, it does not eliminate the need for phenomenal states.

The practice of relying on one's own case in the description of visual experience is essential to the defence of qualia. There is a phenomenon which physicalists frequently draw upon in order to undermine that practice: blindsight. Patricia Churchland is one who has made considerable use of this phenomenon. She describes the work by Weiskrantz and others, in which a patient after surgery claimed not to be able to see anything, at least in a section of the visual field, but nevertheless displayed an ability to locate objects in that visual field and to distinguish between circles and squares. The patient was asked merely to guess his answers to questions about the objects available to be seen:

---

38 A sophisticated account of how this might be done is developed in Perkins (1983), ch. 8, 'The Structure of Sensory Consciousness'.

What is remarkable is that subjects who deny visual awareness can yet be consistently correct in pointing and in determining whether there is a circle or a square in their blind visual field.[39]

Churchland draws the conclusion that we cannot make together two assumptions which are commonly made:

(1) That if someone can observationally report on some current feature of the world, then he has experienced it;
(2) That someone experiences something if and only if he is aware that he has experienced it.

There should, however, be little difficulty in rejecting (1) as a universal truth, and therefore in the case of the blindsighted there is no reason to give up (2). And certainly the evidence provides no reason to give up (2) in the case of those who do not suffer from blindsight. Above all there is no reason to think that what holds true of those with blindsight might be true of everyone, let alone true of myself. As Nicholas Humphrey has pointed out we should be wary even of thinking that assumption (1) should be given up for the normally sighted. For the point about the blindsighted is that not only do they claim not to have visual experiences, they claim not to have perceptions. That is, they do not make observational reports about features in the world at all! They have the ability to locate objects or point to them *if asked,* but not to make observational reports about what they see. As Humphrey writes:

The subject seldom feels an urge to say 'cross' when he sees a cross; what happens on my reading of the evidence is that he feels an urge to grasp it in the appropriate way.[40]

Normal people who make observational reports about circles and squares are able to report not just on the presence of the shapes but also to report, say, that this square is larger than that circle; that the border of this square is black, the border of that circle blue; the border of that square has a gap, that of the circle is unbroken; and so on. Those who have blindsight seem to lack these abilities. In the light of this, it is absurd to think that what is true in the case of such impaired people gives us reason to think that these two assumptions that are commonly made about people who can see are wrong when made about those people.

The problems of relating first- and second-person points of view give rise to an additional objection to qualia, one which goes as follows. The best argument that I can have that other people have qualia is one that

39 Churchland (1986), p. 227.
40 Nicholas Humphrey (1992), *A History of the Mind*, London: Chatto and Windus, p. 70.

uses an inference to the best explanation. It takes as a premise facts about the other person's colour-matching behaviour, including his or her linguistic behaviour, and argues that the best explanation for this behaviour is provided by the assumption that there exist states with qualitative character. As our knowledge of the central nervous system builds up, however, we will in principle be able to construct a robot that can match human behaviour. Ex hypothesi, we will have the same reason to attribute states with qualitative character to the robots as we do to humans. Yet we would be wrong to do so. Since we are wrong in the case of the robots, then for all we know we may be wrong in the case of humans as well. Hence, contrary to what we first thought, we do not have a good argument to support the hypothesis that other people have qualia.

This objection should be rejected. The fact, if it is one, that machines can be built which will mimic human behaviour does not undermine the relevant argument applied to human beings. In the case of the argument about human beings there is a crucial difference. If I am convinced in my own case that I experience qualia, then I use that in applying to others the inference to the best explanation. I appeal to our biological similarities to argue that what is true of me, in this case, is unlikely to be true only of me. The similar behaviour of others, including their ability to construct and defend arguments similar to mine, provides good reason to think that in this case, the existence of states with qualitative character is true not only of me. The fact that robots can be constructed to mimic my behaviour is no reason to think that other humans are mimicking me.

What would I say were I to visit Mars and meet creatures unlike humans in material substance but with a similar intelligent and emotional life? Would I treat them as human-like, or merely as humanoids? One thing I might well do is suspend judgement until I know whether the creatures evolved biologically or were designed and constructed. They might well have a different biological structure from us, but if they are biological creatures that were not manufactured, and if their culture is one that supports similar disputes and worries about qualia as ours, then we would have reason to extend the qualia argument to them.

Finally, there is a more general physicalist objection to qualia, one resting on criticism of the notion of phenomenal content or 'stuff'. The objection is that the use of this notion is incompatible with science, or at least with physics. It should be noted that many physicists themselves have had little problem with this notion. Indeed, historically many of them have insisted on it. The objection usually comes from those who call on the findings of science. One response is to say that such appeals often draw upon nineteenth-century conceptions of science. As J. Eccles and H. Margenau have written, the possibility that quantum mechanics applies at the neural level allows for the handling of problems to do with conservation of energy.[41] As Broad pointed out, it is not at all clear that the content-stuff theory requires loss of energy. Even in the purely physical world certain changes, e.g. from one form of energy to another, take place without loss of energy.[42] Finally, even the alleged unintelligibility of Cartesian interactionism is dubious. As R. C. Richardson has pointed out, interaction between different kinds of physical force would be equally 'unintelligible' if the usual reasons given in the Cartesian case held up.[43] The second response is that, whatever the problem with the two contents, science had better take account of it. For it does occur.

10. CONCLUSION

There are extremely good reasons for holding that in giving an account of colour experiences we must make reference to phenomenal qualities with qualitative character. There are few good reasons for thinking that we can dispense with them or that we can eliminate them in favour of neural states.

The arguments in favour of qualia depend crucially on giving an account of perceptual experience from the first-person point of view. Belief in qualia is not simply an expression of an intuition. Foremost among those arguments is the Phenomenological Argument. Perhaps what marks it out as special is that the appeal to the first-person point of view lies at the heart of the other arguments as well, contibuting heavily to their force.

There is, however, a different sort of reason that can be advanced against qualia. There is a set of social-cultural reasons for thinking that qualia theories are suspect from an explanatory point of view, or that they make reference to private entities of an unacceptable kind. These reasons are in large measure Wittgensteinian. It is the aim of my last chapter to examine them and to show the objections to be unfounded.

41 J. Eccles (1987), 'Brain and Mind, Two or One?' in C. Blakemore and S. Greenfield (eds.), *Mindwaves*, Oxford: Blackwell, pp. 293–307 (see p. 301); H. Margenau (1984), *The Miracle of Existence*, Woodbridge: Ox Bow Press.
42 C. D. Broad (1925), *Mind and Its Place in Nature*, London: Kegan Paul, pp. 103–9.
43 R. C. Richardson (1982), 'The "Scandal" of Cartesian Interactionism', *Mind*, 91, pp. 20–37.

9

The psychological reality of colour

The psychology of colour, like the psychology of anything else – and perhaps even more so – is exposed to two dangers. On the one hand, studies of its biological nature threaten to reduce it to biology, and specifically to neurobiology; on the other hand, arguments that it is essentially social in nature draw it in the other direction. On this side the threat is one of absorption into a theory of social relationships and community.

For those like myself who want to provide an account of colour that is faithful to both the biological and social aspects, the double threat is just as great. My position is likewise set upon by the two opposing camps. For some purposes I have to defend the 'biologists' from the social-leaning theorists; for other purposes I join forces with the social theorists against the attacks of the biologists. The perils of people in this position hardly need elaboration, and no doubt we deserve little sympathy for our plight. For all that, we may still be right.

The discussion of colour has been based on the psychological assumption that there are four unique primary colours – yellow, green, red and blue – which serve as the foci in the construction of systems of colours which have characteristic fourfold structures. The sense in which these colours are primary is the psychological sense. It was also assumed that, independently of the theory of colour that I developed, we could find agreement about the psychological validity of such primary colours, and agreement on the psychological saliency of systems with the fourfold structures. Given these assumptions, it was argued that the explanation of the role colour plays in our psychological lives, which I take to include our social lives, requires making reference to phenomenal qualities.

The picture of colour thus presented is, however, subject to a set of criticisms based on what might be called Wittgensteinian reasons. The first draws on the social aspects of language, especially of colour language, to challenge certain assumptions implicit in the picture of colour. Al-

206

though this criticism is usually levelled at biologically based claims made by theorists with orientations different from mine, it is plausible to believe that these theorists and I share the assumptions which are vulnerable to the criticism.

The second major Wittgensteinian criticism can be taken to be directed against the implication that there are intrinsically subjective qualitative states whose character has a crucial explanatory role to play. According to this criticism, such an implication falls foul of Wittgenstein's private-language argument.

1. WHAT ARE PSYCHOLOGICAL PRIMARY COLOURS?

It is a widely shared assumption that we can identify a set of colours that are primary in the psychological sense and that they form the foci for systems of colour with fourfold structures. One who did perhaps the most to establish this sense was Hering. His influence was strong on Hurvich and on the development of many of the modern colour systems. The HBS system developed by Hurvich and Jamieson, the Munsell system and the Swedish Natural Colour System all presuppose these primaries and claim to capture psychologically salient features.

Not everyone, however, accepts the validity of these assumptions. Critics have raised such questions as whether it is really clear that there are these psychologically primary colours. What is it that makes a colour psychologically unique? In saying that some colours are primary, what is the intended contrast?

In answer to this last question, I take it that the contrast is meant to be between pure colours and colours that are mixed (in some sense). Being mixed in the psychological sense is different from the sense in which lights are mixed or pigments are being mixed. How, though, does one tell that a blue is primary and that another colour, e.g. orange, is not?

The first answer is that it is intuitively obvious which colours are unique. It is obvious when one reflects on one's experience of colours. It cannot be, however, that this intuition is revealed simply by gazing on colours. Orange, brown, olive, purple etc. by themselves are as authentic as red or blue or yellow. It is only because we have wide experience of colours that we can place purple and orange on the negative side of the nonprimary/primary divide.

A more promising answer is the following. Colours can be arranged and ordered in a systematic manner in such a way as to constitute a system in which the unique colours occupy a distinctive role. Purple and orange, in themselves, are as good (as pure) as any others. What makes them different from red, blue, green and yellow is the different kinds of places they occupy in the colour system. It is because of the systematic nature of the relationships that orange and purple stand out as different from yellow, red and blue. It then becomes possible to note that orange is a mixture (psychologically) of yellow and red, and purple of red and blue. It may be true that just as there is an orange halfway between red and yellow, there is also a red halfway between orange and purple, but there is a clear difference between:

(1) The orange is 50% red and 50% yellow

and

(2) The red is 50% orange and 50% purple

We need experience of a large range of colours before we can identify some colours as unique (pure) and others as mixed, but once we have such experience it is clear which is which. If we imagine a world with a restricted set of colours, say, blue, green, blue-greens and orange, but lacking yellows and reds, then in that world orange would reasonably be judged as primary.

The important difference between unique hues and binary hues is captured in a range of colour systems, e.g. the Munsell system, the Swedish Natural Colour System and the Hurvich-Jamieson HBS system. Each system constructs a colour solid which is marked by distinctive positions occupied by the unique hues. That colours can be ordered and arranged in this way is a fact about colours (even if they are virtual properties). It is a fact that needs to be explained. I take it that it is not simply a social construction. It is not because people decide to use colour language in the way they do that colours taken collectively have this structure. For one thing, it comes as something of a surprise to many to discover that there is such a structure and that it has the form that it does (and the structure serves no deep political function).

2. CULTURE AND BIOLOGY

Is the fourfold structure that is characteristic of such colour systems as we have described essential to all colour concepts and to all forms of colour experience? Some writers have thought that it is. One important argument is that there are universal colour categories that hold for all languages and that these colour categories are captured by systems such as the Munsell system. This position is often linked with an account that seeks a biological basis for the colour categories. Such an approach can be found in the book by C. L. Hardin. This argument is not without its critics. One is J. van Brakel who, appealing to Wittgensteinian reasons, throws doubt on some of Hardin's crucial assumptions.[1]

In a section of his book, Hardin discusses the question of whether it is possible to identify a natural, biologically induced set of hue categories.[2] He is persuaded by Berlin and Kay that there is a striking correspondence of colour categories across a variety of unrelated languages.[3] The evidence, they claimed, strongly showed the existence of eleven basic colour categories: (a) three achromatic colours: black, grey and white, and (b) eight chromatic ones: red, orange, yellow, brown, pink, green, blue and purple.

Berlin and Kay then provided evidence that, given these basic categories, colour foci could be determined. The foci are colour points that have special psychological significance. They are 'the best, most typical examples of colour category x'; they are the samples which the subject 'would under any conditions call x'. Whereas colour boundaries were unreliable, it was found that colour foci were reliable. Moreover, the foci for green, blue, yellow and red cluster around the corresponding unique hue loci in the Munsell colour system, they claimed, for normal observers.

It was not claimed that every language had all the basic colour categories. Indeed, some had only two or three. Nevertheless there is a striking pattern that holds for all such languages. First, all languages contain terms for white and black. Second, as the number of basic categories increases, a standard pattern emerges. In order, the following colour terms are introduced: red, yellow or green, green or yellow, blue, brown, and then either purple, pink, orange and grey or some combination. Hardin reasonably says that such regularities cry out for an explanation, suggesting that such an explanation is likely to be biologically based.

There are two crucial issues here. The first is whether Berlin and Kay are right about the cross-cultural evidence. Van Brakel has been strong

---

1 Hardin (1988); J. van Brakel (1993), 'The Plasticity of Categories: The Case of Colour', *Brit. J. Phil. Sci.*, 44, pp. 103–35.
2 Hardin (1988), pp. 155–65, 'Foci'.
3 B. Berlin and P. Kay (1969), *Basic Color Terms*, Berkeley and Los Angeles: Univ. of California Press.

in his criticism of the evidence.[4] He draws attention to competing evaluations of their studies, to criticisms of their methodology and to conflicting evidence.[5] The second issue concerns the relevance of the evidence; that is, it concerns the question of what hangs on whether or not Berlin and Kay are right.

These two issues need to be kept separate. The first is the anthropological issue about the structure of different languages in different cultures. If there are certain distinctive patterns that hold across different languages, then that could provide evidence for biological universals for colour perception. For determining the truth of this issue, it is obviously important to evaluate the Berlin-Kay evidence. Not that the task will be easy. Hardin's recent response to van Brakel acknowledges that there has been considerable research on the subject since the Berlin-Kay evidence was first provided.[6] He forthrightly rejects, however, those of van Brakel's assertions and implications that would lead one to think that the original research was almost worthless, and insists that the central claims of Berlin and Kay (which Hardin had relied upon in his book) are largely unaffected.[7] Quite apart from questions about the research, we need also to be open to the possibility that any linguistic universals are explicable because there are certain cultural, social or even logical universals, and not necessarily biological ones.

There is, however, a separate issue. This concerns whether and to what extent colour discriminations and judgements have their basis in biology or are rather artefacts of language and culture. This is independent of the first concern. For one thing, in order for colour discriminations to have a basis in biology it is not necessary that there be biological universals. For a second, even if there are relevant biological universals, they need not be reflected in linguistic universals.

As far as the first point is concerned, it could well be that in different language groups there are colour-discriminators having significantly different structures which could be explained by genetic differences. As Hurvich has pointed out there are among the subjects studied 'anoma-

4 See van Brakel (1993). This article refers to earlier papers by van Brakel, some in collaboration.
5 See also Jules Davidoff (1991), *Cognition Through Colour*, Cambridge: MIT Press, pp. 147–56, for a more sympathetic, though not uncritical evaluation of the evidence. See also Hardin's response (1993), 'Van Brakel and The Not-so-Naked Emperor', in *Brit. J. Phil. Sci.*, 44, pp. 137–50, which rejects much of van Brakel's criticism.
6 Hardin (1993).
7 Hardin goes further. He claims that neither van Brakel nor the people cited can provide evidence to back up some of van Brakel's claims about research that conflicts with Berlin and Kay.

lous' colour-perceivers who make systematically different, albeit minor, judgements about colour but who are no less proficient in making colour discriminations than normal perceivers.[8] It is possible to construct four-dimensional colour arrays for the anomalous perceivers, but their arrays are skewed relative to the normal. If, as seems plausible, the perceivers are anomalous because they have photopigments with minor systematically different colour response curves, and if that fact is based on genetic differences, then it is possible that there could be greater genetic differences resulting in colour arrays with significantly different structures. Even more important for the soundness of this point, the relevance of biological factors to psychological qualities does not depend upon the existence of biological universals. Law-like universals might occur at the physical/chemical level.

Even if there are biological universals, their role may be subtle and operate at a level lower than what shows up at the psychological and linguistic levels. Take the expectation of Hering and Hurvich that analysis of the psychology (phenomenology) of colour experience can reveal structures that show up at the level of the underlying physiological processes. For example, the existence of the fourfold structure of the psychological colour system and the special relationships between red and green and between blue and yellow suggest the existence of 'opponent' processes.[9] Those processes might occur anywhere between the central (or most central) neural mechanisms and the retinal ones.

If the opponent cells occur prior to the central mechanisms, then it is possible that only in certain circumstances and in certain conditions do perceivers who possess biological cells of the right opponent-cell type exercise the causal powers in the 'right way'. It could be, for example, that the brain's plasticity is such that certain environmental conditions are required in order that the appropriate system of neural states develop and hence that the appropriate psychological experiences be had. Under other conditions, the neural states would constitute a different system, and so would the resulting system of colour experiences. The point is that even if a system of colour classification possessing the fourfold structure, such as the Swedish Natural System, did not hold for certain language groups, then that would not show that, for those groups for which the system holds, that the system does not have a biological basis. It could still be true that for all language groups biology is important – even if the biology is different – at *the appropriate level*.

8 Hurvich (1981), ch. 16.   See Davidoff (1991), chs. 2 and 4.

There could be other evidence that we could appeal to in order to discover how important the biological processes are. For example, it would be relevant, with respect to the Swedish system, to discover how quickly and easily people from other language groups could be trained to use it. It would be important whether they could be fluent in it while absorbing the minimum of a foreign culture.

The further implication of this discussion is that though the Berlin-Kay evidence is interesting, it is hardly crucial. Certainly if it is accurate then it provides some indication of the saliency of biological factors, and at least for that reason it is important that we get it right. If it is false, then very little of significance follows. The biology may still be of great importance in understanding the structure of colour systems.

3. WITTGENSTEIN AND COLOUR CLASSIFICATION

The question of the role of language and culture in theories of colour is brought out in two quotations with which Hardin began his discussion. One is from a social anthropologist, H. A. Gleason, the other from a 'Wittgensteinian' philosopher, Rush Rhees. It is worth repeating them. Gleason:

There is a continuous gradation of colour from one end of the spectrum to the other. Yet an American describing it will list the hues as red, orange, yellow, green, blue, purple, or something of the kind. There is nothing inherent either in the spectrum or the human perception of it which would compel its division in this way.[10]

Rhees:

I cannot learn the colour unless I can see it; but I cannot learn it without language either. I know it because I know the language . . . I can remember the sensation I had, just as I can remember the colour I saw. I feel the same sensation, and that is the same colour, but identity – the sameness – comes from the language.[11]

On the face of it these passages express similar claims: that colour classifications are not natural, either physically or biologically, but are relative to language. It would also seem that each is set against the claims implicit in the Berlin-Kay evidence. But things may be more complex. For one thing, the reasons presupposed by these authors are very different. The quote from Rhees is taken from an article on private language,

10 Hardin (1988), p. 155, quoting Berlin and Kay (1969), p. 159.
11 Ibid., p. 155, quoting R. Rhees (1954) 'Can There Be a Private Language?', *Proc. Arist. Soc.*, Supp. 28, pp. 77–94, p. 81.

which deals with Wittgenstein's views on language, i.e. on ostensive definition, language learning and the possibility of private languages. The kind of reason appealed to by Gleason, on the other hand, could not be countenanced by Wittgenstein. Gleason's position requires that there be a colour continuum and that it have a certain character which is not captured in the American language or in the many other languages which divide the continuum in different ways. This position asserts what the Wittgensteinian one denies: that there are objective similarities and differences that are independent of language and that we can be aware of quite independent of our community-based language. Gleason, it would seem, claims to know what the colour spectrum is really like, the spectrum which Americans and others set about to classify in their distinctive ways.

Quite clearly Wittgenstein could not be happy with what Gleason says. Apart from that, though, is his position in conflict with the Berlin-Kay evidence? There is of course an enormous literature about what Wittgenstein meant or did not mean to say, and whether he asserted any thesis or even presented any arguments at all. Whatever he intended, he surely did not intend to deny any biological thesis, that is, to deny a thesis for which there might be very sound biological evidence. It is more likely that what he intended to do, in the discussion of private language and ostensive definition, was to deny a philosophical or metaphysical thesis. Of course, whatever his intentions, it may well be that the denial of one thesis does not leave the other thesis untouched. That in fact Wittgenstein cannot keep these spheres apart has been persuasively argued by Ralph Walker in an illuminating analysis and criticism of the Wittgensteinian point of view.[12] Walker takes Wittgenstein's views on language, as expressed in the *Investigations,* to be an argument against the metaphysical thesis that

there are objective similarities and differences which exist independently of our practices of rule-following, classification and which we can become aware of and which can help us in language-learning, in the acquiring of concepts.[13]

Walker then argues that Wittgenstein's argument does have commitments that, in principle at least, have biological relevance.

Walker's account is highly valuable in a discussion of the relative biological and linguistic constraints for concepts of colour. It is true that Walker follows Kripke in his interpretation of Wittgenstein's views, and

---

12 Ralph Walker (1989), *The Coherence Theory of Truth,* London: Routledge, pp. 124–45.
13 This thesis is my paraphrase, based on Walker (1989), pp. 17–8, 130–40.

that there are other possible interpretations.[14] For my purposes that is irrelevant. All that matters is that this is a serious interpretation such that if the position can be sustained it will have drastic implications for the study of culture and biology, especially with respect to colour. (Later I discuss another interpretation.)

According to the Walker-Kripke interpretation of Wittgenstein, every application of a predicate, e.g. 'green', beyond the original instances by means of which it was introduced, involves a judgement of similarity, and all our judgements of similarity are determined in the same way by how we group things together, rather than being forced on us by the nature of the things themselves.[15]

If there were objective similarities marked out among things prior to our classification of them ... there seems to be no way in which we could be aware of them. To recognise them as such would again, and inevitably, be to classify, and to classify is again to synthesise: to apply one of *our* rules rather than simply to reflect back the nature of what is recognised.[16]

The argument seems to be that recognition of similarities involves bringing things under rules of classification, and for us to do that there must be standards for correct rule-following available to us. Where are these standards to come from? As Walker states, it would seem that they cannot come from objective similarities; nor can I provide them for myself, or so Wittgenstein argues. The only possible solution seems to be that they are provided by the practice of the community.

Even in the application of the simplest descriptive terms, there is nothing that following a rule can consist in, other than conformity to a general social practice. And the similarities between things that we notice, and mark with such predicates as 'green' are themselves the product of such a practice and are not prior to it.[17]

The important thing, on this account, is that there is nothing for a similarity to consist in apart from the community's readiness to regard the items as similar. There is nothing other than this, for if there were, it could only be some kind of objective similarity amongst the items themselves, and we could never be aware of such things or guide our classifications by them.

Wittgenstein does not have to be taken as denying that there are objective similarities and differences. What he is denying is that we know

14 See S. Kripke (1982), *Wittgenstein on Rules and Private Language*, Oxford: Oxford U.P.
15 The discussion in the next few pages draws heavily on Walker's analysis, especially that in pp. 124–45.
16 Walker (1989), p. 130.   17 Ibid., p. 135.

them independently of our community-based conceptual practices. They exist, but we become aware of them only through our practices. There is an ambiguity here that needs to be resolved. It is reflected in these two different conceptions:

(1) The objective similarities exist independent of conceptual practices, and we can become aware of them, but only through a set of conceptual practices. There is no nonconceptual awareness of them.
(2) There are no objective similarities and differences independent of conceptual practices: there are objective similarities, but only in the sense that they are constituted by conceptual practices.

The crucial question is not whether there are objective similarities and differences, but rather whether they are constituted by conceptual practices or alternatively exist independent of conceptual practices. I take it that Wittgenstein's position is expressed by conception (2).

Given this, however, can Wittgenstein be any happier with Rhees than with Gleason? Rhees says that I cannot learn the colour unless I see it; 'but I cannot learn it without language either . . . identity, the sameness of colour, comes from the language.' Rhees is making the crucial point that language is necessary. However he also says that seeing is important too. What is meant by 'seeing it' (the colour) here? It looks as if it is something in addition to language.

This brings out a difficulty with Wittgenstein's position. Individual people do learn concepts and language, and different individual people in different cultures learn at least some concepts which are different from each other. So he and we are required to allow for some theory of concept-learning. Moreover it is clear that he has one.

He writes that whether or not a judgement conforms to a rule depends on community agreement. A person who uses a language, e.g. applies a concept such as 'green', learns a technique, has mastery of a practice. That is, in applying 'green' the person is conforming to a rule. In the case of some language rules the person obeys a rule but typically obeys it blindly.[18] The person need not apply the rule consciously. What counts is that she is doing something that is right or wrong, and what counts as its being right or wrong is its conformity to judgements of the community. But what is it that explains agreement between members of a community, and what explains how a person acquires a concept?

In attempting to understand how Wittgenstein can respond to such a question, we can see how problems arise. Walker, for example, asks what

18 Wittgenstein (1967), para. 219.

it is that explains the agreement that does in fact so generally obtain? Why is it that we all do judge similarly, and go on judging similarly? All Wittgenstein will say is that it is a matter of how we have been trained.[19]

> If a person has not yet got the concepts, I shall teach him how to use the words by means of examples and by practice.[20]

This, however, makes the agreement completely mysterious. As Walker asks, how does it come about that he extrapolates in the way that others do?

> There would be no serious problem here if we could appeal to objective similarities that exist quite independently of anyone's judgement. For then we could say that he reacts to the new instances in the same way because they are objectively similar to the old instances, the instances by which he was introduced to the word.[21]

And this might be either because he recognised the similarity or because, although he performed no mental act of recognition, the similarity was causally responsible for this natural reaction of his, and my physiological nature makes me react the same way on different occasions, and the same way as others. Wittgenstein has ruled out the first possibility. It may seem that he allows the second, but

> if it is to do the work we require of it, the explanation must draw upon the existence of objective similarities amongst the red things, and objective similarities of a physiological kind between human beings.[22]

There is thus a tension in Wittgenstein's ideas. On the one hand, the community is necessary to rule out a possibility that might otherwise exist, the possibility that one could not learn a concept, because without the community any way one would go on to use a word would count as 'getting it right', which means that nothing would count as getting it right. But then that the new member of the community comes to share the practices of that community is explained by that person's 'being trained', and the practice of a new member's being trained by others is explained in terms of their having 'shared reactions'. Now, this account opens the way for the relevance of a biological explanation. It is a mistake to present Wittgenstein's views as supporting the conclusion that colour classifications are independent of biological factors.

19 Walker (1989), p. 140.
20 Wittgenstein (1967), para. 208.
21 Walker (1989), p. 141.
22 Ibid.

4. PHENOMENAL QUALITIES AND CULTURAL DIVERSITY

I have considered the interpretation of Wittgenstein's views that present him as supporting an anti-realist, constructionist view of colour. It was important to show the tensions that underlie this interpretation, because this interpretation of Wittgenstein's views easily lends itself to an attack in any theory of colours committed to phenomenal qualities (qualia realism). In this section I propose to extend the defence of qualia realism against this Wittgensteinian position.

In considering this and other interpretations of Wittgenstein's views, it is necessary to note that theories of phenomenal qualities and states can be offered for fundamentally different purposes. This is important because the kind of view on colour that I have advanced does not have the kinds of epistemological assumptions characteristic of the philosophical positions that Wittgenstein was trying to undermine, and hence can escape any of his sound language-based criticisms.

There are two very different purposes or roles that phenomenal states or qualities can play:

(1) As providing a foundational basis for 'construction' either of the world or of our knowledge of the world;
(2) As providing the ontological basis which forms part of the explanation of how we perceive the world, or of how we experience and talk of the world.

Examples of philosophers whose interests were of the first kind are Russell, Carnap and (arguably) Descartes.[23] Examples of those in the second camp are Broad and (arguably) Descartes. What is distinctive in the first set of positions are their epistemological assumptions, which very plausibly run counter to the view defended by Wittgenstein. But for a metaphysical realist who sets up quite a different view, who does not seek either certainties or foundations, at least in the ways canvassed by those thinkers, then things will be very different. For the second set of purposes, phenomenal states are 'not the only fruit'. They have a role to play in the full explanatory account, but that role needs to be supplemented.

I hold that qualia exist, that they are real, but I also hold that becoming aware of them as instances of qualia is a sophisticated technique. My view is that the structure of the colour solid (a structure that holds

---

23 Given Carnap's explicitly held views on metaphysics, it may seem strange that I put him on the side of the metaphysical realists. This is not as absurd as it may at first look. Carnap's metaphysics is hidden in the assumptions of his enterprise.

between colour universals) is explained in terms of a structure that holds between (phenomenal) colour qualia. In holding this, I do not claim that these phenomenal features are all noticed by us, or at least that they are noticed as such. What I require is that a token of a colour quale is taken to be an instance of an objective property, one that is open to public access. We are not normally aware of the range of relationships that hold between the qualia. We are, of course, aware of certain similarities and differences.

That there are colour-qualia universals and that there are tokens that instantiate them form part of the explanation for why we take physical objects to have colours standing in the appropriate relationships. This way of looking at things does presuppose that although there are no physical things among which there are the objective similarities and differences in question, nevertheless there are other tokens (of qualia) among which there are objective similarities and differences. To say this is not to say that everyone is aware of them. Moreover in some cultures and for some languages, no person may be aware of the similarities and differences. This does not count against the claim that the similarities are there and could be ascertained. There may be other Wittgensteinian reasons against this, but I shall leave consideration of them until later.

For the moment I concede that there may be cultures and languages for which those objects we count as 'reds' and 'yellows' are divided in a different way from ours. They have no word(s) that pick out all and only reds. Some words pick out reds and yellows. Others pick out one range of reds but not all. Where we may want to talk of red berries, red tomatoes and red blood, they might want to distinguish them. They do not classify them as similar.

This raises an important question. Do they see colours but divide colours differently from us, or do they pick out different qualities, i.e. noncolours? Perhaps they are colour-blind. Alternatively they are simply not interested in colours, but could develop the taste. It may be that in these cultures classifying objects in the way they do involves a complex of properties of which colour is only a minor part. In particular there may well be cultures in which the dimensions of hue and saturation (or equivalents) are not psychologically salient. These people classify together objects which to us are of mixed hues: (a) reds, yellows and some blue-greens; (b) blues, some greens and some reds. Or they divide the blues into different kinds, putting in each kind objects which to us are of the same hue and saturation. Perhaps the more salient classifications have to

218

do with, say, capability of being carried on a horse, capability of being carried on one's back, capability of being put in a purse and so on.

The important question is whether such people born in such a culture can be trained so as to acquire our colour language. I agree that simply taking into such a culture a vast collection of Munsell chips and asking for them to be sorted may be inconclusive (although it might tell us something very important). Without context, such a practice might strike the people as simply bizarre. I agree that colour concepts arise to fit relevant interests, and that therefore different cultures are quite likely to develop different concepts of colour. That fact, though, does not show that there are not for all members of the same species colour universals which are potentially available for all members (apart from the colour-deficient).

If Berlin and Kay are right, then it is clear that the Munsell system has a biological basis. This is compatible with a nonreductionist view of phenomenal colours. For we could follow Hering in claiming that phenomenal qualities provide a key to (certain processes in) the biological level. However, if Berlin and Kay are wrong about the evidence, that does not show that the Munsell Colour System and in particular the psychological primary qualities do not have a biological basis.

Biological relevance would depend on the capacity for human beings from different cultures and different languages to learn the colour systems with facility. Moreover the fact that the colour concepts that have naturally and culturally evolved within similar cultures are capable of being formed into a structured pattern of relationships which was not planned or designed calls out for explanation, and there being a biological basis is plausible as providing part of the explanation. That is, the fact that at least in certain cultures complex colour systems, such as the Munsell system and the Swedish Natural Colour System, can be constructed is something which requires explanation. The systems are cultural artefacts, but that they have the character they do cannot be a cultural artefact.

It is true that in social-cultural contexts there can arise patterns and relationships as unintended and unforeseen consequences of social actions and that these can sometimes be explained as serving some cultural function or reflecting certain cultural interests. It is difficult to see, however, how, say, the character and complexity of the Munsell or Swedish systems reflect any cultural interests. It is true that there have been, in the twentieth century, strong commercial developments related to colour, e.g. in the chemical industry, in dye-making and in colour-photography, but the elements of the colour systems were developed long before, e.g. explicitly in the work of Hering, and at least implicitly in the work of Helmholtz, Maxwell, Goethe and others. In any case the development of commercial and artistic interests in colour can be used just as easily to explain why people came to *notice* pre-existing similarities and differences, as it can be used to explain why they (allegedly) produced such similarities and differences.

That there are biological beings in other cultures with different colour languages allows for the possibility that psychologically primary colours are available for these beings but are not used by them. For it is understandable that cultural interests will make it important to make colour groupings one way rather than another. The fact that the beings do not use the colour categories does not show that the colour categories are not available.

The fact that in the case of shape concepts there are certain illusions that are more common in some cultures than in others and that colour constancy should hold to different degrees in different cultures does not show that biology is not relevant, only that it does not hold all the answers.

5. VIRTUAL QUALITIES AND THE PRIVATE LANGUAGE ARGUMENT

The views on language attributed in Section 3 to Wittgenstein make certain crucial assumptions about the role of language in constructing objective similarities and differences. According to one interpretation, these assumptions lie at the heart of Wittgenstein's Private Language Argument.

There are, however, other interpretations of the Private Language Argument which might allow the argument to undermine any view, such as mine, in which phenomenal states play a vital role. Such interpretations place greater weight on more explicit Wittgensteinian assumptions about the nature of language. The first is that a person can only be said to understand a term if the person can apply it correctly, that is the person can use the term in such a way that what he or she does can be said to be done correctly (or not). In other words, the person must have the ability 'to go on in the right way' in the use of the term. The second assumption is that nothing counts as going on in the right way unless there is the possibility of others' judging that it is the right way.

Clearly, given these assumptions there will be a problem for the account of virtual colour which allows a place for phenomenal qualities and states. For on the face of it, these states and qualities seem private to the person having the phenomenal experiences in question. That person seems to be conscious of them in a way that in principle no one else can be.

There are in fact two important types of objection to the notion of a private language. The first is the Wittgensteinian one about the possibility of a private language. The second is the objection that, whether or not Wittgenstein is right about that, there is nothing in our language that corresponds to the use of a private language. Hence whether or not there could be a private language, the language which describes our perceptual experiences is not private. Language-users learn to describe their perceptual experience by being taught by other language-users. Moreover, the standard way of referring to what one is aware of in perception is by means of predicates and expressions that refer to physical objects or express physical properties.

However, neither of these objections has any force, given my account of colour predicates and virtual qualities. The second objection is the easier to handle. I argue that normal colour predicates express virtual properties, that is properties that are 'objective' and for which the rules are intersubjective. Of course in explanation of certain crucial facts about these colour properties I appeal to phenomenal qualities, but this is irrelevant to the fact which I insist on, that normal colour predicates belong to a public language.

It was the second, weaker objection that I implicitly dealt with earlier, in the section 'Identifying Virtual Colours' in Chapter 2. There I argued that if physical objects only appeared to have colours but never really had them, we would be in exactly the same position in learning colour concepts as we would be if the objects really did have the colours. That is, even if the realists about colour are right, we know about colours because each colour appears in a certain way, and that would be the way we normally identify the colour.

Even the stronger Wittgensteinian argument does not provide insurmountable difficulties. It is true that the virtual redness that I perceive the apple as having is not a property that others perceive it as having. They too, let me hasten to add, will see an apple as having a virtual redness, but in its subjective aspect their virtual redness is different from mine. However, these virtual qualities are not qualities that it is logically impossible for someone else to perceive. The virtual redness is a property that I perceive objects as having: it unfortunately turns out that the objects do not have the property, and hence it cannot be seen by others – but the objects might have had it, in which case others would have seen it. It is true that in order for that to happen the world that we know would have to be very different, with different physical laws and some different causal mechanisms. But this is all right: the Private Language Argument, as I understand it, concerns the meaning of terms that it is logically impossible for others to understand. Hence, to settle doubts raised by that argument, it is legitimate to appeal to logically possible circumstances, however remote. That they are not too remote is shown by the considerable number of direct-realist philosophers who have assumed or defended the kind of possibility that I have suggested.

This answer, perhaps, simply removes the objection to a different level. I have modelled my account of virtual colours on Hering's view of 'visual colours' as being both subjective and spatial. I have tried to provide an interpretation of virtual colours which allows them to be objective but nonexistent. I have argued that the existence of phenomenal qualities explains why virtual colours have the character they do, and that they can do this without the virtual-colour concept's ceasing to be 'objective'. Nevertheless I may well be wrong about this. Perhaps the virtual-colour concept is both subjective and objective, that is it is inconsistent. (Part of the problem here is the difficulty with being clear about what exactly a concept is and how we specify what a particular concept is.) We need not be embarrassed if this should turn out to be the case. In the first chapter I argued that this inconsistency is no objection to there being such concepts or to their serving valuable purposes.

However, the considerations appealed to by the Private Language Argument may resurface at a different level. For even if virtual colours are not essentially subjective, nevertheless what I present as the adequate theory of colour makes reference to phenomenal colours, and these colours are essentially subjective. In explaining why virtual colours have the character they do, I appeal to phenomenal qualities, i.e. phenomenal colours. I have claimed that there are such qualities, ones which in fact are phenomenal but are not thought of as phenomenal. They are taken, normally, to be objective, physical properties of physical objects. They are thought of as intrinsic, nonrelational qualities of physical bodies, typically of their surfaces. (The exception to this will be after-images, but these are special cases.)

Now, if phenomenal colours are essentially subjective, then it will not be logically possible for someone else to be aware of the same phenomenal colour as I am. For if the colour is essentially subjective, then there is no possible world in which that colour exists and someone else perceives it in the way I do. In every possible world that contained that colour, it would be perceivable by me and no one else.

There seem to me to be two important ways in which the Private Language Argument might be dealt with. One is to reject the argument itself, either as lacking in cogency or, more plausibly, as not establishing what it is often taken as establishing. The second approach is to accept the argument but try to show that the argument does not undermine the view of virtual colours and phenomenal colours advanced here.

Let us begin with the second approach, which is the simpler, leaving the former to the next section. Let us grant that if virtual colour is essentially subjective, then it is not logically possible that someone else should perceive the virtual redness that I perceive an apple as having. Nevertheless it is epistemically possible. It could have turned out that virtual colour was not essentially subjective – this is an epistemic 'could' – only it did not. Just as Kripke's desk epistemically could have been made out of ice, or, as Putnam concedes, water might have been a basic element or HO, so virtual colour could, epistemically, have turned out not to be subjective. Now, as far as meeting the Private Language Argument goes, this epistemic possibility is all that is needed.

With respect to the use of terms such as 'gold', 'water', 'this desk' and so on, it is clear that their use is covered by a set of public conventions and rules, and, if Putnam and Kripke are right, it is part of that system of rules that terms such as 'water', 'gold', 'this desk', and so on refer to a certain substance or a certain individual.

The force of the Private Language Argument is that such reference will be secured only if the conventions and rules are public. It is the existence of public rules and conventions governing 'water' that allows us to say that epistemically water could have been HO; so likewise there are public rules and conventions governing 'colour' that allow for the epistemic possibility that virtual colours could have been something different, that is, could have been objective like shape and size. Recognition of this allows us to see that Hering's position is consistent with the results of any cogent interpretation of the Private Language Argument.

Just as terms such as 'water' and 'gold' get introduced into the language and their use is sustained, by means of public rules and conventions, so too do terms such as 'white', 'black', 'yellow' and so on. It is this fact that ensures that there is no flouting of the Private Language

Argument. And just as such facts do not prevent 'water' from referring to H_2O, even though most language-users are not aware of it, neither does it prevent colour terms from referring to subjective qualities, even though the language-users are not aware that they are subjective.

6. PHENOMENAL QUALITIES AND PRIVATE LANGUAGE

The Private Language Argument, it would seem, does not touch the theory of virtual colours, with its inbuilt reference to phenomenal colours. Of course this sounds too easy. It will be argued that the discussion presupposes the wrong interpretation of the Private Language Argument. At least a little more needs to be said.

Exactly what the right interpretation of the Private Language Argument is – and indeed what is the proper conclusion to it is – have been, of course, a matter of great controversy.[24] There are at least two important conclusions that we need to distinguish. The first, which I shall call the weak thesis, entails that there can be no private language which is not, in some suitably strong sense, derivative from or secondary to some public, intersubjective language. The weak thesis is widely accepted. The second, the strong thesis, states that in no circumstances can there be a private language. It is the strong thesis that is far more controversial and, in my view, definitely unproven. An example of the strong thesis is the version discussed by Simon Blackburn in *Spreading the Word*:

The anti-private language considerations aim at this conclusion: no language can contain a term whose meaning (or sense) is constituted by a connection the term has with a private item, which lies, or lay, solely in the mind of the individual who understands the term.

Blackburn labels the doctrine that rules out such a term 'semantic externalism.'[25]

The weak thesis makes the least trouble for the theory of virtual colours. That thesis, which denies that there could occur a private language that was not parasitic on a public language, is compatible with the view that a public language can contain predicates that express phenomenal states or qualities. The theory of virtual colours illustrates this compatibility.

24 Wittgenstein (1967), paras. 199–316.
25 S. Blackburn (1984), *Spreading the Word*, Oxford: Clarendon, pp. 92–3.

Colour terms are learned as terms that apply to virtual qualities. Phenomenal qualities are referred to in the explanation of how this is achieved. It would seem to follow that whereas a colour term such as 'blue' acquires its meaning through the public nature of virtual qualities, it is possible to devise terms to apply to the phenomenal qualities. For 'blue' we can devise 'blue$_{ph}$' to apply to the phenomenal quality. Such a predicate borrows its meaning from the public nature of virtual qualities. It is because people take phenomenal qualities to be objective qualities that they get trained in the application of colour predicates. Having been trained in this way, it is no great problem to go on to make phenomenal application to the colour predicates.

Moreover terms such as 'blue$_{ph}$', 'yellow$_{ph}$' and so on are indexical or relativised to perceivers. We are familiar with the use of terms such as 'environment', 'horizon', 'contemporary', 'here', 'self' and so on. Obviously A's environment may be different from B's even though 'environment' has the same sense. Similarly we may allow that 'blue$_{ph}$' for A is different from 'blue$_{ph}$' for B, though it has the same sense. Just as 'environment' may have the same sense but different reference when used respectively in A's environment and B's environment, so 'blue$_{ph}$' has the same sense but different reference in 'blue$_{ph}$' for A and 'blue$_{ph}$' for B.

What is crucial to providing the sense for phenomenal-blue is not the state's occupying the causal role usually favoured by functionalists, but the 'family membership' role, as specified by three-dimensional colour arrays. Blue, red, green and yellow, for example, have distinctive, specific places in the family of colours. All of us use the same term 'phenomenal-blue' to apply to a state in A, and to a state in B. Reference is to a state which plays similar roles in the two people. It may be a different state but it is referred to in the same way. We can all draw upon the family of colours as providing such a way.

It would seem therefore that the account of virtual colours and phe-nomenal qualities is compatible with the weak thesis of the Private Language Argument. Still, it might well be argued that this is not good enough. For, it might be alleged, the account runs counter to the strong thesis, which disallows the possibility of any private language, even one parasitic on a public language (that is, a fragment of a natural language).

Discussion of the strong thesis therefore seems unavoidable. Such, however, are the difficulties with Wittgenstein's exact intentions, the vastness of the private-language literature and the variety of the interpre-tations available, that it can only be with trepidation that anyone enters such a minefield. It is difficult to imagine that anything one could say in a whole book, let alone a short space, could hope to settle the issues. I have no such grandiose claims. For my purposes, it is sufficient to point out that, given the controversy on what the Private Language Argument is, let alone whether it is cogent, it would not be unreasonable to set the argument aside as too inconclusive. By itself, this response is hardly satisfactory. It is important to go on and indicate how the strongest versions are inconclusive.

First of all there are two major versions, the first concentrating on the material in the *Investigations* up to Paragraph 202, and the second on that succeeding Paragraph 243. Walker, as we have seen, follows Kripke in seeing the latter material as supplementing the earlier ideas. Accordingly Wittgenstein's position is seen as a defence of an anti-realist position against certain metaphysical-realist positions.[26] The problem is said to be that the private linguist makes a metaphysical assumption that he or she is not entitled to: that there exist objective similarities and differences independent of social practices. Insofar, then, as the Private Language Argument depends on a defence of anti-realism (that is, global anti-realism), a view which to say the least is not established beyond serious dispute, the argument is less than devastating.

If we concentrate on the later sections of the *Investigations,* then the difficulty is to reconstruct an argument which is both coherent and cogent. Some versions are ruled out by their appeal, implicit or otherwise, to the Verification Principle. This was persuasively argued by Judith Jarvis Thomson, and reinforced by James Cornman. More recently Simon Blackburn has presented a detailed examination of a different, possibly sounder, version that seems not to depend on the Verification Principle.[27] Blackburn provides a powerful defence of the private linguist against Wittgenstein's argument. The crux of it is that unless the argument simply begs the question against the private linguist, Wittgenstein is forced in his criticism to adopt either of two unwelcome positions. The first option requires putting on the garb of the sceptic and casting doubt on the knowledge the linguist claimed to have formed originally. The problem with this, Blackburn argues, is that the scepticism is likely to be too strong, destroying 'our knowledge of anything, especially of public meanings'. Nor is the second option much

26 Walker (1989), analyses and criticises this interpretation, pp. 124–45.
27 Judith Jarvis Thompson (1964), 'Private Languages', *Amer. Phil. Quart.,* 1, pp. 20–31; J. Cornman (1971), *Materialism and Sensations,* New Haven and London: Yale U.P., pp. 84–96; Blackburn (1984), pp. 92–103.

better off. It rests on an assumption that runs counter to an important principle that Wittgenstein himself had rejected, and had shown to be implausible:

that there should be a fact of our being guided by a previous intention which can, as it were, be laid out to view in the form of an image in the head or other guide.[28]

An even more general criticism has been produced by Edward Craig.[29] By drawing parallels between Wittgenstein's argument and a similar one used by Michael Dummett, Craig persuades us that the two arguments suffer similar defects and that as a result the argument for the crucial assumption that a private ostensive definition is impossible does not go through.

In the light of these considerations, there are strong grounds for thinking that no coherent version of the Private Language Argument has been provided that does not beg the question, rely on the verification principle or propose some controversial and unproven metaphysical or epistemological thesis. This thought is only reinforced by reading the detailed analysis presented by Crispin Wright in a defence of the Private Language Argument. First, he cites three of the most plausible interpretations, saying that though none of them provides a fully cogent argument, nevertheless 'collectively they suggest that a defender of private language had better be anti-verificationist, anti-Cartesian, and a proponent of the propriety of groundless belief.'[30] Though he wonders whether these make a consistent set of beliefs, it is not clear to me that there is any great problem. Each claim seems plausible and defensible, and Wright certainly provides no argument against their joint consistency. Wright goes on to propose yet another interpretation, the conclusion of which is to force the defender of the private language into a dilemma:

One way or another he has to draw the 'seems right'/'is right' contrast. If he accepts the need to do so operationally, by reference to practical criteria, our finding was that he was able to do so in a satisfactory way only in very special, at best unlikely circumstances; and that an element of contingency will thereby intrude into his central claim which is quite foreign to his original conviction. If, on the other hand, he claims the distinction need not be operational but may be drawn purely truth-conditionally, he commits himself to the unwelcome

28 Blackburn (1984), p. 103.
29 Edward Craig (1982), 'Meaning, Use and Privacy', *Mind*, 91, pp. 541–64.
30 Crispin Wright (1986), 'Does *Philosophical Investigations* I 258–60 Suggest a Cogent Argument Against Private Language?', in P. Pettit and J. McDowell (eds), *Subject, Thought and Context*, Oxford: Clarendon, pp. 209–66, p. 222.

consequence that the private linguist can have no satisfactory basis for his belief in his general competence to practise the private language.[31]

Neither fork of this dilemma is threatening to the position that I have advanced. This dilemma would count at best against a position that insisted on the viability of a private language and that depended on knowing that the language was indeed private. It would not be effective in a context in which it was argued that someone who held a certain philosophical position was *committed* to the existence of a private language. Such a position is threatened not by an argument that we cannot know that we have a private language if we have one, but rather by an objection that there cannot be such a language, whether or not we know about it. My position is such that at best it follows as a consequence of this position that it is possible for there be a private language, or more accurately a private fragment of a public language.

Finally, there is reason to doubt that the Private Language Argument, even if it were cogent, implies what it is often claimed to do, and in particular that it rules out theses that refer to phenomenal qualities and states. What it excludes is that the meaning of a term is constituted by a connection the term has with a private item, e.g. one 'in the mind of the individual who understands the term', where this item is logically private. The phenomenal qualities and phenomenal items that I have discussed are 'in the mind' and are private. But it is not the case that they have to be essentially private, in the sense that it is logically impossible for another being to experience them. Of course, things being what they are, there are no human beings who are in any such position, and hence in practice the phenomenal states are private. Nothing in my account, or in the representationalist account, requires that the phenomenal states be logically private.

Can we describe the logical possibility of another being's experiencing the same phenomenal states as I do? Yes. First, let us remind ourselves that as far as my visual experiences are concerned, I am not just a being that has visual experiences. I am a being that acts and in particular does so by having control over my body. Among the things I have control of are the eyes, the organs from which I look. Normally I see objects relative to a point of view, and that point of view is the place occupied by my eyes. However, there is an exception to this. The use of TV cameras, e.g. at a cricket ground, enables me to sit at home and watch a match at the ground. Now the point of view from which I look is a

31 Ibid., p. 258.

point in the stands. That is how things are at the moment. We are in a quickly changing world, however. Perhaps one day I could have control of the cameras at the ground. Furthermore the TV set could be attached to my eyes. In such a way we can imagine my acquiring the ability to see from a range of points of view.

Once we have started on this science fantasy, we can imagine it to be extended. We could imagine further technological progress of such a kind that another person could have access to the visual centre of my brain. I hear a voice over which I have no control correcting some of the claims I make from time to time. Indeed, if we can take seriously the claims of some neurologists, this fantasy has already been achieved – in split-brain patients and in split personalities.

Hence it is not unreasonable to hold that phenomenal states and qualities are private but not logically private. This may make it look as if the Private Language Argument is trivial. This appearance is misleading. It is true that it leaves quite untouched a wide range of theories that it is often taken to undermine. Nevertheless it would still rule out certain views in the philosophy of mind and the philosophy of language, e.g. certain Cartesian views. It would seem to rule out the attempt by Carnap in *The Logical Structure of the World* 'to provide a rational reconstruction of the concepts of all fields of knowledge on the basis of the concepts that refer to the immediately given'. Included among these concepts that were to be reconstructed were the concepts of the self and of other selves. If Wittgenstein is right, this project is misconceived. In addition Carnap uses as a key term in his system the relation of 'part similarity'. This relation, he says, can be defined in terms of one of its constituent relations:

This constituent relation is also epistemically more fundamental. If it is recognised that two elementary experiences x and y are part similar, then a memory image of the earlier of the two, of say x, must have been compared with y.

'Recollection of similarity holds between x and y' means: x and y are elementary experiences which are recognised as part similar through the comparison of a memory image of x with y.[32]

Whether or not Wittgenstein had Carnap in mind, one can clearly see the implications Wittgenstein's arguments would have for Carnap's position.

32 Carnap (1967), *The Logical Structure of the World*, 2nd ed., London: Routledge and Kegan Paul, p. 127. Note that each of these sentences is put by Carnap inside special quotes, c-quotes and p-quotes, to indicate whether the symbols are of the constructed language or of psychological language.

7. INTUITIVE AND ABSTRACT KNOWLEDGE

There is a far more radical strategy that a defender of the subjectivity of phenomenal qualities might follow to counter the Private Language Argument. This entails making a distinction between two purposes of language. One, perhaps the primary one, is for the purpose of communication. Here the speaker-audience relationship is crucial to the notion of language. A key concept, furthermore, is that of the audience's understanding or knowledge. What is meant by an utterance depends on what a standard audience can be expected to understand by the utterance. The second purpose of language is for thought. Now, there is no doubt that the development of public language and the resulting powers of communication enormously expand the powers of thought. It is not so plain however that all thought requires such language: the abilities of animals and babies give some evidence that it does not, even if the evidence is far from compelling.

The private language might fulfil the function of satisfying this purpose – at least in a restricted domain. Now, it may well be that the linguist can do this only if she can formulate the purposes in a public language and judge its overall success in a public language, but there is no good reason why the private linguist cannot do so consistently. This possibility may be ruled out if we think of the private linguist as being engaged in the epistemological tasks of Descartes, Russell or Carnap, but not if she dissociates herself from such tasks (as I have done in this exercise). As well, we should be extremely wary about ruling out Descartes, Russell and Carnap, for it is not all that clear why each of this group cannot help himself to certain assumptions in setting up a system, even if with the system those assumptions will be set aside. I have no particular interest in this context in pursuing this thought, but it strikes me as not at all out of the question for it to be done.

The suggestion I am making is that it is possible to formulate private thoughts and private knowledge which might be expressible in a private language. It need not be the case that the linguist decides to set up the private language with a certain conscious purpose in mind. It could be that the private linguist simply develops the language (is caused to develop it) and retains the language because it is successful. The linguist did not develop the language for that or any other purpose.

The best illustration of how to follow the strategy can be found in Russell and Schopenhauer. Russell drew what he thought was an obvious distinction between knowledge by acquaintance and knowledge

230

by description. This distinction mirrors an earlier distinction made by Schopenhauer between intuitive and abstract knowledge.[33] Such distinctions seem to be between conceptual and nonconceptual knowings, or between propositional and nonpropositional knowledge. Propositional or conceptual knowledge is knowing *that* so-and-so is the case.

In the latter part of twentieth-century philosophy, such distinctions seem to be almost universally rejected. Through the influence particularly of Wittgenstein, the nonpropositional knowledge favoured by Russell and Schopenhauer is rejected. It is accepted that there are other forms of 'knowing', e.g. knowing-how, but not intuitive knowledge or knowledge-by-acquaintance. Dretske has argued that there are epistemic and nonepistemic forms of perception but presupposes that in this context there is only one relevant form of knowing.[34]

There is one response to these critics which provides a partial defence of Russell and Schopenhauer. This is to say that there is an important distinction that they were aiming at but failed to capture. They were aiming at something that most of their critics simply ignore. The proper distinction is not between conceptual and nonconceptual ways of knowing, but between two different kinds of conceptual knowings, reflecting different kinds of concept. Gareth Evans, for example, after drawing a distinction between individual concepts and general concepts, argues that each embodies a different kind of knowledge which can be combined in a single judgement.[35] To illustrate: take a judgement that is expressible in language in a sentence such as

That cup is white and made of porcelain

where this is said in the presence of such a cup which is clearly visible. A person who uses the sentence with understanding is making a judgement which employs two kinds of knowledge:

(i) She *knows which* individual 'that cup' is (or which individual 'that cup' refers to);

(ii) She *knows what* it is for something to be white and for something to be made of porcelain.

33 B. Russell (1912), 'Acquaintance and Description', ch. 5 (pp. 46–59) of *The Problems of Philosophy*, Oxford: Oxford U.P; A. Schopenhauer (1969), *The World as Will and Representation*, trans. E. F. J. Payne, New York: Dover, esp. sections 3, 4, 8, 12, 14, 16.

34 F. Dretske (1969), *Seeing and Knowing*, London: Routledge and Kegan Paul, esp. pp. 4–77. Whatever Dretske's purposes, we might construe his nonepistemic perception, which is manifested in certain abilities, as a certain kind of knowing, e.g. the intuitive knowing discussed below.

35 G. Evans (1982), chs. 2–6.

These two pieces of knowledge are put together in the single judgement above. We could thus take these two kinds of knowledge to embody the distinction that Russell and Schopenhauer were obscurely aiming at.

It is not clear, however, that, even in their own terms, Russell and Schopenhauer are defeated by the arguments often given against them. Let me give as an example an argument presented by Robert Solomon in his commentary on Hegel. Solomon provides a paraphrase of an argument of Hegel's.[36] The crucial thing from my point of view is that Solomon wishes to bring out that Hegel was anticipating an argument that is widely accepted in twentieth-century philosophy and that, in Solomon's view, is rightly accepted.

Hegel argues against 'sense-certainty', which is taken to imply that there can be a form of knowledge that is immediate, in the sense that it is unmediated by concepts. What this is supposed to mean is that we can gain knowledge 'by ap-prehending an object without com-prehending it through concepts of the understanding'. The argument presented by Solomon is this: there are no uninterpreted experiences; sense-certainty is not only an inadequate form of consciousness, it could not possibly be a form of consciousness at all. The attempt to say what the object is that one is conscious of, in this form of consciousness, leads one to say it is a 'this' and finally to expel a grunt.

Hegel argues that our identification and knowledge of particulars does not precede but presupposes our knowledge of universals – our use of language and our ability to apply concepts – and that whatever the sensory basis of knowledge may be, there are no uninterpreted (unconceptualised) experiences, and even if there were, there could be no knowledge of them without concepts and interpretation.[37]

But is it so clear that this is an argument against intuitive knowledge or knowledge-by-acquaintance, rather than simply the presentation of an alternative view? In other words, does the argument simply beg the question? The argument seems to be that insofar as one tries to describe knowledge by acquaintance without using descriptions, one is left making a grunt: pointing or gesticulating in the air. But does not this simply beg the question? Russell and Schopenhauer say that it is important to distinguish between knowledge by acquaintance and knowledge by description. Critics ask them to translate knowledge of the first kind into

---

36 Robert Solomon (1983), *In the Spirit of Hegel*, New York: Oxford U.P., pp. 321–37. See G. Hegel (1977), *The Phenomenology of Spirit*, trans. A. V. Miller, Oxford: Oxford U.P., 82/58 to 89/64.

37 Solomon (1983), pp. 336–7.

knowledge of the second, and when they fail – they can only 'grunt' – they say that there isn't any such thing as knowledge by acquaintance.

Schopenhauer makes a distinction between abstract thought and intuitive thought. Perception is thought of as both intellectual and intuitive. It is not that perception does not involve understanding, for the understanding is both intellectual and intuitive. Schopenhauer wants to say that there are cognitive, intellectual processes involved but that they are not ones that involve abstract concepts. There is a nonconscious automatic application by the understanding of what he calls the Principle of Sufficient Reason that automatically produces the world-as-representation:

As with the appearance of the sun, the visible world makes its appearance, so at one stroke does the understanding through its one simple function convert the dull, meaningless sensation into perception.[38]

Schopenhauer's view contrasts with Kant's. For Kant the role of the understanding in perceptual experience is to apply concepts and categories in the making of judgements (to which the sensibility contributes intuitions), and the role of reason is to make inferences. For Schopenhauer the understanding does not provide concepts; it is the role of reason to apply abstract concepts. Whereas for Kant sensibility provides the forms of space and time to the incoming data to produce sensible intuitions, for Schopenhauer the understanding provides forms of space, time and causality to produce perceptual objects. These perceptual objects are representations-for-a-subject.

It may be doubtful whether Schopenhauer can provide a coherent account of this process. The understanding, in order to construct representations-for-a-subject, must start with things other than representations, and it is difficult to see, on his account, what these items could be. He explicitly says that they are bodily effects, but it is not clear that he can coherently say this. On the other hand, it is questionable whether Kant's view is any more coherent. (Different philosophers reconstruct Kant to fit their own favoured account.)

The interest in Schopenhauer's view is that it has the following characteristics. First it provides a 'naturalised' theory of how perception works (which in my view is not to say that it is reducible to biology or physics). Second, it provides a unified account of humans and animals, as far as perception and the understanding are concerned. The difference between humans and animals rests on humans' use of abstract concepts,

38 Schopenhauer (1969), p. 12.

characteristically in language. Third, there is a distinction drawn between intuitive knowledge and abstract knowledge.

Schopenhauer holds that the processes involved in perception are intellectual and cognitive but are also intuitive and nonconceptual. In philosophy over the last forty years such a view has been almost universally rejected. The orthodox view has been behind Kant (and Hegel) in holding that the processes are conceptual. One form this doctrine about the centrality of concepts takes is in the language-of-thought thesis: that the cognitive processes underlying the mind, that is thought, perception, language use and intentional action, are best understood as requiring mental representations, where these representations are understood as linguistic or sentence-like or conceptual. The cognitive processes involve forming such representations or transforming one representation into another. Schopenhauer can be understood as coming down on the side of those opposed to the language-of-thought thesis, e.g. those supporting connectionism.

It seems to me that the proper way for someone to defend the view that perception is intellectual but not conceptual is as follows. Perception of objects and their states involves the perceiver's forming perceptual representations of objects and their states. Forming such perceptual representations does not require rule-following in the manner of concept application. Spatial properties and relations, and colour properties and relations, are represented within a characteristic representational system. Physical states x, y and z are represented by states x_r y_r and z_r. The perceiver uses the representational states to get bearings on x, y and z. That the representational states form collectively a system of states that stand together in the right kind of way explains how that system of states will work as a representation of, say, spatial states and relations or of colour states and relations or whatever.

The representational states play a role in allowing the perceiver to fix on objective states of affairs and objects. They manage to perform this role successfully if they match objective states of affairs. The way to think of this is in terms of a map. The states of a map enable one to negotiate the terrain successfully if the map states collectively match the states of the terrain (at least broadly).

Once the model is in place, it can be modified. In some cases the representational states work successfully without collectively matching existing objective states of affairs. They match intensional states of affairs, i.e. states of affairs that do not exist. This is not as crazy as it sounds at first, and for two reasons. One is that by matching intensional states of

234

affairs they can match dispositional states, and such dispositional states, as we have seen in the case of colours, can be highly significant. Secondly, if different observers agree on the intensional states of affairs (for whatever reasons), then for many purposes *it is as if* such states exist. It is plausible that sociocultural objects are in such a position. What makes it true that kings, parliaments and prime ministers exist is that people believe that they exist, or at least have the appropriate intensional attitudes. Apart from such intensional attitudes, they do not exist. (Of course with different attitudes, something else might exist in their place.)

Let us return to the judgement used earlier to illustrate Evans's position. It was one expressible in a sentence such as

that cup is white and made of porcelain

spoken in a context in which the expression 'that cup' is a demonstrative phrase used to refer to a cup which the perceiver is seeing. A person who uses the sentence with understanding is making a judgement which employs two kinds of knowledge: individuating knowledge of which cup is referred to, and general knowledge of what it is for something to be white (and for something to be made of porcelain). These two pieces of knowledge are put together in the judgement. Let us concentrate on the piece of knowledge contained in knowing what it is for something to be white. One form such knowledge may take is knowing what it is for '*a* is white' to be true. This involves knowing, under the right conditions, that *a* is white. But this is not the only form such knowledge can take. It is possible for some language-users to have the knowledge in another form. Such people have either of these abilities:

The ability to recognise something as white (red, blue . . .)
The ability to identify something as white (red, blue . . .)

With respect to at least some properties, it is necessary that some language-users (experts) have the knowledge in this form.

It is not clear to me that to say of a person that he has such abilities requires saying that he possesses the linguistic concept 'red', that is, that he applies and understands the expression 'red'. It seems to me that a person may exemplify this ability through his behaviour, that is in what might be called red-oriented behavings.

If we think of the biology of colour judgements it seems to me that *one* form this knowledge can take is as follows:

P knows what it is for *x* to be red

235

is equivalent to

> P has the capacity to represent x as red in P's colour-representing system

which is to say:

> P has the capacity to represent x by means of its red-representations

that is,

> P has the capacity to place x in the 'red' locus in the colour-representing system.

It should go without saying that having such a capacity requires having a load of other capacities that are related to it, capacities to locate blue, yellow, brown, olive etc. in their places in the same system.

Animals, babies and people have spatial thoughts and colour thoughts. They locate objects in space: x is close to y, x is nearer to me than z, x is yellow, y is a darker red than z, and so on. These colour thoughts are representations of x, y and z in the space-representing system and the colour-representing system. What makes them thoughts and representations of x, y and z, and of their spatial and colour properties, is not just that they match publicly observable objects and qualities but that they guide the organism's behaviour towards these objects and properties.

I agree with Wittgenstein that to recognise x as red is not to conjure up a mental image of red and to compare it with x. Such a technique would presuppose that I recognise the memory image itself as red. Instead to recognise x as red is to treat it as red. This does not, however, require performing a public act. It may be achieved by placing x (or the x representation) in the place reserved in the colour-representing system for red things.

8. CONCLUSION

In the last section I examined the possibility of a radical defence against the Wittgensteinian arguments on language. As stated earlier, I prefer to rest the defence of my position on the less radical strategy described earlier, but it is certainly worth considering the stronger position. For one thing, it has prospects for showing how a comprehensive account of perception can be developed, one that can accommodate the biological and social aspects of perception. Central to any such account, I submit, will be the kind of account of colour developed in these pages.

Bibliography

Aaron, R. I. (1971), *John Locke*, 3rd ed., Oxford: Oxford University Press.

Agoston, G. (1987), *Color Theory and Application in Art and Design*, Berlin: Springer.

Armstrong, D. M. (1969), 'Colour-Realism and the Argument from Microscopes', Brown and Rollins (1969), pp. 119–31.

Austin, J. C. (1962), *Sense and Sensibilia*, ed. G. Warnock, Oxford: Clarendon Press.

Averill, E. A. (1985), 'Colour and the Anthropocentric Problem', *Journal of Philosophy*, 82, pp. 281–303.

Baldwin, Thomas (1992), 'The Projective Theory of Sensory Content', in Crane (1992a), pp. 177–95.

Beck, J. (1972), *Surface Color Perception*, Ithaca, N.Y.: Cornell University Press.

Berlin, B., and Kay, P. (1969), *Basic Color Terms*, Berkeley and Los Angeles: University of California Press.

Blackburn, S. (1984), *Spreading the Word*, Oxford: Clarendon Press.

Blakemore, C., and Greenfield, S. (eds.) (1987), *Mindwaves*, Oxford: Blackwell Publisher.

Block, N. (1980), 'Troubles with Functionalism', in *Readings in the Philosophy of Psychology*, Vol. I, ed. N. Block, Cambridge, Mass.: Harvard University Press, pp. 268–305.

Block, N., and Fodor, J. (1972), 'What Psychological States Are Not', *Philosophical Review*, 81, pp. 159–81.

Boghossian P. A. and Velleman, D. (1989), 'Colour as a Secondary Quality', *Mind*, 98, pp. 81–103.

Boynton, R. (1978), 'Color in Contour and Object Perception', in Carterette and Friedman (1978), pp. 173–98.

Bradley, M. C. (1964), Review of Smart, *Philosophy and Scientific Realism*, *Australasian Journal of Philosophy*, 42, pp. 262–83.

____ (1969), 'Two Objections Against the Identity Theory', in Brown and Rollins (1969), pp. 173–89.

Broackes, Justin (1992), 'The Autonomy of Colour', in Charles and Lennon (1992), pp. 421–66.

Broad, C. D. (1925), *Mind and Its Place in Nature*, London: Kegan Paul.

Brody, B. A., and Grandy, R. E. (eds.) (1989), *Readings in the Philosophy of Science*, 2nd ed., Englewood Cliffs: Prentice-Hall.

Brown, R., and Rollins, C. D. (eds.) (1969), *Contemporary Philosophy in Australia*, London: Allen and Unwin.

Burnyeat, M. (1979), 'Conflicting Appearances', *Proceedings of the British Academy*, 65, pp. 69–111.

Campbell, J. (1994), 'A Simple View of Colour', in Haldane and Wright (1994), pp. 257–69.

Campbell, Keith (1969), 'Colours', in Brown and Rollins (1969), pp. 132–57.

Carnap, R. (1967), *The Logical Structure of the World*, 2nd ed., London: Routledge and Kegan Paul.

Carterette, E. C., and Friedman, M. P. (eds.) (1978), *Handbook of Perception*, vol. 8, New York: Academic Press.

Chamberlin, G. J., and Chamberlin, D. G. (1980), *Colour: Its Measurement, Computation and Application*, London: Heyden.

Charles, David, and Lennon, Kathleen (eds.) (1992), *Reduction, Explanation and Realism*, Oxford: Clarendon Press.

Churchland, Patricia (1986), *Neurophilosophy*, Cambridge, Mass.: MIT Press.

Cornman, J. (1971), *Materialism and Sensations*, New Haven, Conn.: Yale University Press.

Cottingham, John (1990), 'Descartes on Colour', *Proceedings of the Aristotelian Society*, 64, pp. 231–46.

Craig, Edward (1982), 'Meaning, Use and Privacy', *Mind*, 91, pp. 541–64.

Crane, Tim (ed.) (1992a), *The Contents of Experience*, Cambridge: Cambridge University Press.

(1992b), 'The Nonconceptual Content of Experience', in Crane (1992a), pp. 136–57.

Davidoff, Jules (1991), *Cognition Through Color*, Cambridge, Mass.: MIT Press.

Dawkins, R. (1986), *The Blind Watchmaker*, Essex: Longman Scientific and Technical.

Dennett, Daniel (1992), *Consciousness Explained*, London: Lane, Penguin.

Descartes, R. (1954), *Philosophical Writings*, trans. Anscombe, G. E. M. and Geach, P., London: Nelson.

Diogenes Laertius (1925), *Lives of Eminent Philosophers*, trans. R. D. Hicks, London: Heinemann.

Donington, R. (1962), *The Instruments of Music*, London: Methuen.

Dretske, F. (1969), *Seeing and Knowing*, London: Routledge and Kegan Paul.

(1981), *Knowledge and the Flow of Information*, Cambridge Mass.: MIT Press.

Dummett, M. (1979), 'Common Sense and Physics', in Macdonald (1979), pp. 1–40.

Eccles, J. (1987), 'Brain and Mind, Two or One?' in Blakemore and Greenfield (1987), pp. 293–307.

Ellis, B. (1992), 'Scientific Essentialism', Victorian Centre for History and Philosophy of Science, preprint 1/92, August.

Evans, Gareth (1980), 'Things Without the Mind', in Straaten (1980), pp. 76–116.

(1982), *The Varieties of Reference*, Oxford: Clarendon Press.

Evans, Ralph (1974), *The Perception of Color*, New York: Wiley.

Feyerabend, P. K. (1989), 'How to Be a Good Empiricist', in Brody and Grandy (1989), pp. 104–23

Garfinkel, Alan (1981), *Forms of Explanation*, New Haven, Conn.: Yale University Press.

Gaukroger, S. (ed.) (1980), *Descartes: Philosophy of Mathematics and Physics*, Brighton: Harvester Press.

Gellner, E. (1979), 'Concepts and Society', in Wilson (1979), pp. 18–49.

Gibson, Eleanor (1969), *Principles of Perceptual Learning and Development*, Englewood Cliffs, N.J.: Prentice-Hall, pp. 363–8.

Gilinsky, A. S. (1955), 'The Effect of Attitude upon the Perception of Size', *American Journal of Psychology*, 68, pp. 173–92.

Green-Armytage, Paul (1983), 'Brightness, Whiteness and Lightness', Colour Report F26, Scandinavian Colour Institute.

Green-Armytage, Paul (1984), 'The Specification of Colours', invited paper at the Illuminating Engineering Society of Australia, 30th National Convention, Perth.

Guerlac, H. (1986), 'Can There Be Colours in the Dark?' *Journal of the History of Ideas*, 47, pp. 3–20.

Hacker, P. M. S. (1987), *Appearance and Reality*, Oxford: Blackwell Publisher.

Haldane, John, and Wright, Crispin (eds.) (1994), *Reality, Representation and Projection*, Oxford: Clarendon Press.

Hard, Anders, and Sivik, Lars (1981), 'NCS-Natural Colour System: A Swedish Standard for Colour Notation', *Colour Research and Application*, 6, pp. 129–38.

Hardin, C. L. (1988), *Color for Philosophers*, Indianapolis, Ind.: Hackett.

—— (1992), 'The Virtues of Illusion', *Philosophical Studies*, 68, pp. 371–82.

—— (1993), 'Van Brakel and the Not-so-Naked Emperor', *British Journal for the Philosophy of Science*, 44, pp. 137–50.

Harman, Gilbert (1990), 'The Intrinsic Quality of Experience', in Tomberlin (1990), pp. 31–52.

Harre, R., and Madden, E. H. (1975), *Causal Powers: A Theory of Natural Necessity*, Oxford: Blackwell Publisher.

Harrison, B. (1973), *Form and Content*, Oxford: Blackwell Publisher.

Harvey, John (1992), 'Challenging the Obvious: The Logic of Colour Concepts', *Philosophia*, 21, pp. 277–94.

Hegel, G. (1977), *The Phenomenology of Spirit*, trans. A. V. Miller, Oxford: Oxford University Press.

Hering, E. (1964), *Outlines of a Theory of the Light Sense*, trans. L. Hurvich and D. Jameson, Cambridge, Mass.: Harvard University Press.

Hilbert, D. R. (1987), *Color and Color Perception*, Stanford, Calif.: C.S.L.I.

—— (1992), 'What Is Colour Vision?', *Philosophical Studies*, 68, pp. 350–70.

Holt, E. B. (1912), *The New Realism*, New York: Macmillan.

Honderich, T. (ed.) (1985), *Morality and Objectivity*, London: Routledge and Kegan Paul.

Horgan, Terrence (1984), 'Functionalism, Qualia, and the Inverted Spectra', *Philosophy and Phenomenological Research*, 44, pp. 453–69.

239

Hughes, Robert (1988), *The Fatal Shore*, London: Pan.

Humphrey, Nicholas (1992), *A History of the Mind*, London: Chatto and Windus.

Hurvich, L. (1981), *Colour Vision*, Sunderland: Sinauer.

Jackson, Frank (1977), *Perception: A Representative Theory*, Cambridge University Press.

    (1990), 'Epiphenomenal Qualia', in Lycan (1990), p. 469.

Jackson, Frank and Pettit, P. (1988), 'Functionalism and Broad Content', *Mind*, 97, pp. 381–400.

Johnston, Mark (1992), 'How to Speak of the Colours', *Philosophical Studies*, 68, pp. 221–64.

Judd, D., and Wyszecki, G. (1963), *Color in Business, Science and Industry*, 2nd ed., New York: Wiley.

Katz, D. (1930), *The World of Colour*, trans. R. B. Macleod and C. W. Fox, London: Kegan Paul.

Kraut, Robert (1992), 'The Objectivity of Colour and the Colour of Objectivity', *Philosophical Studies*, 68, pp. 265–88.

Kripke, S. (1980), *Naming and Necessity*, 2nd ed., Cambridge, Mass.: Harvard University Press.

    (1982), *Wittgenstein on Rules and Private Language*, Oxford: Blackwell Publisher.

Land, E. H. (1983), 'Recent Advances in Retinex Theory . . .', *Proceedings of the National Academy of Sciences*, 80, pp. 5163–9.

Landesman, C. (1989), *Color and Consciousness*, Philadelphia: Temple University Press.

Lehrer, K. (1989), *Thomas Reid*, Arguments of the Philosophers, London: Routledge.

Lehrer, K., and Beanblossom, R. (eds.) (1983), *Thomas Reid's Inquiry and Essays*, 2nd ed., Indianapolis, Ind.: Hackett.

Locke, J. (1961), *Essay Concerning Human Understanding*, ed. J. Yolton, London: Dent.

Lowe, E. J. (1992), 'Experience and Its Objects', in Crane (1992a), pp. 79–104.

Lycan, G. (ed.) (1990), *Mind and Cognition: A Reader*, Cambridge, Mass.: Blackwell Publisher.

MacAdam, D. L. (1985), *Color Measurement*, Berlin: Springer.

Macdonald, G. (ed.) (1979), *Perception and Identity*, London: Macmillan.

McDowell, J. (1985), 'Values and Secondary Qualities', in Honderich (1985), pp. 110–27.

    (1986), 'Singular Thought and Inner Space', in Pettit and McDowell (1986), pp. 137–68.

McGinn, C. (1983), *The Subjective View*, Oxford: Clarendon Press.

MacIntyre, A. (1984), *After Virtue*, 2nd ed., Notre Dame, Ind.: University of Notre Dame Press.

Mackie, J. (1976), *Problems from Locke*, Oxford: Oxford University Press.

Margenau, H. (1984), *The Miracle of Existence*, Woodbridge : Ox Bow Press.

Maull, N. (1980), 'Cartesian Optics and the Geometry of Nature', in Gaukroger (1980), pp. 23–40.

Maund, J. B. (Barry) (1981), 'Colour: A Case for Conceptual Fission', *Australasian Journal of Philosophy*, 59, pp. 308–22.

(1986), 'The Phenomenal and Other Uses of "Looks" ', *Australasian Journal of Philosophy*, 64, pp. 170–80.

(1991), 'The Nature of Colour', *History of Philosophy Quarterly*, 8, pp. 253–63.

(1993), 'Representation, Pictures and Resemblances', in Edmond Wright (1993), pp 45–69.

Mulligan, Kevin (1991), 'Colours, Corners and Complexity', in Spohn (1991), pp. 77–102.

Mundle, C. W. K. (1971), *Perception: Facts and Theories*, Oxford: Oxford University Press.

Nassau, K. (1983), *The Physics and Chemistry of Color*, New York: Wiley.

Peacocke, Christopher (1984), 'Colour-Concepts and Colour Experience', *Synthese*, 58, pp. 365–81.

(1992), 'Scenarios, Concepts and Perception' in Crane (1992a), pp. 105–35.

Perkins, Moreland (1983), *Sensing the World*, Indianapolis, Ind.: Hackett.

Pettit, P., and McDowell, J. (eds.) (1986), *Subject Thought and Context*, Oxford: Clarendon Press.

Putnam, H. (1977), 'Meaning and Reference', in Schwartz (1977), pp. 119–32.

(1978), *Meaning and the Moral Sciences*, Boston: Routledge and Kegan Paul.

(1981), *Reason, Truth and History*, Cambridge: Cambridge University Press.

Reid, T. (1970), *An Inquiry into the Human Mind*, ed. T. Duggan, Chicago: Chicago University Press.

Rhees, R., (1954), 'Can There Be a Private Language?' *Proceedings of the Aristotelian Society*, supp., 28, pp. 77–94.

Richardson, R. C., (1982) 'The "Scandal" of Cartesian Interactionism', *Mind*, 91, pp. 20–37.

Robinson, Howard (1993), 'Dennett on the Knowledge Argument', *Analysis*, 53, no. 3, pp. 174–7.

Ross, J. J. (1970), *The Appeal to the Given*, London: Allen and Unwin.

Russell, B. (1912), *The Problems of Philosophy*, Oxford: Oxford University Press.

Schopenhauer, A. (1969), *The World as Will and Representation*, trans. E. F. J. Payne, New York: Dover.

Schwartz, Stephen (ed.) (1977), *Naming, Necessity and Natural Kinds*, London: Cornell University Press.

Sellars, W. (1963), 'Empiricism and the Philosophy of Mind', *Science, Perception and Reality*, London: Routledge and Kegan Paul, pp. 127–96.

(1968), *Science and Metaphysics*, London: Routledge and Kegan Paul.

(1971), 'Science, Sense-Impressions and Sensa', *Review of Metaphysics* 23, pp. 391–447.

Shoemaker, S. (1975), 'Functionalism and Qualia', *Philosophical Studies*, 27, 1975, pp. 291–315.

(1982), 'The Inverted Spectrum', *Journal of Philosophy*, 79, no. 7, pp. 357–81.

(1991), 'Qualia and Consciousness', *Mind*, 100, pp. 507–24.

Smart J. J. C. (1961), 'Colours', *Philosophy*, 36, pp. 128–42.

(1963), *Philosophy and Scientific Realism*, London: Routledge and Kegan Paul.

(1971), 'Reports of Immediate Experiences', *Synthese*, 22, pp. 346–59.

Sober, Elliott (1990), 'Putting the Function Back into Functionalism', in Lycan (1990), pp. 97–106.

241

Solomon, Robert (1983), *In the Spirit of Hegel*, New York: Oxford University Press.

Snowdon, Paul (1992), 'How to Interpret "Direct Perception" ', in Crane (1992a), pp. 48–78.

Spohn, Wolfgang (ed.) (1991), *Existence and Explanation*, Dordrecht: Kluwer.

Straaten, Z. van (ed.) (1980), *Philosophical Subjects*, Oxford: Oxford University Press.

Strawson, P. F. (1979), 'Perception and Its Objects', in Macdonald (1979), pp. 41–60.

Thompson, Evan (1992), 'Novel Colours' in *Philosophical Studies*, 68, pp. 321–50.

Thompson, Judith Janis (1964), 'Private Languages', *American Philosophical Quarterly*, 1, pp. 20–31.

Tomberlin, James (ed.) (1990), *Philosophical Perspectives*, 4, Alascadero: Ridgeview.

Tye, Michael (1992), 'Visual Qualia and Visual Content', in Crane (1992a), pp. 158–77.

van Brakel, J. (1993), 'The Plasticity of Categories: The Case of Colour', *British Journal for the Philosophy of Science*, 44, pp. 103–35.

van Frassen, B. (1980), *The Scientific Image*, Oxford: Oxford University Press.

Walker, Ralph (1989), *The Coherence Theory of Truth*, London: Routledge.

Wasserman, G. (1978), *Colour Vision: An Historical Introduction*, New York: Wiley.

Westphal, Jonathan (1991), *Colour: A Philosophical Introduction*, 2nd ed., Oxford: Blackwell Publisher.

Whitehead, A. N. (1925) *Science and the Modern World*, Cambridge: Cambridge University Press.

Wilson, B. R. (ed.) (1979) *Rationality*, Oxford: Blackwell Publisher.

Wittgenstein, L. (1967), *Philosophical Investigations*, 3rd ed., trans. G. E. M. Anscombe, Oxford: Blackwell Publisher.

(1978), *Remarks on Colour*, ed. G. E. M. Anscombe, trans. L. L. McAlister and M. Schättle, Oxford: Blackwell Publisher.

Wood, Alexander (1962), *The Physics of Music*, 6th ed, London: Methuen.

Wright, Crispin (1986), 'A Cogent Argument Against Private Language', in Pettit and McDowell (eds.) (1986), pp. 209–66.

(1987), *Realism, Meaning and Truth*, Oxford: Blackwell Publisher.

Wright, Edmond (ed.) (1993), *New Representationalisms*, Aldershot: Avebury.

(1993a), 'More Qualia Trouble for Functionalism: The Smythies TV-Hood Analogy', *Synthese*, 97, pp. 365–82.

Wright, W. D. (1967), *The Rays Are Not Coloured*, London: Adam Hilger.

Zeki, S. (1983), 'Colour Coding in the Cerebral Cortex', *Neuroscience*, 9, no. 4, pp. 741–81.

Index

243

pluralist framework of colour, 65, 148,
  161–2, 171–3
psychological colour-space, 141, 190–2
psychology of colour, 206
psychophysical colour, 143–6
primary colours, psychological, 141–2, 145,
  206, 207–8, 211, 218–20
primary qualities
  appearances of, 72–4, 77
  intrinsic concepts, 72–4, 77
private language, 212–3
Private Language Argument, 207, 224–9,
  230, 236
  and phenomenal qualities, 224–9
  and virtual qualities, 38–9, 220–4, 224–
  6
Putnam, H., 52–4, 56–62, 64–8, 77–83,
  124, 200, 223–4

qualia, 42–3, 101–2, 175–7, 184, 191–2,
  193, 198, 202–4, 217–8
  and functionalism, 175, 177–82
  open-qualia, 43, 45, 101–2, 174–5
  phenomenal, 42–3, 45–6, 101–2, 174–5
  phenomenological character, 175–6
  physicalist challenge, 174–5, 201–5
  realism, 177, 181, 184–90, 191–2, 193–
  4
Quine, W. V. O., 200

real colour
  real and apparent, 130–3
  'real' by convention, 133–7, 151
Reid, T., 88, 90–4, 106, 149n
representations
  clear and confused, 7–8, 19–24, 47–8
  of colour, 21–4, 47–9, 75–7, 105, 174–5,
  198, 234–6
  sensory, 21, 47, 75–6, 104, 105, 172,
  174–5, 197
Rhees, R., 212–16
Richardson, R. C., 205
Robinson, Howard, 180
Ross, J. J., 15
Russell, B., 217, 230–3
Ryle, G., 13

Schopenhauer, A., 230–6
Sellars, W., 7, 13, 57
sensory qualities, 184–90, 192, 202
Shoemaker, S., 177, 179–182
size, concepts of, 109–11
Smart, J. J. C., 126–30, 154–5

Smythies, J., 27
Snowdon, Paul, 194n
Sober, Elliott, 177–8
Solomon, Robert, 232–3
spectrum inversion, 177, 179–82, 199
standard conditions for colour, 133
  variety of, 135–7, 147
standing colour, 116
Strawson, P. F., 89
supervenience, of colour, 124–6

theories of colour, 50–3
  commonsense, 9, 88–9, 90–4
  dispositional-analytic, 50–3, 68–72, 79,
  140, 154, 160, 162–3
  naive, 68
  natural, 7–12, 43, 68, 85–7, 88–90, 94,
  155
  objectivist, see objectivist accounts of
  colour
  plain-man's view, 37–8, 88
  pluralist, 105, 106, 111, 114–15, 128,
  149, 168, 171–3
Thompson, Evan, 190–2
Thompson, Judith Jarvis, 226
transitory colour, 116
Tye, Michael, 176, 182, 185, 188, 190,
  193–194

van Brakel, J., 209–12
van Frassen, B., 124
virtual colours, see colour as a virtual property
virtual natural kinds, 36, 78
virtual properties, 36, 78
visual experiences, 6, 21, 26, 44–6, 105,
  178–87
  act-object analysis, 185–6
  adverbial analysis, 186
  conceptual content, 181, 187–90
  diaphanous character, 185
  functional role, 178–82
  intensional object, 187
  intrinsic qualities, 182–8
  nonconceptual content, 181
  representational content, 187–90

Walker, Ralph, 213–16, 226
Wasserman, G., 27–8
Westphal, Jonathan, 27, 31, 51–4, 56–62,
  69–70, 84, 106, 135, 137, 149n, 151–
  2, 163
Whitehead, A. N., 9, 11

window model of perception, 14, 98
Wittgenstein, L., 15–16, 61, 95, 173, 190–2, 206–7, 212–19, 220–9, 230–1, 236
Wood, Alexander, 29–30

Wright, Crispin, 227–8
Wright, Edmond, 178
Wright, W. D., 28

Zeki, S., 29

CPSIA information can be obtained
at www.ICGtesting.com
Printed in the USA
LVOW07s1955141217
559743LV00001B/132/P